I0629366

NO LONGER PROPERTY OF
FALVEY MEMORIAL LIBRARY

Forbidden Territory

THE MEMOIRS OF

Juan Goytisolo

1931–1956

Translated by Peter Bush

NORTH POINT PRESS

San Francisco 1989

Copyright © Juan Goytisolo, 1985
English translation copyright © North Point Press and
Quartet Books Limited
Printed in the United States of America
Library of Congress Catalogue Card Number: 88-61171
ISBN: 0-86547-337-4

Coto vedado was originally published in Spanish by
Editorial Seix Barral, S.A., Barcelona, 1985.

Forbidden Territory

*La lucidité est la blessure
la plus rapprochée du soleil.*

RENÉ CHAR

PART 1

T HE WRITING OF genealogies, according to the ironic narrator of Biely's *Petersburg*, comes down to tracing the origins of well-to-do families right back to Adam and Eve. Beyond this important, undeniable discovery, the foliage and branches of maternal and paternal family trees do not usually extend—with the possible exception of a few aristocratic families—into that original limbo going by the pompous name of the dark night of time. I am an offshoot on both sides of exemplary bourgeois stock; the information that I obtained during my childhood about my ancestors does not go beyond the first half of the nineteenth century. This did not prevent my father, in one of those dreams of greatness that always acted as a prelude to one of his disastrous enterprises, from fashioning a family coat of arms that comprised, if I remember rightly, fleurs-de-lys against a red background. He traced the shield himself on parchment that gleamed from its frame on the verandah of our house in Torrentbó and was, he said, irrefutable proof of our noble lineage. On those long summer evenings that favored the evocation of the intimate details and long-lost anecdotes of family life, my uncle Leopoldo would greet the explanation of our so-called family shield with a wry, skeptical smile: no sooner had his brother turned his back than he would confide his suspicions that Great-grandfather's journey of no return from Lequeitio to Cuba, where he went as a youth and quickly made a fortune, was perhaps the result of his need to break from an environment hostile because of the initial stigma of his birth as a bastard. Why otherwise had this triumphant success settled down with such pomp in Catalonia and not in his native Basque country? That alienation and rupture from the rest of the family is and will always be a riddle. In any case, he would conclude, the shield and noble origins were products

of my father's wild fantasy: our Basque forebears were but country gentle-
men.

Whatever the truth of the matter, Great-grandfather Agustín, whose imposing, lordly image presided over the ghostly collection of Torrentbó portraits during my childhood, had become one of the magnates of the Cuban
sugar industry thanks to his merciless exploitation of a cheap, abundant labor force: namely, the slaves. The way in which he amassed enormous capital over a few years reveals his harsh, authoritarian character, endowed with
the ambition and pride that go with power—a man entirely convinced of his
rights. As the owner of the San Agustín sugar refinery in the municipality of
Cruces, next to Cienfuegos, he also acquired numerous properties on the island and in the metropolis. We owe to the orderly habits of his son Antonio
the preservation of a real archive of documents—personal letters, bills,
checks, commercial correspondence, receipts, photographs—which would
enable a historian interested in the business practices and way of life of a
prosperous family of Spanish settlers in South America to unearth the ideology, beliefs, aspirations of the old sugarocracy and the impact on them of
the political vicissitudes of the colony, from the first independence struggles
and abolition of slavery to the events that culminated in the blowing up of
the *Maine* and the direct intervention of the United States. From the letters
sent to and from Cuba one can reconstruct Great-grandfather's hectic movements between Barcelona, Havana, and Cienfuegos; his decision to entrust
the care of the refinery and other interests on the island to his son Agustín,
while my grandfather-to-be Antonio and "little Trina" settled into their luxurious accommodations on their properties and estates in the principality of
Catalonia; his wife's numerous ailments, which she, Great-grandmother
doña Estanisláa Digat y Lizarzaburu, eased only by devout practices and religious feelings. The reader can get an idea of the effect the belated discovery
of these papers produced in me by leafing through the pages of *Señas de identidad* and, especially, the first chapter of *Juan sin tierra*. The family myth,
carefully nourished by my father, vanished forever after the naked revela-
tions of a world of abuse and robbery, outrages hidden behind pious phrases,
excesses and violence beyond belief. A constant, repressed feeling of guilt, an

obvious residue of a long-since defunct sense of Catholic morality, was added to my already heightened awareness of the iniquities of Spanish society and the irrevocably parasitic, decadent, and vacuous world to which I belonged. I had just discovered Marxist doctrine and its detailed descriptions of the crimes and privileges of the bourgeoisie matched perfectly the reality evoked by those faded bundles of letters.

That is how at the age of twenty-three or twenty-four I became a fellow traveler of the clandestine Communist party—coinciding, to be true, with one of my father's financial disasters, which brought us to the brink of ruin. My decision owed as much to a hasty reading of the pamphlets and books that began to circulate undercover in Spain as to the conclusive evidence I found for their theories in the daily life, history, and ups and downs of my own family. I then lived through the Cuban revolutionary process, which was initiated a few years later. It was a liberating experience, historically sanctioned by the past crimes of my family, and my enthusiastic participation would soon help me to cast off my heavy burden of guilt. The letter included in the last chapter of *Juan sin tierra* is authentic although I made a few changes in transcription to adapt it to the novel. I still retain others that are equally wounding and accusing. Without any wish to labor the matter, just to arouse the emotions that they stirred in me, I will copy those whose eloquence will free me of the need to comment.

Cienfuegos, Sep. 5, 1873

Dear Don Agustín Goytisolo

Dear master, this letter is to inform you that yesterday the 24th i gave young Agustín 300 gold pesos to give me the letter and he say that he can't give it me i no use to you because of my illness as your honor know and i hope your honor speak to him about this i with Vizente and he keeping me, paying my sickness costs and i hope your honor tell young Agustín to give it me to see if I move somewhere else where i get better since i very sick and if your honor want to make sure of this just ask people you can trust in nothing more to say may god bless you, little Trinidad and the rest of your family, your servant Factora Goytisolo.

Remember your honor that you promised me the letter and when i see how your honor delayed i got into debt but they still not give it me. I not know what to do and if you want me work in the fields and sleep on the ground you tell me that be my reward for toiling i hope and hope you and the Virgin of Charity will send me the letter your servant girl F. G.

Cienfuegos, 30 July 1882

Dearest sir with the deepest sense of sorrow i write to give you the sad news of the loss of your beloved black Cándido, my beloved husband, who passed on to a better life on the 23rd of this month and just as the loss of his likeable character has plunged friends and family into terrible grief i am convinced that you will suffer equally and i beg you to pray for him and to this end i put myself at your disposition and pleasure May God preserve you for many years
Ceferina Goytizolo

Cienfuegos, April 22, 1884

Dear Don Agustín Guaitisolo
My dear friend, I hope this letter find you and all your family enjoying perfect health and that your life is all happiness. Blessed be little Fermina Trina Luisita Josefita may God be with her for a thousand years and i give thanks to your son Agustín for the favors he bestows on me in a misfortune which befell me and from which he, after God, has saved me and please call your servant who would much rather see you than write to you and please answer this letter so i may kiss it in place of yourself who is not my master but my father.
Vicente Goitisolo

But I am anticipating a reading that took place many years later. During the summer holidays in my early school years, the glorious past of my father's family was centered above all on the rather faded tobacco-colored photographs that were evidence of their magnificence and splendor. The scenes of the refinery—the sugarcane train with the Goytisolo and Montalvo nameplate, its trucks ready for the crop, the sugarhouse and the stores, the dwellings of the blacks, the machine room where the sugar was purified—and

Great-grandfather's substantial possessions—the Cienfuegos mansion, the sumptuous Moorish residence he had built on the Barcelona Ensanche, his establishment on the Plaza de Cataluña at present owned by the Bank of the Basque Country were graphic proof of a greatness that even if faded could confer and still did confer on my father an immanent sense of superiority. The bound collection of the old *Ilustración Española y Americana* with its wealth of prints of the period, engravings and daguerreotypes, contributed to the development of my simpleminded fantasies within the parameters of space and history that framed the family epic. The colonial images of Cuba, the rebels' clothes and appearance, mass farewells to the volunteers embarking for Havana are an integral part of a kaleidoscope of memories that are closely linked to my childhood. The myth of Cuban adventure would thus assume for me, until adolescence erupted, the form of a paradise lost, of an Eden glowing before my eyes only to vanish afterwards like a mirage.

In Cuba Grandfather Antonio had married the daughter of rich settlers of Anglo-Menorcan origin: the sweet, pure, distant Catalina Taltavull y Victory whose puberty portrait reveals a melancholy resignation to her fate. After selling off the West Indian heritage, the Taltavulls also settled in Barcelona where my grandmother's brother led a life of ostentatious leisure that was heavily criticized by the parallel branch of the family. In *La Habana para un Infante difunto* Guillermo Cabrera Infante, while listing the inhabitants of the block of flats in which he was brought up by his parents and brother, mentions an Afro-Caribbean called Tartavul who must in reality have been a Taltavull descended from some slave belonging to my other paternal great-grandfather and entered in the register under his master's name as was the custom at the time. These Goytisolos and Taltavulls still exist in Cuba and my brother José Agustín was photographed with one of them who by chance bore the same name as me. In 1962 during a brief visit to Trinidad's villa, near Cienfuegos, I heard of another Juan Goytisolo, famous for his magical arts, who had just taken refuge in the hills apparently fleeing the fury of some husband he had deceived.

It is much easier to reconstruct the Barcelona life of my Basque-Cuban family: one can add to Grandfather Antonio's well-organized documents

and letters the decanted memories of the peaceful summertime reminiscences of my father, his brother Leopoldo, and sister Catalina in the house in
Torrentbó. From their endless gossip in the garden or on the verandah, I
know that my great-aunt Trina, a formidable mustachioed Catholic spinster, who looked like a guardsman according to Leopoldo, lived surrounded
by a small band of curates and canons. They accompanied her in her life of
leisure and benefited from her generous charity. In their decorative lapdog
role, they would come to her society gatherings, give her an arm when she
crossed the street and obsequiously hold her sunshade. In this way, Uncle
jokingly concluded, these pious leeches inherited all her wealth when she
died. Aunt Catalina would pretend not to hear his comments and, stretched
out on her eternal chaise longue, would mumble and count her rosary beads.
The useless, extravagant life of Great-uncle Juan Taltavull was also the object of much comment and speculation: on one occasion in a typical fit of
megalomania he had reserved a special train for his guests in order to enter-
tain them in his luxurious mansion in Caldetas. He and Aunt Angeles had
lived a leisurely life on their income and, as this diminished, they gradually
sold off their property until they reached the uncomfortable, if not desperate, state in which I met them: imprisoned in a huge elegant flat on the Ram-
bla de Cataluña, incapable of sustaining the extravagant follies to which, in
their misfortune, they had become accustomed. Both died after the war and
I only met two of their four children: Aunt Mercedes and a male, Juanito,
who followed in his father's erring footsteps to the shame and scandal of his
family. In the dining room at Torrentbó hung a child portrait of Great-uncle
Juan ridiculously dressed in a tight jacket and dark underpants, seated on a
kind of red stool or bench: his furtive, scowling expression, the solemnity
and effort on his face, the suspicious nervousness of his position could lead
an evil-minded observer to suppose that the artist had caught him in the
humble act of defecation.

    The figure of Grandmother—parallel and symmetrical in the unchang-
ing order of pictures that decorated the room—in no way resembled him.
Catalina Taltavull reveals the image of a gentle, delicate adolescent girl,
condemned by the patriarchal code of the society in which she lived to the

shadowy existence of a faithful, obedient partner, the victim of a relentless succession of births that would prematurely destroy her life. Grandfather Antonio made her pregnant with great regularity and she left him ten heirs, both male and female, when she died in childbirth at the age of thirty-seven. As a widower, her husband devoted himself with Christian resignation to the careful management of his wealth and the strict upbringing of his children. While his brother Agustín took over the patrimony in Cuba and sold off the Cruces refinery, which was costly and unproductive after the great political and economic changes wrought by the independence struggle and the North American invasion, he spent his time maintaining an elevated social position against the gradual erosion of time and the changes in his fortunes, since he lacked his father's drive and infallible business sense. A large part of the correspondence at the beginning of the century is taken up by relations with Cuba. One letter from his lawyers just after the end of the war with the United States gives a revealing insight into the state of mind of one segment of the wealthy classes after the shock of Spain's defeat and the threat of radical revolution led by the rebels: "even when the country is being slowly rebuilt and there are still many hotheads talking of machetes and gunfire and terrifying children, the positive fact remains that the country is advancing. Large companies are changing hands every day and foreign money will soon revive life and well-being in the fields of Cuba watered by so much blood and tears. Whatever the future of the country politically speaking, if the Americans intervene one way or the other in its destiny, it will prosper."

Although the exchange of letters with Cuba becomes infrequent after the division of property between the two brothers, the documents concerning Spanish life still present considerable interest. They allow us to re-create the daily existence of a wealthy, conservative, rigidly pious émigré back from South America. His behavior, feelings, and ideas fill me and have always filled me with deep antipathy. His proverbial miserliness—vouchsafed by all who knew him—allowed only one exception and that was in the sphere of religion. When Uncle Leopoldo commented that he preferred to spend his money on parties and mistresses like Uncle Juan Taltavull to ruining himself as "others" did for love of the Church, the dart was clearly aimed at this wasted largesse. Such exceptional generosity was not altogether disinterested: like a good merchant's son, he pursued a rate of profit that if not immediate and tangible was at least metaphysical. In payment for his faithful, assiduous service to the ecclesiastical cause, Pope Leon XIII had deigned to grant a plenary indulgence *in articulo mortis* to him, his relatives, and descendents for three generations. The certificate bearing his photograph, stamp, and signature gleamed pompously from its frame on the wall at Torrentbó. Although one can echo my uncle's rather pedestrian view that absolution of sins, whose benign cloak protected me (whatever my crimes) from the punishment of hell, must have cost him a small fortune, the tremendous rewards of eternity were infinitely more worthwhile to a believer like my grandfather. To secure eternal happiness for oneself and for one's family assumed the proportions of a highly profitable investment. The rigidities of a favorable social system were extended beyond the present like the paradise dreamt of by Egyptian nobles buried in the Valley of the Dead, whose hypogea contain the most beautiful drawings of the life of plenty— flowing with food, drink, servants, and offerings—that awaits them when they depart from this world. To reproach him for such foresight—a real insurance policy against death for himself and his family—would be superfluous and unseemly and a shocking example of ingratitude.

Grandfather's severe, haughty character, his sad life as a widower, the insistence with which he submitted his sons and daughters to the rigors of a harsh, religious education are clear from his correspondence with them during their years as boarders with the Jesuits or nuns of the Sacred Heart. The religious manuals of the time, which were compulsory reading for my aunts and uncles during their summer holidays, reflect a curious Manichaean conception of the world divided between God and evil, much closer to Genesis than to the Gospels, and are far more revealing than any analysis of the ultramontane thought of our ruling classes during the Restoration. A much-handled copy of a *Prayers to St. Joseph*, which I just happen to have with me as I write these lines, meticulously gathers together a series of miracles in which Divine Justice fulminates indiscriminately against freethinkers, blasphemers, trade unionists, Republicans, masturbators, and enemies of the Pope: "In one town there was an example of Heaven taking revenge. At about midday the priest was taking Holy Communion to a sick man. After leaving the church he walked in front of an inn where there were three men seated at a table. Two got up and took their hats off as they saw the most holy sacrament. The third man, rather than imitating them, began to mock them, and, as an example of his courage and wit, he blasphemed horribly against Jesus Christ and the Virgin Mary. Hardly had the wretched man uttered his blasphemy than he fell unconscious to the ground in the presence of his terrified companions. A doctor was called, so was the parish priest, but all to no avail: on three separate occasions the priest came to confess the dying man, but always in vain. That blasphemy was his last word on earth. He shook with horrible convulsions for ten hours; delirious, he cut his tongue with his own teeth and then expired. . . . Another individual who was very fond of reading immoral newspapers saw his daughter, dressed in white about to go to a neighboring village where the bishop was administering the sacrament of Confirmation; flew into such a rage that he tore off her veil, snatched away the bouquet she was carrying and shut her up in a room. After a few days a wild horse ran through the village without hurting anyone, went in the thoughtless father's house, knocked him down, and stamped on him till he was dead."

A man of order worried by the convulsions that shook Barcelona on the eve of the *Semana Trágica*, my grandfather enthusiastically supported the repressive policies of Antonio Maura against the agitators and revolutionaries who dared to disturb the social order. I recently found among his papers a letter, dated the first of February 1904, on the official stationery of the President of the Council of Ministers in response to my grandfather's of which there is unfortunately no copy. Maura thanked him sincerely for his kind support: "From the growing number of letters of encouragement which I receive daily from people of all social classes, I can see that upright moral public opinion is gaining ground and this spurs me on to finish the work I have begun." This unholy exchange of opinions between my grandfather and the grandfather of my friend, Jorge Semprún—as I said to him when I shared this amusing find with him—would perhaps have been interpreted by Santiago Carrillo, the former general secretary of the Spanish Communist party, if he had known of it when Semprún broke with the Party and I unwittingly became involved through a letter I published in *L'Express*, as a distant antecedent of our evil alliance aimed at undermining the unity of the organization and the morale of its members. This surprising link between the two grandfathers—seen after an interval of almost eighty years from the privileged vantage point of our different political experience—strikes me as one of those chance events in history that often lead people to believe in the presence behind the scenes of a sly, mocking genius skilled in the art of paradox and the subtle use of irony.

In the second decade of the century the correspondence decreased in size till it dried up completely. Grandfather's final years in his mansion on Majorca Street are thus lost to the realms of conjecture and gossip: the university studies of his elder sons, marriages, summer holidays in Torrentbó, the slow, implacable decline from wealthy patrician to greedy, mean financier, reduced by the natural inertia of life to an empty, decorative existence. The date of his death coincided with the betrothal of my father and apparently delayed for a few months the celebration of the wedding. The classic family cycle of success, splendor, and decline, already evident in his old age, must have filled him with bitterness and anxiety. The sharing out of his still considerable fortune among his ten sons and daughters, and their lack of ambition and fighting spirit, augured a difficult period of uncertainty in an era characterized by social mobility and political upheavals. When the bond that held them together disappeared, his heirs would quickly disperse: their coexistence in the anachronistic mansion, already dwarfed by the surrounding flashy apartment blocks of the Ensanche, would soon become expensive and useless. While some married and set up homes, others, like Leopoldo, Luis, and Montserrat, sought out pleasant modern flats suited to their tastes and needs. The Moorish villa was sold and soon disappeared under the demolition gang's hammers, swept away by the wave of property speculation in those years that would change forever the peaceful, romantic appearance of the city.

If any of my aunts and uncles played an important role in my childhood, most of them quickly disappeared or appeared fleetingly in the shadows like a group of bit-actors. My memories of Aunt Rosario, her husband, and her children are almost entirely bound up with my first experience of life, when their family and ours lived as refugees in the village of Viladrau during the war. I have a hazy picture of Aunt María, a widow with seven children: a visit with my mother to a rather Gaudí-style house in Dominicos Street in the upper reaches of Bonanova. I never met Aunt Magdalena: sick and neurotic, because of her protracted suffering, she had got addicted to drugs and died in a clinic when I was a child. Her brothers and sisters would avoid mentioning her and all I know about her I learned indirectly or in whispered conversations. I once discovered in Torrentbó a little book of hers much underlined in pencil: its title, *The Deceptions of Morphine*, suggests that it was recommended to her by a doctor during one of her cures. The work, which was supposed to warn of the dangers of drug abuse, included the "divine" Marquis de Sade in a strange list of famous addicts: so this first mention of the creator of Justine and Juliette reached me through that pseudomedical prose riddled with lies and errors. It had the predictable result of arousing in me a strong desire to get to know his life and work, which was portrayed with such unhealthy fascination by the horrified propagandist. Uncle Joaquín, who qualified as a doctor like Leopoldo, emigrated to Argentina before I was born, after his marriage had been roundly condemned by our family because of his wife's humble origins. Once there he devoted himself with sudden, unsuspected energy to an enormous cattle-farming enterprise until he made a fortune that elevated his economic status well above his brothers' and sisters'. The hardships of civil war and the shortages in the Republican zone supplied him with a pleasant opportunity to remove the stain on the family honor with regular shipments of food supplies to his father, brothers, and sisters who received them like water in the desert. He was given a hero's welcome when he, Aunt María, and our cousins arrived in the port of Barcelona in the late forties. The whole family came to embrace the ex-black sheep and my father, forgetting his active role in dispatching him to Patagonia, held him up as a paragon of virtue, an example to be followed. While he and his brothers struggled as best they could through the hard times of postwar Spain and the decline in their fortunes, the reviled Joaquín emerged strengthened from the test, an object of respect and admiration. My father, whose obsession with the dangers of Communism at times bordered on the pathological, encouraged us to make our fortunes far from Europe, learning from the experience and advice of Great-grandfather's worthy rival in the quest for glory and adventure. Uncle Joaquín and his wife took only moderate pleasure from their revenge and overwhelmed us all with their affection and simplicity.

Grandfather Antonio's younger offspring, Ignacio and Montserrat, also made sporadic appearances in my childhood. Ignacio was an industrial engineer and inventor of patented improvements to the railway system. During the war he had become a passionate supporter of Franco and had heated discussions with Leopoldo when the latter forecast the inevitable defeat of the Germans after the battle of Stalingrad. Montserrat belonged to an entirely different world from that of her brothers: with neither mother nor father, she adopted an independent, carefree style of life, the very opposite of the puritanical piety that had dominated her upbringing. She smoked, drank, was a pioneer of the Charleston, split skirts, and sunbathing before marrying, in her thirties, one Federico Esteve with whom she settled in Majorca before the Civil War. I remember them visiting the house in Pablo Alcover to ask my father (in his capacity as elder brother) for permission to marry. The marriage turned out to be very unhappy and, after years of suffering and humiliation, finally led to her ruin.

I will write later about Uncles Leopoldo and Luis and about Aunt Catalina: all three played their part in my life's development. The rest of the paternal stock—twenty or so cousins who included or include a Salesian father, an Opus Dei worthy, a missionary in Chad, and a Marxist worker-priest—will also emerge in these pages as required by the narration of the facts. While the idea of the family has for years ceased to have any meaning for me, the strangeness of our surname and a purely atavistic reflex action can explain my mania for consulting the telephone directories of the cities I visit in the vague hope of happening upon a remote member of the clan.

However, except for Mexico City and New York, I have never discovered any trace of distant relatives by this means. My connection with the Goytisolos, beyond the circle of my brothers and sister, has in the last decades been a product of chance: in the first place, there was a strange non-meeting with a Madame of my name in a Marrakesh hotel because of a telegram dated in Bordeaux from this most mysterious lady cancelling her and her companion's reservations on the same day as I arrived; this caused understandable confusion and the incredulous comment of the hotel manager convinced that the message was mine and that I was pulling his leg—"vous ne me ferez pas croire tout de même, Monsieur, qu'un nom pareil court les rues!" There was the equally unlikely but real, tangible poster advertising a Goitisolo brandy displayed, to my amazement, in a window in the Great Bazaar of Istanbul, by a Turkish trader who was a fan of Atlético Bilbao and an admirer of all things Basque. As I do not suffer from hallucinations and had not smoked kef, I only had to stand for a few seconds with my nose pressed against the shop window set out with Basque national flags before I was convinced that it was true.

IMPERCEPTIBLY, THE SIGNS *accumulate. Scattered insidiously, treacherously, at irregular intervals, as if spaced out deliberately to make it difficult for you to read them. Not just the physical deterioration you hardly notice in daily life, the greater efforts required in all the routines and petty rituals, not even the anger and surprise, the instinctive rebellion—quickly suppressed—when you are suddenly confronted with a faded photograph from your youth: rather the brutal blow that strikes, at a carefree, happy moment, smashing through plans and calculations, and delivers you without defenses to awareness of inevitable decrepitude.*

*You are driving, for instance, at daybreak through a quiet, luminous countryside, along a peaceful, almost deserted side road and have forgotten, in fact, as you later discover, that it is Friday the thirteenth and that you are also in French dé-*partement *thirteen: all of which anyone remotely superstitious could interpret, albeit mistakenly, as an act of provocation. You brake at the stop sign by the junction with the main Saint Rémy-Tarascon road in response to a call from a middle-aged individual carrying a battered old suitcase on the other side of the crossroads: he wants a lift to a nearby town and once you realize it's on your route, you cross the road, after a brief exchange of words, forgetting even to look left, and suddenly hear a violent screech of brakes, seconds before the crash reduces your car to a sad heap of scrap metal. You stagger out of your car, confront the truck driver's waxen face, contorted by fear, an innocent bearer of a warning from destiny and Arab into the bargain. You say a few soothing words to him in his own language and then listen as he stammers out—not at all surprised by the fact that this seemingly injured European speaks his language—a half-whispered recitation of the* Kulchi fi yid Allah *and other respectful formulas from the Scriptures interwoven with exclamations of thanksgiving. An unlikely dialogue on the glass-strewn* road. You don't yet feel any pain from the thumbnail that is hanging off, as you notice the indirect cause of the accident running off at top speed, suitcase on shoulder, and the shopkeeper at the crossroads lets you telephone the friend with whom you were staying and then pockets the price of the call without a murmur. Only confusion at your presence in this hazy, ghostly world, an object of the pity or idle chatter of the inevitable spectators, next to the aged, skinny figure of the helpless Moorish fruit-transporter who, after the shock, is also striving to establish the simple facts of the case—what damage, whose responsibility, the need to inform his boss, while you await the arrival of the police.

Or fifteen months later in the course of a sentimental journey to a region you have written about, after visiting the lonely, rural landscape, the setting for the plot of one of your novels, returning to the spot as the guilty man always revisits the scene of his crime, engulfed by a noisy, high-spirited throng of fans who have come from every corner of the province to witness, like you, the cruel, expiatory ceremony of the penning of the bulls. You perch on the wooden barrier in the lower square in Elche de la Sierra, through which the beasts will soon pound with their retinue of oxen and farmhands to a chorus of shouts and exploding fireworks, running away, attacking, climbing, delighting, and exciting the motley crowd; you move away from the human swarm, walk on up the street with your friends behind the rear guard, toward the parish church, trying to predict from the screams and hastily beaten retreats when the horns will come back from the square, the fenced-off square where the bulls will be fought and executed hours afterward in the bloody, collective ritual: after a long wait, you go down a side street that has been barricaded off, deaf to the warnings of your friend from Albacete who knows the lay of the land better than you—the length of the walk to the church, the lack of refuge points and barriers over which to climb in case of dire necessity—intent on reaching the stockade where the bulls are kept: you get to the opening onto the square and from the gap in the upright, wooden palisade, assess the difficulty of clambering in without drawing the attention of one of the animals, which already excited by the exploding firecrackers and the noise of sticks and clubs is pawing the ground, gazing stubbornly at the exit, anxious to attack, break through, and take revenge on the wily gang of boys who mock and mistreat it; you look for a safe place on your left as the beast lowers its head, charges quickly at the opening in the *fence, and thunders past the farmhands, you hear the cries of terror when it catches one of them in full flight, throws him on the floor, gouges the body with its horns, and then abandons him for dead, facedown, and continues its outraged chase; again you hear the uproar announcing the second bull and notice your neighbors sneak away and climb up the barricades on the right, hauled up by the people above them, for a second time, you cling rashly to the left corner, trapped between a wall and the vertical logs of the barricade; suddenly realize that the bull has crossed the opening and instead of moving forward to attack those speeding off into the distance, it has turned round and is squaring up to you, barely two meters away, it stares at you for endless moments, just time for you to consider calmly, in pure amazement, the unthinkable situation you are in: your back to the corner, no way of getting over the barricades, aware of the absurdity of the scene, in suspense, your mind in a thick fog of disbelief; you try slowly to move toward the gate, con-vinced it is impossible this is really happening to you, that you are the protagonist in some sort of daydream, the usual, nightly, opaque, exhausting, persistent night-mare; yet you feel the blow from its head that knocks you down, drags you on your face across the ground, all notions of time and place disappear, seconds, unimagin-able seconds, no panic, no pain, no anxiety, only, only, only an overwhelming sense of unreality; you then hear a friendly cry, your name howled rather than shouted out, moments before anonymous hands pull you up by your arms, sit you up, res-cue you; as you look up, you can see Abdelhadi between the horns of the bull, hoisted up like an empty carton by the furious beast, about to be flung backward by a toss of its head until, whipped by youths after a brief, spectacular fall to the ground, the animal gets up, forgets your savior, half turns and races, enraged, after the gang. There is movement, concern, belated, untimely offers of help from those huddled around you and Abdelhadi; you are almost flown through the air to the nearby first-aid post, both wanting with the wounded pride of someone who has just tripped in public to stop people from taking pity, to be removed as quickly as possible from their curious gaze; you grasp at once, far from the surrounding bus-tle, the grotesque, comic twist of fortune that has hit you on exactly the same day as a wretched spur-of-the-moment torero died impaled on a bull's horns in the ring at Albacete in front of millions of future televiewers; you are determined to hide this humiliation from Monique, especially from her, before it is consumed,*

digested, exorcised, days, weeks, months, or years later, thanks to that slow, grad-
ual, internal process leading secretly to the act of writing; you are identified,
treated, your bumps and bruises disinfected with Mercurochrome and cotton and
like sleepwalkers acknowledge the admiring homage of a corporal in the Civil
Guard, witness to the accident, who slaps Abdelhadi on the shoulder several times,
tries in vain to communicate with him, and then turns to you and clumsily for-
mulates his compliment: your friend, though an Arab, is noble and brave.

Just like a frustrated mother after an unwelcome miscarriage wishes to over-
come her trauma and impatiently searches for a suitable opportunity to become
pregnant again, you suddenly feel in the bedroom where you are recovering from
the blow the violent urge to write rise up after months of sterility, the urgency and
need to write, express yourself, not to allow all that you love, your past experience,
emotions, what you are and have been, to disappear with you, determination to
fight tooth and claw against oblivion, that black abyss with open jaws that lies in
wait, you well know, around any corner, to capture the precious gift of life, the
human miracle, the reluctant concessions of existence and reality, you delight in
your five senses' confirmation that the daily portent is being extended, that a
chance postponement allows you to be yourself, sudden, repeated floods of mem-
ories, flashes in the pan, snapshots, will-o'-the-wisps, an intoxication with seeing,
touching, smelling, stroking, evoking the past, History, histories, the linking of
facts, imponderables, circumstances that have changed you into this misused body
stretched out on your back on the bed in the narrow room where you are staying,
a moment relived now almost two years later at the touch of a pen when you begin
to order your impressions and feelings, shape them on the blank page, abridged
reminiscences, like waves breaking, subject to your wandering memory, impera-
tive to tell others and yourself what you were and are not, whom you might have
been and have not become, to clarify, correct, complete the reality elaborated in
your successive fictions, the single book, the Book you have been creating and re-
creating for twenty years and as you invariably note, at the end of each of its chap-
ters, that you still have not written.

T HE SHADOWS AND darkness on my mother's side are even deeper. Grandfather Ricardo rarely mentioned them and Grandmother Marta's confidences, heard as a child, have largely been erased from my memory. I know for certain that my great-great-grandmother was Andalusian, was called doña María Mendoza and wrote a novel, *The Silver Bars*, inspired by the stories of Sir Walter Scott: we kept a copy of the book bound in red in the house on Pablo Alcover Street but my curiosity never tempted me to read it. There was also a portrait of her, a lady of severe, majestic appearance, although infected by the gift or insane desire to write. Novel and portrait disappeared when my father died or perhaps before, victims of the confusion of those years; furniture and belongings were moved from the house and the family scattered everywhere. The vestiges of the past were annoying interferences in my youth and it was only later that I thought again about that possible, distant, genetic transmitter of the literary vocation that would mark my life and my brothers'. Who was she, what was she like, why did she write? And other such questions, unanswered and lost in the limbo of oblivion.

When I was three or four I did see my great-grandmother, her daughter-in-law, in her mansion in Pedralbes: she was dressed in mourning and wore yellowish, perhaps dyed, ringlets above her ears. Her name was Pastor, she came from military stock and had been widowed by José María Vives y Mendoza, a notary with humanist leanings. This great-grandfather possessed a historical-military library, some volumes of which—Latin dictionaries, an illustrated chronicle of the *almogávares*—ended up in our house. Grandmother Marta used to tell us stories from the career and service record of members of the family, and describe her feelings as a child when the cor-

net sounded and the guard formed to welcome their arrival at the barracks.
Her family's legalistic, military traditions had, however, very little in common with the anomalous, rebellious, Catalan nationalist attitudes of her
brother, the poet and translator Ramón Vives Pastor. My great-uncle Ramón, as I indirectly discovered much later, had led a bohemian existence in
his youth, dedicated to literature, dandyism, and dissipation. Contemporary
accounts present him as a skeptical, passionate character: his Catalan version
of the *Rubáiyát* of Omar Khayyám is dedicated to his lover, the Irish Bertha
St. George, *filla tristoia i dolça d'aquella verda Erin, esclava, com ma terra, d'una
llei opressora*. The translation, based on the one by the French Orientalist and
diplomat M. Nicolas had a prologue by Joan Maragall and includes some
lines that I used to read with enjoyment through discreet recourse to the dictionary when at the end of my schooling I began to lose my religious faith:

> I sent my soul far to the Invisible
> to search out the message from the After-life:
> And soon my soul calmly returned
> to tell me: I am my own Heaven and Hell.
>
> Woman: I don't want your prayers. God will
> have his way without them, and the power
> of his forgiveness and pity, vast like the ocean,
> will cover over Omar's great sins and not notice them.

His hostility to religion and militant nationalism must have caused a
scandal even in the liberal, cultivated milieu where he was brought up.
Grandmother Marta often spoke of him: the jokes he used to play when they
were children, his trip to Geneva where he went in search of a cure for the
tuberculosis that would drag him years later to the grave. He had thrown a
piece of paper on the ground there, in the middle of the street, and a passerby
had reproached his carelessness, unworthy of a civilized country, and invited
him in a friendly manner to pick it up. It is one of the few anecdotes I remember and was always accompanied by the comment: the Swiss are very
clean and tidy. Some of his books were on the shelves in the bookcase in the
hall in Pablo Alcover, in French, Castilian, and Catalan: a beautiful edition

of *La regenta* was among them. There was also a pile of folders full of his manuscripts. With the cruel indifference of a child, I had used the blank side of the pages to draw and scribble, so condemning his dramatic works to destruction and to oblivion. When I think now of my action, it surprises me to realize that, even in my unconscious state, I was capable of such a lamentable deed: of dealing a crushing blow to the precious object of his efforts and reducing to ash the testimony and justification of one life. But, incredibly, at home we hadn't been inculcated with the slightest respect toward his writings. Apart from Grandmother's string of family anecdotes, nobody referred to him, from which I deduce an attitude of reproving caution. Those who knew him—my mother, Aunt Consuelo—had died or kept a prudent silence like Grandfather. As for my father, I know that he professed a frank, stubborn antipathy toward him. His Catalan nationalism and bohemianism were in direct opposition to my father's traditionalist convictions, his attachment to the Basque region and liking for patriotic values; then there was the irrational ingredient, the suspicion voiced on several occasions, times when he was looking for a universal cause for calamities and misfortunes, that Great-uncle Ramón had been the source of the tubercular meningitis that had killed my brother Antonio at the age of seven, before I was born. This fact, and his unrestrained dislike for Grandfather Ricardo for reasons that I will later reveal, explain why his relationship with my mother's family was at best cold and distant. The work and memory of Ramón Vives were damaged beyond repair in that domestic atmosphere traumatized by the disaster of war in years of vertical salutes and imperial language, attachment to religious norms and eternal essences, a sacrificial victim of circumstances in which the mere mention of his name was upsetting, and they were abandoned unprotected to the caprice of an irresponsible, ignorant child. My unhappy contribution to his second death fills me today with sadness and embarrassment. Little, very little, survives of the work of this rebel thrust by an untimely birth into a society traditionally hard on dissidents and whose harsh therapy in times of crisis would find an unfortunate complicity within the heart of his own family. His *Notes poetiques*, subtitled *Poesia es llibertad*, printed at the beginning of the century, have never reached my hands and I know nothing about them apart from the odd passing reference by his nephew, my mother's first cousin, Professor Josep Calsamiglia. In spite of that, the few details I have to construct his history and character convert him into one of the few ancestors with whom I feel affinity and a moral closeness beyond the fortuitous, uncertain ties of blood, an affinity stained in his case with remorse and melancholy. The writing destroyed and torn to shreds by me as a child has perhaps unconsciously infected me and insidiously emerged in all I have written and write. Whether true or not, the idea of that possible transmigration consoles me for my unredeemable action, which it transforms into a rebirth if not a gentle form of afterlife.

The same aura of mystery envelops the life and personality of my Aunt Consuelo. My mother's younger sister was also blessed with a luminous beauty; her expression, captured in a number of photos, reveals a defenseless fragility barely disguised as modesty and charm. She was fond of the violin and had lessons in interpretation until she could play tunefully. She wrote a delicate poem on Maurice Ravel, which was published in the magazine *Mirador* and jealously guarded by Grandfather among his papers. Her records of Bach, Mozart, Schubert, Brahms, Debussy, preserved in an album that came to us after the war, put me in contact for the first time with the peaceful realm of music; but, although she died when I was nine years old, I never got to see her. Before I was born, she had married the lawyer Eusebio Borrell and was widowed without children. This short-lived marriage and the nature of the disease that finished off her husband were never mentioned in the family circle. A portrait of the couple, taken in front of one of the monuments of the first Universal Exhibition, I'm not sure whether on San Juan Avenue or in Citadel Park, reveals him as one of those individuals with bland, shrinking features who, for some mysterious reason, are so plentiful in the ranks of the petty bourgeoisie of Barcelona. As a result of his premature death, Aunt Consuelo had gradually lost her sanity. When I began to open my eyes and notice what was happening around me, she never came to our house and was probably already confined to a nursing home. During the civil war, her parents took her into the flat where they sought refuge after the militia requisitioned the Pablo Alcover mansion. There, the bombing raids of Franco's

planes, sirens, terror, shortages swept away her last traces of lucidity. After
the conflict, she was shut up again and died soon afterward of an illness the
nature of which I am ignorant. I can only remember her funeral, which I attended with my brothers and sister, wearing a black arm band. Although
Uncle Eusebio's family lived in the same district of Bonanova where we were
brought up, and we passed his house daily—a dark, damp villa at the top of
Anglí Street—on our way to the Jesuit school, for some unknown reason we
had no contact with them. My grandparents referred to the other mother-in-
law by the nickname of Shorty and the pejorative character of the term
added to this strange distancing suggests that some bitter, unresolved con-
tention existed between the two families. Were there also political motives,
linked to possible Catalan leanings or the possibility, suggested by my father,
that Uncle Eusebio had passed on to his wife some shameful, incurable disease? Again as in the case of Ramón Vives, the erosion of time and death of
contemporaries prevent any certain answer. When I read history books, the
intrepid sureness with which their authors establish what happened thousands of years ago produces in me an insuperable sensation of incredulity.
How is it possible to reconstitute a remote past if even the most recent past
appears to be sown with doubts and uncertainties? The darkness over the
destiny of a good part of my family illustrates perfectly to me our power-
lessness to discover and exhume after a few years the tangible reality of what
happened.

Grandfather Ricardo's branch of the family offers less variety and melodrama: originating apparently from the Ampurdán, it includes among its
members the lawyer and publicist Gay de Montellá, the author of a number
of works on legal matters. Who his parents were or what they did is a memory he took with him to the grave. Grandfather had two brothers, Víctor and
Laureano, whom I got to know before the war: they dressed with austere elegance and ceremoniously took off their hats as they entered the house. I
couldn't say, however, exactly when they died: both left family, and Aunt
Lola, the widow of one of them, used to visit us with her offspring in the forties. She was a baroque lady covered in cosmetics, whose figure is associated
in my memory with a world of porcelain jugs and tasselled lampshades. Her

children and nephews and nieces bore their difficult, precarious existence with dignity: but social decline hurt their pride and good manners. Grandfather was in their eyes the wealthy man of the family but, so far as I understand, they rigorously observed the rule against complaining or testing out his very doubtful feelings of generosity. These distant relatives gradually deserted the family sphere: the last time I saw them at home, at the end of my school career, was when they came to say hello on the pretext of the departure of one of them to seek his fortune in the kinder, more prosperous land of Venezuela.

The gradual, definitive eclipse of my mother's side was especially important for my brothers and me because of our future status as writers. To answer the question so often repeated in recent years of why don't we write in Catalan, I feel compelled to spell out the circumstances in which our life as a family developed. While grandparents Marta and Ricardo spoke that language to each other, they addressed us in Spanish on the express instructions of my father. Although Grandmother had taught us some nursery rhymes and often mixed up expressions and phrases from both languages, at home—with my father and Eulalia—and at school—in class and with friends—we only used Spanish, an impoverished, diluted Castilian as I later discovered, when I extended the circle of my acquaintances and friendships beyond the insipid, conventional Barcelona bourgeoisie. Under strong pressure during the several years in which the "language of the Empire" had by decree to be cultivated, Catalan survived with difficulty in the intimacy of people's homes. A fruit of this would be my meagre knowledge of the language beyond the polite formulas, greetings, and swear words that I learned every summer from the Torrentbó peasants. Father, from the nirvana of his anti-Catalan phobia, would delight in contrasting the lineage, distinction, and euphony of the language of Castile—the resonant sonority of its toponomy—Madrigal de las Altas Torres, Herrera del Duque, Motilla del Palancar—with the plebeian coarseness of some grotesquely pronounced Tarrasas, Mollets, or Hostafrancs in order to round off his most singular course in comparative etymology and phonetics with the obligatory reference to the mysterious beauty of the term *luciérnaga* as opposed to the miserable obscenity of the local *cuca de llum*. For one reason or another, the truth is that my mother tongue—vanished forever with my mother—became with her death deeply alien to me: a language within which I would move uncomfortably and could hardly read fluently until, once I was established in France, I took the trouble to study it in my spare time in order to get to know its works without using a dictionary. Thanks to that effort I can now enjoy reading writers like Foix, Ferrater, or Rodoreda, but after almost thirty years of remoteness everyday common phrases do not spring easily to my lips.

In the present period of "linguistic normalization," my situation—like that of my brothers and a dozen or so friends and writers—is marginal, on the outside, in a double sense. In Madrid we are mistakenly thought of as Catalans, as Alberti is Andalusian, Bergamín was Basque, or Cela is Galician. But our colleagues and compatriots quite rightly do not welcome us into their midst to the extent that our basic activity—writing—links into a language and culture different from the ones they identify with. Spaniards in Madrid and Castilians in Barcelona, our location is ambiguous and contradictory, threatened with being ostracized by both sides and yet enriched through this mutual rejection by the precious gifts of mobility and rootlessness.

As proof, my own case: the inclination toward one or other language by a potentially bifid writer is not the exclusive result of individual free choice but rather the result of a series of social and family conjunctions that are grasped later. The early disappearance of my mother, the conservative, religious Franco-ist milieu in which I was reared, were no doubt essential factors in my insertion into a culture that, fifty years earlier, Uncle Ramón Vives had termed "oppressive." But, more significant than that historical determinism in favor of one of the languages in the field is, in my case, the passionate relationship I developed from the day when, far from Spain and Catalonia, I discovered that it was my true country and the object simultaneously of love and hate. My late passion for Castilian culture and language, already suffered by a series of writers who developed their masterpieces in conflict with them, by dint of bitter inner turmoil, was at once a lustral identity bath and defense mechanism against the emptiness of a lengthy exile. To say that I did not choose the language but that I was chosen by it would be the simplest way of conforming to the truth. The wavering between two cultures and languages is fairly similar to the child or adolescent's sensual and emotional indecision: dark, underlying forces will one day channel his future erotic orientation without his agreement. The blind impulse toward the male physical form will thus be as mysterious as the one that will lead him to fall in love forever with a language fit for Quevedo or Góngora. A choice that is all the more meaningful and valuable for being expressed in a forum or meeting of cultures, the clash of which implies ideas of crossbreeding, bastardy, and contingency. Castilian in Catalonia, Frenchified in Spain, Spanish in France, a Latin in North America, *nesrani* in Morocco, and a Moor everywhere, as a result of my wanderings, I would soon become that rare species of writer not claimed by anybody, alien and opposed to groupings and categories. The family conflict between two cultures was the first indicator, I now think, of a future process of dynamic breaks and tensions that would put me outside the bounds of abstract ideologies, systems, or entities always characterized by their self-sufficiency and circularity. The fruitfulness of all that remains beyond entrenched walls and fields, the vast domain of latent aspirations and silent questions, the fresh, unfinished thinking, the interchange and osmosis of cultures would gradually create the sphere in which my life and writing would develop, on the edge of values and ideas that were castrating rather than sterile, linked to the notions of creed, country, State, doctrine, or civilization. Nowadays, when Hispanic bluster daily reproduces celebrations of our artistic and literary glories in small, medium, or large regions of the land, the silence, alienation, and emptiness that envelop me and several others, far from saddening me, convinces me that the opposition loyalty/rootlessness in relation to language and country of origin is the best indicator of aesthetic and moral value fortunately beyond the reach of the organizer of Homages. Freedom and isolation will be the reward of the creator immersed to his eyebrows in a multiple, frontierless culture, able to migrate as he pleases to the pasture that suits him and without becoming attached to any. The intimate civil war of my sexuality and language, perhaps the prelude to my literary and phallic orality, was directed underground through the cultural conflict fought by my family. After the death of my mother, the ground was to remain clear, but the victory of Spanish, returning boomerang-like, occurred a good few years after my youthful dedication to writing: it was the work, not of an imagined parthenogenesis of Catalan, but of a temporary but necessary defense against the cunning Gallicist invasion. My stubborn conquest of a language intensely proud of its difference took place then in dialectical opposition to the fertile stimulus of other languages: without this dynamic interrelation with French, English, or Arabic at the rich crossroads of several opposed cultures, I would not have been able to contribute my modest, respectful homage to the Archpriest of Hita in the here and now of Xemáa el Fna.

Awareness of the *complete inanity of the enterprise:
amalgam of your motivation and inability to make up
your mind about your aim and would-be destination: a lay substitute for the sacrament of confession?; an unconscious desire to justify yourself?: to make a statement that nobody asks you for?: a statement for whom, from whom?: for you,
everybody else, your friends, enemies?: the wish to make yourself better understood?: to awaken feelings of affection or pity?: to feel yourself accompanied by
future readers?; to struggle against the oblivion of time?; purely and simply an ex-
hibitionist impulse?: impossible to answer these questions and yet attack the task,
the daily torture of confronting the page, putting your life on the drawing board,
the unmentionable material reality of your body, not the one hidden by masks and
disguises in daily ritual farce, projection of a false image aimed at the gallery, inopportune guest who usurps your voice and contracts it in the endless muttering
of a ventriloquist, no, the other one, which within hours, days, weeks, scared, bent,
on its knees, defenseless like a fetus, will repeat the sucking gestures and mannerisms, internal feeding, a polymorph of the distant maternal cloister, the silent, pro-
scribed truth, deprived of the power of speech, that other ego whisked out of the
sight of their neighbor or of themselves by those aspiring to the tinsel of fame,
spokesmen for future power reason dogma ideology, not daring to bring into public gaze their desires great or small, the misery, disloyalties that litter the sinuous
path of their lives with pebbles, competing for a History that excludes and destroys
histories, professional swindlers or bemedalled pachyderms, counterfeiters, at any
rate, of a past subject to considerations of long-term strategy of petty self-interest,
even if it is not submitted, when they take up their pen and strike the official,
hieratic pose of their glorious portraits to a merciless lobotomy operation. to
be distinguished from them, what they leave out, half-truths, two weights and*

two measures, forgetful memoirs, grotesque hagiographies, inner, private cen-
sorship in order to concentrate on what is most painful and difficult to express,
what you haven't yet said to anybody, an odiously vile or humiliating memory, the
bitterest blow in your life: to find in the internal resistance to laying it bare the
moral canon of your writing, that bull's horn that is not simply metaphoric but
real, as real as the one that dragged you along during the celebration of the
encierros, a metaphor, like those of Don Quixote, lived from within, not wind-
mill-giants nor basin-helmets, a total fusion of both levels in the material text, a
deliberately accepted risk of being turned over and gored, no outside sanction if it
is unfulfilled, only the wounding awareness of your infringing the rules of your
personal game, of not being up to the effort required, of throwing in the towel
half-way, pitifully unfaithful to yourself and everyone else.

S CENARIO: AN AGED mansion in the Bonanova district, number thirteen Raset Street. A house since demolished, the long, narrow garden of which was terraced down to the Vía Augusta, separated by an enormous ditch from the open stretch of the Sarriá train, between the Muntaner and Ganduxer stations. You remember its appearance because you often ran around there on the way to your schoolfriend's house: an ugly, ramshackle building, which is also preserved in some family photos taken before your birth. You do not, however, retain any memory of your stay there: according to your calculations, it must have been short, since at the age of three or four you had already moved to the Tres Torres, to number forty-one in a street to be rebaptized in the postwar period with the name of Pablo Alcover.

Time: date of birth was the fifth of January 1931. Although the exact time it happened is recorded on the certificate of baptism, you have forgotten and are not interested in finding out. It probably happened at dusk or well into the night: during your childhood your parents would say that you were a present from the Three Kings of the Orient and you thought you belonged to the day of the Magi until some public document straightened you out years later. As you don't have too much faith in the stars or in their possible influence over our destiny, this lack of precision on the moment you came into the world does not cause you any concern. Your Capricorn character is beyond doubt, and in some popular books on that subject you easily recognized various traits and elements of your character. But, instead of investigating the influence of the planets or giving yourself over to the electronic science of some Astroflash, you prefer to invent, like the Archpriest of Hita, a fantastic ancestor from Venus with the help of Al Biruni or Alí Abenragel. Cured of your father's obsession with distinguished lineages, you find it more pleasant to manipulate at will the jovial compilations of ancient astrological treatises. Venus-Zuhara, whose cheerful, libidinous patronage would mark with her stamp those born in lands of Islam, would be the best antidote against the obstinacy, self-absorption, and harshness of your official sign and a plausible explanation for the irreducible rigor of your dichotomy.

Prehistory: eventually restored through photographs seen in childhood and, sometimes, later lost from sight. In the first place, the wedding photo: unusual portrait of the couple who twelve years later would procreate you. He's standing up, wearing a morning coat, slim, mustached, incredibly young: no similarity to the sick, worn-out old man you would later know. She's sitting on a sofa, wearing a snow-white veil and bridal gown, caught in the glory of her unfaded beauty. The man's hand resting protectively on her shoulder. A serious, absorbed expression on the woman's face, perhaps distant or removed from the ancestral rite that she was fulfilling.

The wardrobe and mirror behind them both similarly reflect them from a tangent: the aquiline outline of the bridegroom, invested with a certain intellectual air by the light, metallic frame of his spectacles; the soft, gentle silhouette of the betrothed, captured in a pose whose daring spatial harmony we could describe as à la Velázquez were it not for the absence from the picture of the anonymous author of the photograph.

Surprise: the material nature of the love between those two beings, visible in the careful, punctilious trouble with which the portrait-painter, your father, fixes the serene beauty and expression of the eternally mysterious youthful woman, as if, foreseeing her sudden disappearance, he was unconsciously collecting proof of that future existence soon to be swept away.

Blurred images of the Torrentbó terrace, its eucalyptus trees, balustrade, pond with frog-mouthed fountains, the stone bench, the extravagant, rustic pavilion. Her, always her, still her, in half boots, long loose skirt, summer bodice and blouse, her carefully gathered-up honey-colored hair.

Sometimes, Pedralbes, with Aunt Consuelo in the enormous garden of orange trees or on the tennis court, radiant, confident, spontaneous, with a racquet in her hand, happy and windswept.

Later: the short-lived family trinity.

Antonio, the firstborn, thus baptized in Grandfather's honor, alone or with her, at the age of six or seven, in his blue-and-white sailor-suit, looking as if he has received Communion, just a bit proud and arrogant and, at a distance, fragile, awkward, unreal, retrospectively pathetic.

Enlargements dispersed by the monotony of time, framed in purple or grey card: images of the twenties, hoops, bicycles, toys, mutual affection, smiles, derisory testimony of the suddenly incomplete trio.

First experience of grief, to which your parents' loss of affection for and rejection of the loving practice of photography no doubt dates back.

THE OPAQUE LIMBO *of childhood: tunnel darkness broken momentarily by patches of light, fleeting images: fixed by chance in a tender, adaptable mind or simply a product of some later, now forgotten process?: an irregular, slow succession of black-and-white and color pictures painfully rescued from the mists of my dreams and then projected by a magic lantern: difficult to link them together in the right order, insert them in the place they happened and endow them with possible meaning: seminal nucleus of future memories or a passing impression captured in shadows?: avoiding, above all, tricks and traps, anachronisms that lie in wait, the temptation of a palimpsest interpretation: merely sifting the sparks of light, the voltaic arc created by the break in the electric circuit, picking them out of the shapeless, porous night caught in the bubble of their modest splendor.*

A parallel between the scarcity of the first images that you retain and your experience on the night when you absorbed an enormous dose of maaxún *dissolved in a glass of mint tea: sitting in a café by the fortress in Tangier, surrounded on your long trip by soothing cardplayers and the becalming aroma of kef while a ridiculous television broadcast a muted version of the political-cum-bullfighting disquisitions of an overweight announcer from your species. Nothing at the beginning except for waves, currents, rushes to the brain that either intermittently or in syncopation crossed its yielding surface, gently unifying it, as if under the burning breath of the sirocco. Awareness of the importance of the moment, the palpable material nature of the place, your central presence in the weft. Then, suddenly, a rapid, almost hurtling succession of literary images: similes, tropes, daring verse, dazzling, airborne metaphors, light feathery levitation, slow gliding, dizziness, furious flights. An ecstasy of concepts, sinuous baroque, captivating phrases, coiled up snakes: the creative paroxysm of someone who has scaled the peaks of poetic art but realizes the avaricious precariousness of his gifts. Then the metaphors overlap, rest on each other, combine with maddening rapidity, flow liquid through your fingers, rival Góngora's light subtlety: they appear, gleam, burst, mock your efforts at retaining them, drag you along with them tied to their tail. Attempts to set buoys, scatter pebbles in that feverish flux, gradually becoming frenetic, provoke only verbal collisions, semantic fractures, sudden derailings. Powerless, you will see how the brilliant display of words vanishes like a firework. Nothing, absolutely nothing, remains of it: sparkles, verses, genial inventions rush into oblivion. Your brain is present at the procession and constant replacing on its murky surface of dozens of miraculously forged masterpieces and, just like those overrefined dreams that hardly leave a tattered web when you wake up, so your fleeting control of the creative mechanism like the child's distant awareness of the adult world is reduced to a few words and images emptied of all meaning, mere indicators of a previous chain, now lost. The floating names of Góngora and Borges, rising up like small islands after an endless night beset by anguish and exultation; the childish remnants and snapshots, similarly free from context and seam, must be, in both cases, the sad vestige of impressions and facts whose extreme poverty completely rules out any attempt at interpretation.*

I MAGES FILTERED AS if through a skylight: you are sitting in the dark on the floor of a room, possibly under the dining room table, and, from your hiding place, you look at the adults moving about and talking in the kitchen, clearly visible, unaware of this future description of the scene and the tiny presence of an observer. The memory could perhaps relate to your first home in Raset Street or, more likely, to some family visit to Great-grandmother in her Pedralbes villa.

Summer holidays in Llansá: while he is swimming toward the small island or headland opposite, she sits on the beach reading a book or newspaper. You are playing with your younger brothers, you make sandpies and castles, you join in a neighbor's frustrated attempts to get going a kind of float that he has invented but it lets in water everywhere and finally capsizes. Neighbors' conversations around your mother: Mr. and Mrs. Isern, Pascualín Maisterra's parents, and, as you will discover later in Mexico, the family of Ramón Xirau, the writer.

Trips in the buggy with Ciscu as far as the Font de Gat in Pedralbes. Visits to the grandparents, Marta and Ricardo, in their house in the nearby Doctor Roux Street. The exact distribution of the rooms in your memory, the exact layout of the garden. Sometimes you sleep there and, when they take you to see your mother, who has just fallen ill with dropsy, you are told you have got a baby brother. You go into the room where the baby is sleeping and pinch him, unsure whether you are curious or envious, you want to be certain, you say, that "he's real."

You have learned how to feel yourself and, when alone, you usually slip your fingers along your groin and caress your penis. Once your mother caught you, gently moved your hand and told you that you shouldn't do it. The wet nurse feeds Luis and, often, if you bother her, she laughs, squeezes her breast and splashes you with her milk. One day, José Agustín and Marta dress you up in a big skirt and you enter the dining room in Pablo Alcover in the disguise; your father's reaction is unexpected and energetic: he pulls the skirt off you and smacks the guilty parties. Someone said you might die through lack of air. The idea terrifies you and for a few moments you take deep breaths in and out so as not to risk the same unhappy fate as Antonio. When you go to bed, you gasp and pray to the holy Guardian Angel asking him to protect you.

Your father has bought a grey DKW and is learning to drive in the Tres Torres district. His instructor tells him to pull the grey knob up and down and Marta and José Agustín laugh in the backseat: take your knickers off, put them on. You go to the convent run by nuns of St. Teresa's Order in Ganduxer Street built by Gaudí: Mother Delfina gives you sweets and, on the way home, maids and the girls accompanying the infants talk about Paquita Marín: a very beautiful girl, in a higher form at the school, who sings *Rocío*, flirts with the boys, uses powder and lipstick. Expressions of admiration and horror. Someone asks you if you want to be her boyfriend and you proudly say that you would.

Friends of the house: Ciscu and his buggy; Paquita the dressmaker; Miss María Boi. Family conversation about the English working week, the war in Abyssinia, Gardel's tangos. As you are being fussy over your food, your father puts you on a fruit diet: after the first minutes of euphoria, you are in tears demanding the previous diet. One day you go to Torrentbó in the DKW, sitting on the front seat on your mother's knee. As the car twists round the slope at San Vicente de Montalt, your father is distracted, momentarily loses control of the steering wheel, and crashes against a plane

tree. Your head hits the windshield, you suffer deep cuts on your skull, fore-
head, the bridge of your nose: scars that will mark you forever. A vague
memory of shouts, pain, your mother crying, the chemist's shop and chemist
who fainted when he saw you. The return to Barcelona, bandaged up, surrounded by toys and pampered: sitting on the floor, with your presents, you
have the pleasant impression of being king of the world.

The wooden chalet in the Gulf of Puigcerdá: the meadows, streams, cows,
unmistakable smell of cowpats and grass that would come back to you a long
time afterwards, in the Haute Savoie, during the shooting of a film written
by Monique. Walks through the town, the lake, the Cabrineti square, an ex-
cursion to the frontier spot of Bourg Madame. A Sunday Mass, the sermon
of which would be the object of mysterious commentaries. Uncle Ignacio
came to see you and you heard for the first time on his lips the sinister name
of the *rabassaires* and the ominous initials, FAI.

I N SPITE OF the atmosphere of disruption and agitation, my memories, which are confused until then, seem to get clearer and settle down at the beginning of 1936. My family lived in the house in Pablo Alcover and, while my mother went about her domestic chores, my father would leave very early in the morning for the ABDECA office—the Barcelona Gum and Fertilizer Company—of which he was the main shareholder and whose factory was in Hospitalet. After the trauma of Antonio's death, I think that both their lives followed a pleasant, calm routine. Marta, José Agustín, and I went to the St. Teresa school, and the Galician maid took over care and responsibility for Luis. To an outside observer, we were the typical bourgeois family of the time: an economy model car, involvement in a small industrial enterprise, a rented villa in the Tres Torres district, a brand-new chalet in an upmarket residential area in Puigcerdá. I cannot say for sure whether the comfortable, unpretentious channels of that existence corresponded to my parents' taste and aspirations. After getting a degree in the Chemical Sciences my father had sought a way to combine his undoubted talent and inventiveness in that field with a much more doubtful skill at running a business: unlike his brothers Leopoldo and Luis—the latter, handicapped by his deafness—he aspired to be a man of action, an offshoot worthy of the Cuban stock begun by the tough, tenacious lad from Lequeitio. Although I haven't any reliable evidence, I presume that things weren't going badly for him at that time: our style of life was not extravagant like that of the already bankrupt prodigals of the family, but probably suited its nature and needs. He really swung between two opposite extremes: a rather Prussian love for an austere, orderly way of life and an impatient thirst for fame, to rival grandfather's exploits, which swept away all the restraints and caution of his usual miserliness and led him to invest money rashly in absurd, risky ventures. His first forays into industry had worked successfully, but the world economic crisis and the violent unrest during the Republic soon caused him problems. At this time, in the key year of 1936, which opens the doors to my story, my father was, in purely social terms, a decent employer of longstanding right-wing persuasion, ready to ride out the storm that would finally be unleashed over the country with unprecedented violence to the misfortune of him and everybody else.

I think my mother's position is more problematic. Daughter of a family in which the liberal professions abounded, with a greater concern for the world of culture, she had adapted without any apparent difficulty to life with a man whose intellectual interests and ambitions were quite at variance with her own. The titles of housewife, model consort, mother of four were absolutely in line with all that traditional society represented by her husband expected of her but did not entirely fit in with her emotional sensibility and insatiable desire for books. The placid image of the still youthful woman with her elegant hairstyle, wrapped round with a fur boa, captured in a portrait in the passage in the Pablo Alcover house does not express in its hollow conventionality the deeper, more complex reality that is, however, revealed by the list of her favorite books. While my father was unaware of the existence of literature until the publication of my first novel, *Juegos de manos*, hit him like a cold shower, my mother, perhaps with the help of her uncle the poet, had created for herself a vast, out-of-the-ordinary literary culture. When at the age of nineteen or twenty I began, dictionary in hand, to explore the array of French books that made up her library, their content— plays, novels, memoirs, volumes of poetry—and the catalogue of authors— Proust, Gide, Ibsen, Anouilh—showed me the range of a passion that, in its turn, would have a decisive influence on my life. A new image of her as a secret, solitary reader, in a typical bourgeois household full of children shouting and constant to-ing and fro-ing, replaced the one made up till then of incoherent memories and shallow recollections. The young woman who gave birth to me, suckled me, looked after me, my brothers and sister, externally bound to her role as mother of a family, was she the same one who, as I would discover much later through the confidences of one of her cousins, had secretly written a text entitled *The Wall and Madness*, the morbidity of which made a strong impression on her?* What was the relationship between the two? How could the second, hidden existence have tolerated the pedestrian, mediocre life of the first? The compromise between the two must have been real, since I can see nothing to indicate that she endured marriage and domestic life as an annoying burden. She had probably fashioned for herself an inner, spiritual life where she could take refuge through writing and reading. My father and the rest of us were no doubt the pillar of her life: but it was a life with its hiding places, havens for rest and meditation, pleasant, protective shade.

The build-up of political, social, and economic factors that polarized the February election campaign from one end to another and gave an overwhelming victory to the Popular Front candidates must have shaken the foundations of my family's peaceful routine. My father was a Catholic monarchist with a gut opposition to Catalan nationalism not only to the radical branch of Macià and Companys but also to the moderate one of Prat de la Riba and Cambó: he had voted for the right-wing coalition of the CEDA as a lesser evil. I can remember the day when, after a Mass in the Josephine convent, I went with my parents to the local electoral college, situated in a house on the corner of Ganduxer, close to the Vía Augusta. As we went in, someone was giving out propaganda for the left-wing parties and my mother refused it in a dignified fashion. "He was really disappointed," they said afterward in the DKW. Unfortunately, I do not remember any detail of the intense months of agitation that preceded the military uprising and the outbreak of the revolution.

In June we went to our chalet in Puigcerdá and the adults' mood of anxiety impressed even a child my age. As I found out later on, my father had planned to send us to France in order to be able to defend his interests in the factory knowing that we were in a safe place but for some reason the plan was not carried through. Later on, the sick, ruined man inexorably associated in my memories with the Viladrau period would continuously lament this

*Mentioned in a letter to Monique written about 1962.

mistake that had had such disastrous consequences for the family. The closeness of the frontier, he would say, could have saved his wife from the destiny that awaited her. The idea that it would soon be over, that things would soon be sorted out, decided their return to the lion's mouth: bloody, gun-ridden Barcelona in the hands of the ideals and excesses of revolutionary struggle. On the return journey, a militia control stopped the car to inspect their papers and, after the brief questioning, my parents commented ironically that the group leader, when he got the identity cards, had looked at them upside down.

Days afterward we were in Torrentbó with my mother and the maid. Uncle Ignacio followed the course of events from there with his wife and children, but vanished one morning with his family after hurriedly hiding the holy objects from the chapel in an ivy hedge. On the surface things had not changed: we played in the garden, read "Mickey Mouse," said our prayers; only María's whispered words about the Antichrist and my parents' discussions hinted at the abnormal situation. Mossèn Joaquim, the chaplain from the church of Saint Cecilia in Torrentbó, sometimes came to see us. He was an open, friendly man who chatted to my mother on the verandah and, as he said good-bye, would give us his hand to kiss. Once, to our great surprise, he appeared in the house grotesquely dressed as a civilian, wearing a beret to hide his tonsure: he was going away, he said, and had come to say good-bye. My mother handed him some money and a parcel of food for the journey and, when she was wishing him good luck and he, in turn, was blessing us, I noticed that María was crying. Mossèn Joaquim disappeared into the depths of the wood and was not seen again by any of his parishioners. Although he had asked us to pray for him and no doubt we did, he was immediately caught as he tried to escape and died soon afterward, a victim of an extremist gang.

Our maid's apocalyptic prophecies were fulfilled: the last issue of "Mickey Mouse" had come out splashed in the black-and-red colors of the FAI; churches were burning one after another as under the Roman Empire. From the garden pavilion we observed the lorry of the "reds" parked next to Saint Cecilia, the thick column of smoke rising over the tiny white building.

Had someone been gossiping mischievously about our family chapel? Although the hypothesis, later formulated by my father, does have some grains of truth, the fact is that our chapel, completely visible from the place the arsonists were, would have been a tempting target without the need for any informers. Whether the result of a chance or careful planning, when minutes later the men from the lorry suddenly burst into our garden we were terrified. María was sobbing: her favorite book was a religious primer made up of biographies of child saints and perhaps she was inwardly flirting with the exciting possibility of approaching martyrdom. My mother, who had looked out of the window when the invaders got the farmers to open the chapel door, was ordered (at revolver-point) to withdraw to her living quarters. We took refuge on the verandah and listened to shouts, hammering, and voices. My mother kept us quiet and the maid was silently telling her rosary beads.

In spite of the fact that there are some dark spots and gaps in my memory of how this episode developed, I well remember the moment after the intruders left and we ventured into the garden to see the damage. The marble statue of the Virgin, the work of Mariano Benlliure, had been knocked down from the altar and was lying outside the chapel with its head knocked to pieces by a mallet. A variety of liturgical objects was still burning on a bonfire. In marked contrast to our sorrow, the farmer and his family were examining the destruction impassively, in silence.

The events I have just related took place in my father's absence. When he finally reappeared after we had waited in a state of nervous tension and anxiety, it was with an escort of two bodyguards: Clariana and Jaume. I found out later that they both carried FAI cards and, in exchange for a hefty reward, assured his physical well-being and freedom against the threats to which he was subject. Every day they went with him to the factory and, in Torrentbó, they slept in the house and watched over the peace and quiet of the family. Jaume was a nice, dark young man whose natural ways and open character at once won my heart. He always carried a revolver, which he showed to me and let me touch when he walked with me to the Lourdes and Santa Catalina wells. Alongside his kindness and patience with children, he enjoyed a curious, praiseworthy respect for the beliefs of others: one day he discovered the black box in which Uncle Ignacio, in his rush to depart, had hidden the chalice and paten in case of a possible militia raid. He informed my mother of his find and advised her to look for a better hiding place. This act of trust increased his standing with all of us. As for me, I think that for the first time in my life I experienced a passion that could be described without exaggeration as amorous toward someone totally outside my family. Jaume's presence, his warm simplicity, our wanderings through the wood, the immense prestige his revolver bestowed on him in my eyes, embellish the images of that summer full of changes and surprises until the day when, for some reason, we were forced to abandon Torrentbó and move into a more modest house in the neighboring town of Caldetas.

Was the position of the house the decisive factor in the move?—its isolation and vulnerability in those dangerous times was obvious. Or was it requisitioned, as I heard later, to accommodate refugees from the Basque country?* Whatever the reason, autumn passed in the house in Sentema opposite the small hot-water spa on the edge of the *riera*. Our new home had a terraced garden at the back climbing the slope of the mountain to the ruined tower of els Encantats. María Boi was still with us, but her untimely religious fervor in a period of furious anticlericalism worried my mother deeply. Had she tried to win us to the idea of martyrdom, as I was later told, or was there some other weighty reason to justify her sudden sacking? Although I cannot answer with any certainty the fact is that she vanished from our sight overnight. My mother aired her empty room and her only comment was that it smelt badly.

It was our first year without school and we spent most of the time in the garden or in the street. The effects of the war were still not evident at home: we had regular meals prepared by two servants. María was always singing *Rocío*; the other preferred *María de la O*. My mother taught me to read and I eagerly went through the geography books. One day, I was looking at the map of Europe with her and she asked me which country I preferred. I pointed at the enormous pink mass of the Soviet Union and she said curtly,

---

*According to a recent account by the farmer's son, José Antonio Aguirre, president of the Basque government, and his family stayed in the large house for several months.

"No, not that one." Another time, my father was visited by the committee that was running the factory: a group of five or six men who awkwardly kissed the "lady's" hand, talked a while very noisily, and then started drinking. When they left, one was tottering, and the lavatory was full of sickness. While my father apologized to his wife for the incident, she was indignant and I could hear them at a distance arguing loudly.

A few months passed and we returned to Barcelona. We were back at the house in Pablo Alcover where some foreign soldiers, probably members of the International Brigades, were lodging on the top floor. There I heard the whispered news of my father's arrest (why? by whom?) and his subsequent release thanks to the timely intervention of the trade-union leaders from his factory. They came for him at night, as he later told me, but he had foreseen the danger of the *paseos* and used to sleep in our grandparents' house, preferring to give himself up to the legal authorities. His stay in prison was brief, but he fell ill after he left. The doctors diagnosed pleurisy and he went into Dr. Corachán's clinic.

From then on we visited him daily with my mother, walking through the Tres Torres district. The clinic had an enormous leafy garden where we played for hours waiting for her to return from the room where they were caring for him. My brothers, sister, and I still didn't know how serious the illness was and, particularly, the method used to cure it: the infection of the initial pneumonia had forced the doctors to drain the pus from the pleurisy by putting a rubber tube between the pleura and an orifice in the ribs. For years, my father stayed in bed or was semi-immobilized by that terrible pipe sunk into his chest and leading to the glass jar into which his humors poured. This new image of my father was only imprinted on my memory in Viladrau; but, gradually, it spread to the one forged in my childhood—that of a man who was active although getting on and whose difference of age with my mother did not seem alarming—and destroyed it altogether. The admiration and respect I felt for him were thus damaged irreparably. The despondent, prostrate figure, hypostatically united to the pipe and the jar of pus, began to fill me with an unjust but real feeling of repugnance. Imprisoned by cotton wool, bottles of medicine, bandages, jars of fluid in a room

smelling like a hospital, that pathetic man in no way fulfilled my idea of a
father's role or acted as a possible source of support. Without recourse to hyperbole or any retrospective manipulation of the facts, I have long since
reached the conclusion that, months before my mother's departure, the protective family shell had begun to shatter around me.

The reason for our move to Viladrau also remains somewhat obscure.
The mountain air, no doubt recommended to my father by his doctors,
could provide one key. The growing difficulties over supplies in Barcelona,
the street battles between rival factions, the first bombings by Franco's
planes, and finally the presence there of Uncle Ramón and Aunt Rosario
could be other reasonable explanations to throw light on the choice of that
summer holiday village set in the skirts of the Montseny mountain. According to my calculations, we must have moved in the autumn of 1937: first to a
dark, damp villa, with a garden covered in yellow leaves; later, to a much
smaller house where we only occupied the top floor. The building was part
of a group of four houses that shared a garden: the owner, an octogenarian
smallholder who cultivated the adjoining land, would later be the butt of our
jokes and mischief. We had bid farewell to Conchita, and María Cortizo, the
Galician servant, cooked and did the household chores while my mother
acted as nurse and looked after us as best she could. Downstairs lived a
woman named Angeles, accompanied by her daughter: the former used to
complain to us about everything, especially the way she was persecuted by
her sister, Encarnación, a strong, stout woman, married to a Madrid taxi
driver and whose only son, Saturnino, looked abnormal because of slight hy-
drocephalus and a squint. Encarnación and her husband lived in the house
next door and one night we heard shouting and cries for help after which we
saw Angeles appear bleeding and dishevelled, blaming her sister for the attack. The rest of the neighboring properties were big villas with stone walls:
we soon stealthily penetrated one that was unoccupied; another one, which
took up a whole block, was the provisional shelter for the Archive of the
Kingdom of Aragon.

Our life in Viladrau that winter prolonged the holiday period that had
started a year and a half earlier. The shortages began to show their effects and

I remember my mother going round the nearby farmhouses in search of food. During my father's illness, the factory committee paid his salary regularly; but the money was gradually losing its value and as the war advanced and the situation in the Republican camp got worse, the ancient barter economy reappeared. We would go with my mother and brothers and sister to visit Aunt Rosario's family in her flat in the main square in the village or we would walk round the outskirts, taking the road to Espinelves, the path to la Noguera, or one of the shortcuts that curled down to the hidden springs nearby. We often got together to play hide-and-seek with other children in the spacious garden of the Bioscas' villa or we would go to their house for a Charlie Chaplin film show from a Baby Pathé projector. I can remember a soirée of film and poetry when someone pathetically inspired declaimed poems by Gustavo Adolfo Bécquer. At home, I read the illustrated stories my mother gave me and I began to draw and write "poetry" in an exercise book. My future career as a writer was thus inaugurated at the age of six: the lines poured out and, once adorned with my own scribbled illustrations, I was quick to show them to visitors with a precocious feeling of pride.

While I write these lines, I am trying to hold steady the few, faithful memories of my mother: the time she had an argument with father—I don't know why—and she wiped her nose with her handkerchief; the day I was feeling uncared for by her and I said that I would like to fall ill too, since she was entirely absorbed in caring for her husband, and, unable to restrain herself, she gave me the smack I deserved; the afternoon at my aunt and uncle's when I learned of the accident in which cousin Paco, Aunt María's son, had lost a leg, cut off by a tram while he was roller-skating: Aunt Rosario asked me to tell her only about "some bad news," without giving any specific detail what it was about and, while my mother got dressed and ran with me to her house, I selfishly enjoyed my momentary power over her gradually suggesting, in my own way, all I knew about the drama.

Until then the civil war and its disasters had distant, indirect repercussions on my awareness. The small colony of well-off Barcelona bourgeois lived in Viladrau provisionally on the margin of the conflict and maintained a public attitude of prudent neutrality. Only a few ironic comments—the obligatory reference to the fact that Bono, a well-known ladies' hairdresser who had also taken refuge in the village, was picked up weekly by an official car in order to do the hair and beautify the wives of government and *Generalitat* ministers—allowed one to read their real feelings. But, out of earshot of any indiscreet listeners, tongues would be unleashed. At night, we used to be visited by Lolita Soler, a woman in her forties, a gaunt spinster from a monarchist military family, who had lived the siege of Madrid before being evacuated to Catalonia to be stranded like us in that isolated mountain spot. Her bloodcurdling tales of murders, executions, deportations, heroic martyrdoms, recounted in whispers so that we children could not hear her, mingled with encouraging news of the other side's progress, which she apparently intercepted via a crystal radio on the Burgos wavelength. Her tribulations and adventures—which my family thought were exaggerated—aroused endless discussions in the dining room, which continued long after her departure. The precarious situation in which my grandparents lived, the helplessness of Aunt Consuelo, shut up with them in a flat on the Diagonal, the ever more frequent bombing of the city, intensified my mother's state of anxiety, and she was already overwhelmed by four children and a sick husband with no hope of a quick cure. In a letter, which my sister found years after, she told her parents of her fear and worry because of a lack of news after an air attack. Every two or three weeks she would get on the coach that took her to the railway station of Balenya and, after spending the day with them and doing a little shopping, she would return to Viladrau at night. These ever so brief visits did not stop her worries, however, and after several months they became a kind of ritual.

On the morning of March 17, 1938, my mother started her journey as usual. She left home at daybreak and, although I know the tricks that memory and its fictitious re-creations play, I retain a clear memory of looking out my bedroom window while that woman, soon to become unfamiliar, walked with her coat, hat, and bag, toward the definitive absence from us and from herself: destruction, emptiness, nothing. It no doubt seems suspicious that I should wake up precisely on that day and that, forewarned of my mother's departure by her footsteps or the noise of the door, I should have got up to watch her leave. However, it is a real image and for some time it filled me with bitter remorse: I should have shouted to her, insisted that she give up the visit. It was probably the fruit of a later guilt mechanism: an indirect way of reproaching myself for my inertia, for not having warned her of the imminent danger, and for not attempting the gesture that, in my imagination, could have saved her.

My memory of the frustrated waiting for her to return—my father's growing anxiety, our comings and goings in search of news to our aunt and uncle's house or to the village coach stop—is much more reliable. Two days of tension, anticipatory anguish, unbearable silence, visits from our uncle and aunt, Lolita Soler's sobbing, a round of whispered conversation in my father's room until that sad St. Joseph's holiday when the three brothers and sister were brought together on the outside staircase that descended to the garden and Aunt Rosario, with occasional feeble interruptions from Lolita Soler, told us about the bombing, its victims, how she too had been caught, very seriously injured, leading us gradually, like that bull that has just been stabbed by the *torero* and is now pushed skilfully by his team onto its knees so that the fighter can finish it off with one quick thrust, to the moment when, her voice drowned in tears, ignoring the other woman's pious protests, uttered the unutterable word, leaving us in a state of bewilderment not because of the grief immediately expressed in sobbing and wailing but rather the inability to take in the brutal truth, still untouched by the bare reality of the fact, and especially its definitive, irrevocable nature.

How her death happened, in exactly which place she fell, where she was taken to, at which moment and in what circumstances her parents recognized her is something that I have never known nor will I ever know. The unknown woman who disappeared suddenly from my life, did so discreetly, far from us, as if to temper delicately the effect that her departure would inevitably have, but thickening at the same time the shadows which would envelop her in the future and turn her into a stranger: the object of guesswork and conjectures, incomplete explanations, and doubtful, undemonstrable hypotheses. She had gone shopping in the center of the city and was caught there by the arrival of the airplanes, near where the Gran Vía crosses the Paseo de Gracia. She was a stranger, also, to those who, once the alert was over, picked up from the ground that woman who was already eternally young in the memory of all who knew her, the lady who, in her coat, hat, and high-heeled shoes, clung tightly to the bag where she kept the presents she had bought for her children, which the latter, days afterward, in suits dyed black as custom ruled, would receive, in silence, from the hands of Aunt Rosario: a romantic novel for Marta; tales of Doc Savage and the Shadow for José Agustín; a book of illustrated stories for me; some wooden dolls for Luis that would remain scattered round the attic without my brother ever touching them.

The empty black bag: all that remained of her. Her role in life, in our life, had finished abruptly before the end of the first act.

O NLY TWENTY YEARS *later—during the prepara-tions for the editing of Rossif's film,* Mourir à Ma-drid, *the day you and some French friends were viewing a series of Spanish and foreign news and documentary films on the civil war—did the horror that dominated her last moments impose its sharp outline on your consciousness. A weekly news film from the Republican government, in its denunciations of the enemy's aerial attacks on defenseless civilian populations, shows the results of the one suffered by Barcelona on that unforgettable seventeenth of March: alarm sirens, noisy explosions, scenes of panic, ruins, destruction, desolation, cartloads of corpses, hospital beds, wounded comforted by members of the government, an endless line of bodies laid out in the morgue. In the foreground the camera slowly pans the victims' faces and, soaked in cold sweat, you suddenly realize the harsh possibility that the face you fear may suddenly appear. Fortunately, the absent one, with a sense of elegance and modesty, hid in some way to spare you the traumatic, ill-timed reunion. But you were forced to rush from your seat, go to the bar, drink a glass of something, just the time necessary to hide your emotion from the rest and discuss the film with them as if nothing had happened.*

The bond linking that death and the meaning of the civil war would not be apparent to you until the day when, now interested in politics, you began to be fascinated in eye-witness accounts and books on the recent history of Spain. Your religious and family education in the forties had succeeded in breaking the link between the two events. On the one hand, after the collective rosary that followed supper, you quickly prayed in a mechanical, routine fashion three Lord's Prayers for the eternal rest of the absent one's soul; on the other hand, you accepted without any reservations whatsoever the official version of the conflict as rehearsed by ra-

dio, newspapers, teachers, relatives, and all around you: a crusade undertaken by healthy, patriotic men against a Republic stained by all kinds of crimes and abominations. The stark, undeniable reality that your mother had been the victim of your side's strategy of terror, a product of cold, hateful calculation, was ignored by your father and the rest of the family. The setbacks the former suffered—imprisonment, illness, widowhood—were, according to him, the work of a band of enemies generically labelled as "reds." Deprived of its context, clean and disinfected, your mother's death was thus transformed into a kind of abstraction that, although it exempted the real guilty ones from their responsibility, emphasized conversely for you the unreal confusion of their fate. Although the ease with which this whitewashing operation was carried out may seem suspicious, the closed, conservative circle in which you live, the silent complicity of your home, the difficulty in getting objective information, spotlights once more the uncritical acceptance of the facts. It was only at university, when you befriended a student with ideas hostile to the regime and, thanks to him, got to know the books that told the story of the civil war from an opposite point of view, that the bandage fell from your eyes. Imbued with crude but refreshing Marxist principles—hostile to the reactionary values of your class—you began to focus on the events you experienced marginally from childhood from a very different perspective: Franco's bombs—not the innate evil of the Republicans—were directly responsible for the break-up of your family.

To tell the truth—apart from that belated feeling of historical indignation— the early date of your mother's departure took from her exit any real degree of grief. What was snatched from you then would weigh heavily on your destiny, but the consequences of your orphanhood would only appear later: alienation from the father figure, insipid religiosity, lack of patriotism, an instinctive rejection of any kind of authority, all the elements and features that later would fix your character no doubt have a close relationship to that state. However, to the extent that the affection for your mother vanished with her, you can say quite rigorously that rather than her son, the son of a woman who is and always will be unknown to you, you are a son of the civil war, its Messianism, cruelty, and anger: of the unhappy accumulation of circumstances that brought into the open the real entrails of the country and filled you with a youthful desire to abandon it forever.

*You remember now, in the light of what you have just written, the episode with
the axe: the destructive rage that overpowered you one morning in Barcelona, a
few months after the war, when you were wandering through the house along
with Luis.*

*At the back of the garden, in the space between the garage and a room used as
a junk room, there were two cubbyholes for storing wood and coal beneath the
space under the staircase that led to the terrace on the first floor. The junk room was
crammed with furniture belonging to the family, awaiting, you suppose, the probable move to Torrentbó. You can remember a number of sofas, armchairs, consoles, corner shelves covered in dust and cobwebs where you used to hide to play at
ghosts, happy in the midst of that mixture of valuable objects and broken or useless
bric-a-brac. This spot had been transformed into your favorite hiding place when
you came back from school until the day when, out of temper or whim, you took
the axe from the woodpile and with your brother's help proceeded to destroy its
contents with ferocious enthusiasm.*

*Piece of furniture after piece of furniture, with no quarter given, you began to
cut legs, arms, backs, chop tables, rip the stuffing out of chairs, break decorations,
pull springs, bash chairs, possessed by a cheerful, absorbing sense of inspiration
that you would not meet again, you think today, except in the act of creation, the
exultant vandalism of adult writing: the pleasure of exorcising the symbols of a
society, the conventions of a code suddenly perceived as an obstacle; an intense desire for vengeance against an ill-formed universe; the effusive, primeval impulse
linked to the binomial of creation-discreation. What meaning can be given to this
sudden, excited, enjoyable act of two brothers who were normally calm yet suddenly overtaken by a plan of destruction whose ultimate explanation was beyond
them? A protest, accumulated rage, a desire to retaliate? Or boredom, pure lack
of awareness, an attempt to imitate the grown-ups? The original cause of the
scene, the swiftness and audacity of its execution, will always be an enigma impossible to resolve. You will then focus your memory on the image of those small
boys who, with the blows of the axe, liberate in some way mysterious inner energy,
perhaps the unconscious, secret desire to make their voices heard.*

ARKED OUT BY the holy signs of mourning, we were the object of much weeping and sympathy. The daily visits of consolation soon became a ritual: Aunt Rosario, her husband and our cousins, Lolita Soler, friends, or just acquaintances from the colony took their turns in my father's bedroom, worried by the helpless state of the sick widower with four children. From now on, who was going to look after us? The question was not posed directly but could be discerned on the anxious, verging on aghast, expressions of his devotees. My father's illness, moreover, required constant care and it was necessary to have recourse to the services of a nurse. Someone mentioned a "right-wing" midwife who had also taken refuge in the village and a few days afterwards old Josefina, a massive, thickset woman with coarse features, settled down with her suitcases and belongings into a spacious room in the front of the house.

Strangely, I do not retain any image of my father during the days following the catastrophe. He stayed shut up in his room while the visitors came and went at his bedside preaching Christian resignation or mumbling the rosary. My brothers, sister, and I, after our shock and despair at the news had gone, got by as best we could and began to savor the advantages of our absolute freedom. At first our black-dyed clothes distanced us from our mates. Some village lads pointed at us and made jokes about our disguise. Any possible attempt on my part to play the victim and win the pity of others was thus a deplorable failure. Life—with its growing difficulties—war—with its suite of horrors—continued their usual course indifferent to and removed from my family's drama. We escaped instinctively from the atmosphere that reigned at home and went off far to play with the village children and organize expeditions to the hills in search of chestnuts.

The general shortage of food became more pronounced: shops and gro-
cery stores lacked the most basic goods and displayed windows and counters
empty except for a few odd sweets, cleaning cloths, brooms, and other un-
necessary leftover objects. Without reaching starvation point, our family diet
worsened daily. María, the servant, would often come back with her bag full
of turnips and greens: the only articles sold in the market. The parcels that
arrived from time to time from Argentina or France—sent by Uncle Joaquín and our relations in the Gil Moreno de Mora family—were a real feast.
We opened them at home or in Aunt Rosario's flat and shared out their contents—sugar, coffee, chocolate, tinned meat, condensed milk—with the
same restrained anxiety which the authors of a dangerous, daring raid later
share out their booty. Then the deficiencies in the post and the frequent loss
of parcels forced us to search out other sources of supplies: direct purchase
from the peasants, the breeding of domestic animals, happy fruitful hunting
through garden plots and chestnut trees.

A hunter from the neighboring area of Puigtorrat would often be around
at home with the spoils of his forays: hares, partridges, and squirrels. One
day he even brought a strange, skinned animal that, in spite of his denials
and protests of good faith, turned out to be a vixen. In the periods of greatest
scarcity, Marta, José Agustín, and myself would steal watercress or the stalks
of wild marrow from the edge of the cultivated fields or would spread out
fanwise through the nearby chestnut trees until the cries and threats of the
owner or tenant put us to flight. In the attic, we bred rabbits and a dozen
hens: their eggs, mixed with greens or marrow leaves, comprised the usual
dish for our lunch or supper except on those happy days when we received
food from France or Argentina. The chestnuts—raw, boiled, or roasted—
were the second source of sustenance. Consequently, and perhaps as a result
of the scares I had when getting them, I have always hated them and have
not tasted them since the war ended and we left Viladrau.

As soon as she moved in, Josefina the nurse had elaborated a strategy
aimed at domination based on a pretense of motherly affection, and on cunning and intimidation. Her first victim was Lolita Soler: her repeated visits
to the widower's bedroom singled her out in her eyes as an immediate rival

and Josefina dispatched her rapidly after a violent row. After removing that awkward presence, she began to adopt with us the role of the caring mother: in the dining room, in front of my father, she used to sit me on her lap and embrace me tightly with lots of kisses and tender, loving gestures. Luis's indifference to her endearments irritated her and, when alone, she was quick to reproach him for it. She had also taken charge of the running of the kitchen and she used the few goods for her own benefit: in spite of her robust constitution and good color, she pretended to suffer from continuous "weakness" and did not stop eating throughout the day. Thinking she was indispensable to my father, she gradually intensified her pressure on him. During the rosary after supper and the prayers for my mother, she exhibited extreme piety, which soon seemed hateful to us. Her attempt to replace my mother, evident in many details, no doubt finally opened my father's eyes, despite his prostrate, dependent state. Did she perhaps hint clumsily at some sexual advance that could only repulse him, obsessed as he was by his wife's memory? Or did she somehow suggest to him the suitability of remaking his life, of looking for an adoptive mother for those poor orphans? Her crude ways, hypocritical behavior, and coarse, obscene physical appearance did not favor her plans for conquest. But something must have happened between them since my father, taking strength from his weakness, suddenly threw her out of the house. I can remember Josefina's tears as she saw her dream destroyed. Still hoping for some possible intervention by us, she tried in vain to win us to her cause: now living away from us, she got me to her lodging with the bait of some sweets and tried to wheedle from me news of my father's health and temper. But from then on he forbade us to have any contact with her. One day when we spotted her in the distance, on the way to the market, José Agustín and I sang an indecent ditty to her, and she went into a fury, insulted us, and threw large stones after us.

After she left, Lolita Soler and my uncle and aunt resumed their visits. My sister, Marta, now carried out the onerous duties of nurse to my father and looked after him patiently. The room's bitter smell, the cannula and stained cotton wool, the spittoon, bedpan, and jar of pus created for me on the other hand a circle around the invalid that was difficult to cross. When I went to bed, I furtively touched the thin outstretched hand with my lips and, as far as possible, tried to avoid his outpourings and embraces. The rosaries and Lord's Prayers that we prayed together in his room were the most trying moments in the day. One night when he was reading us a passage from the gospel that makes reference to an ass accompanied by its jenny, this last word sent us into inexplicable fits of laughter. My father was forced to interrupt his reading and in a rage he ordered us out of the room. I remember that as a result of this incident I spoke for the first time of my lack of affection for him, I am not sure whether alone or to one of my brothers or my sister. The idea of being adopted by Uncle Joaquín and accompanying him to Argentina captivated me for some time. Moving in with any member of the family seemed more desirable than living with that sad, embittered man whose grief and frustration I did not share. On another day, I suddenly entered my room and found him sitting on my bed, crying, with my mother's photograph in his hand. Ashamed at discovering something I did not wish to see, I quickly tiptoed out, without uttering a word. Today, this lack of filial pity and understanding of course seems shocking to me. The tests to which my father had been submitted went beyond the limits of his endurance and did not deserve my attitude of rejection. I do not wish to absolve myself in any way but, to explain my behavior at the time, one would have to consider my tremendous disappointment when I realized that the all-powerful, magnificent character praised to the heavens in my mind as a child was not only a flesh and blood being like the rest but senile and helpless to boot. The spite that followed my disillusion should clarify to an extent the precocious, unjust manifestations of cold detachment.

Around this date—the summer or autumn of 1938—I experienced my first sexual emotions. Until then I was completely ignorant of the matter; not even contact with domestic animals had taught me like other children. The time when, at one of the farmhouses near the village, I saw a goat give birth, I accepted my mother's explanation that it had swallowed a sandal and was ejecting it, to the point that, many years later, I related the anecdote to my brothers and sister without realizing my gullibility nor the simplicity of the deceit. In the attic, I would similarly keep a watch on the rooster's attacks on

the hens and armed with my rod of justice, I would pursue the supposed per-
petrator of these insults. Still my ingenuousness did not stop me, José Agustín, and a gang of kids from playing at showing each other our parts and,
with our penises out, dancing a kind of conga to the cry—incomprehensible
to me—of "girls, do you want to have a stroke?" My brother declared that
he had let María caress him and one day he showed us an enormous damp
patch on the front wall of the house, the product, he said, of a militia man
who went out with the servant. The mental image of the individual pissing
had an indelible impact on me: when I found out later that one of the boys
in the gang held down our neighbors' abnormal, hydrocephalic son and ur-
inated over his head, the news overwhelmed and excited me. I went down to
the garden anxious to repeat the deed and, when I didn't come across the
child, I spat and pissed outside the door to his house, filled with a passionate
emotion, the dark causes of which would flower in my writing much later.
As for my imaginary victim, I didn't hear of him again: Encarnación and her
family moved to another village and their house stayed shut until we left Viladrau.

I do not propose to interpret this violent outburst in the light of my present experience—that is, as a possible forerunner of my future sensuality—
but to situate it in the context of immediacy and innocence in which it took
place. My desire to physically humiliate the backward, squint-eyed boy was
a spontaneous, isolated act that did not rouse in my mind any guilt feelings
and soon fell into semi-oblivion. When sometime after, on one of those evenings organized by Lolita Soler and my uncle and aunt, a priest came in civilian dress and, before celebrating mass and giving communion to the
adults, he called me to his side and said he wished to hear me confess. Although I followed to the letter his instructions and searched out, bewildered
and confused, anything that might give cause for reproach, I never conceived
the idea of establishing a connection between that act and the nebulous notion of sin. I evoked or invented some theft or fib and received absolution
from that man without feeling any emotion. The concentration and sorrow
of the communicants, the priest's Latin, the getting up and kneeling down,
the blows to the breast that I had forgotten since before the war seemed like

a mere charade lacking meaning or substance. At the end, the adults ordered us to keep quiet about it. Above all, said my father, not one word to the servant.

Although María had always behaved most discreetly, Lolita Soler and my family distrusted her as a red. On Saturdays and Sundays she went out to dances with militia men, she had won a UGT or PSUC badge in a *tómbola*, and I well remember that, when she commented on the news from the front with us, she said: "With Durruti dead, the war's lost." During Christmas, her pessimism intensified. While my father, Lolita Soler, and my uncle and aunt hardly disguised their joy, she, the poor, illiterate woman who believed in the cause of the Republic and generously offered her body to the soldiers, rightly suspected the arrival of difficult times for her, and she obsessively repeated the legends about the Moors. Her stories—of rapes, chopped-off ears, heads kept in rucksacks for their gold teeth—unearthed in fact under the gloss of antirebel propaganda the old Hispanic phantasmagoria forged in the centuries of the ill-named Reconquest. As for many Spaniards of my generation, the term "Moor" was associated within me, from an early age, with vague, disturbing images of violence and terror. It would be necessary for twenty years to pass before I overcame the imprints of that period and succeeded in establishing a fruitful personal relationship with the Arab world in its triple dimension of space, body, and culture, a relationship that would soon be transformed into the basic axis of my life. Sometimes, in my wanderings through the Islamic world I have thought remorsefully and affectionately about that humble woman from Carballino whose ancestral fantasies, anchored in my subconscious and then doubly exorcised, both in life and writing, would become the source that would later nourish the Moorish inspiration of my work. The ways that make us what we are are tortuous and unpredictable: for my part, I do not have the slightest doubt that in my move toward and sympathy for the Life unto Islam, the fascinated imaginings of the servant I listened to as a boy played through unpredictable twists and turns that initiatory, baptismal role destiny had mysteriously conferred on them.

T HE FRONT WAS getting closer to us: the road had filled
up with soldiers on foot and on horseback, official vehicles, motorcycles with sidecars, Supply Corps lorries. Then we could see
from our windows long, interminable strings of prisoners of war file by;
their guards rounded them up like cattle outside the local parish church
and gave them their watery rations. Exhaustion, illness, despondency were
painted on all their faces: they left behind them a trail of defecations, dirty
paper, and empty tins. Lolita Soler and Aunt and Uncle watched them go
with tears in their eyes and tried to furtively give them a crust or some other
help. José Agustín and I dared to talk to them and we presented one with a
cigarette made from dried maize leaves. A small nationalist reconnaissance
plane appeared one morning and a captain took his pistol out of its holster
and fired a few shots well-seasoned with curses and oaths at it. Our father
told us Barcelona had been liberated by Carlist troops.

The village provided daily scenes of panic and disorder. Cars packed with
refugees, lorries stuffed with soldiers, passed through heading north followed by hundreds of people on foot, all dirty and unkempt, soldiers, civil-
ians, children, old men and women, all loaded with suitcases and bundles,
absurd bits of lumber, saucepans, furniture, an absurdly outlandish sewing
machine, a diaspora of insects after the death of the queen or the unexpected
destruction of the ants' nest. There were the wounded carried on stretchers,
cripples on crutches, arms in slings. The nationalists had just cut off the railway line and José Agustín announced that he had seen a dead body. Some
officers visited us one afternoon. After making himself comfortable in the
dining room, the captain noticed the existence of a chicken coop in the attic

and, with remarkable brazenness, invited himself to dinner. María sacrificed a couple of hens and, while my father strove to maintain an empty conversation with his guests, one of the latter inspected the house curiously and displayed a sudden interest in Aunt Consuelo's violin case. He insisted on examining the instrument, plucked the strings, said that his aide was fond of music. After the meal they said good-bye politely and, belying our fears, did not take anything. The following day, however, the doorbell rang loudly and there was the orderly. The captain had asked him to requisition the violin, he told us; but he was thinking of deserting and begged us to help him. Rather than carry out his orders, he wanted to remain hidden in our house awaiting the arrival of the nationalist troops. My father agreed to his request. The last Republican soldiers were evacuating the village and there was no longer any risk that the officer would retrace his steps to find out where his subordinate had got to. The deserter's name was Veremundo Salazar, and he came from the Rioja area: he hid in the attic for the whole morning waiting for the sudden appearance of the scouts of the enemy army. We could hear the muffled, intermittent echo of gunfire. The reconnaissance planes continued their flight northward. After a few hours, Veremundo came down from his hiding place, gave us a yellow-handled campaign knife, and bid us farewell. My father had forbidden us to go out but, soon after, without asking his permission, José Agustín and I slipped out to the garden. One of our neighbors had come out to have a look as well and she told us that the village now belonged to "our fellows."

We heard the bells ringing and ran to the plaza. The entire colony of Barcelona refugees seemed to have agreed to meet there: men and women in tears embraced and kissed each other, waved flags, cheered Franco, intoned the "Oriamendi," gave free rein to their emotions. My uncle and aunt with my cousins were also exultant, in ecstasy. Somebody wore a red beret and was surrounded by admirers. They had thrown open the doors of the church the Republicans had converted into a warehouse. People were discussing whether the Carlists or the Falangists would arrive first.

These were busy days, full of changes: new money, food supplies, speeches and hymns broadcast over the loudspeakers. Wearing blue shirts and red berets, José Agustín and I had queued for hours outside the Social Welfare offices where they distributed free fizz and omelette sandwiches. The military were camping in the mansion that had been a shelter for the Archive of the Crown of Aragon: they kept bags of beans and sugar there and, taking advantage of the carelessness or the blind eye of the Supply Corps, a neighbor and I filled two saucepans with their precious contents. My father dared to venture briefly out of the house and made friends with two NCOs: an Italian, Mr. Lupiani, and the man we called "Sergeant Fatty." While we played with cartridge cases, he spoke to them of his widowhood, the misfortunes of life under red domination, his traditionalist, Catholic views. One day he invited them to lunch and, at the end of the meal, perhaps strengthened by their dashing military presence, he sacked María. The red housemaid, bedmate of Communists and militiamen, obeyed the sentence of the court without a murmur of protest. Dejected and flushed, she went off to her room to collect her wretched belongings and put them in a bag: not one of us, still sitting in front of the dishes she had cooked and served, got up to say good-bye or show her any sign of sympathy. With her bag over her back, resigned to her fate, she disappeared forever from our sight.

What happened to her in those days of merciless control and repression, when arbitrary arrests and denunciations were an everyday occurrence? Did she try to find a job in Barcelona—a difficult task lacking as she did references or recommendations from a family that was "beyond reproach"? Did she go back to her own village to suffer misery and hunger? Did she suffer reprisals like so many other women and go through the humiliation of purging courts, spoonfuls of castor oil, and sinister head-shaving? A feeling of retrospective shame overwhelms me as I write these lines. I think that it is incredible that even as an eight-year-old I experienced no remorse or shame at that contemptible settling of accounts. Our María served as the sacrificial goat to the real sufferings of my father: yet she had in no way been responsible for them. Of all the unpleasant, sad episodes in the war, this one is no doubt the most difficult to digest.

Mr. Lupiani had created a children's brigade of the Falange and, in his baritone voice, with his chest proudly puffed out, he would teach us to stand to attention, salute, march in step. We sang verses of "Cara al sol," the hymn of the Youth Front: "with ranks closed, strong and warlike, our troops go forward to the morning that promises us our country, justice and bread." A village boy who had received a corporal's stripe would strut in front of us with his uniform and beret. The priests had reappeared also in full dress: they celebrated Mass in the parish church and I received catechism classes from Mossén Rovira to prepare myself for Communion.

Outside these religious and military activities, we enjoyed complete freedom. Schools were not yet open: we walked along the Espinelves road still littered with vehicles either burnt out or reduced to scrap metal; we hunted birds with slingshots and ganged up with the village children. We looked like real savages. I remember the day a large car stopped next to us and a lady offered Luis and me some almost rotten oranges. We refused to take them and the vehicle's occupants resumed their journey surprised and upset. Our dirty, neglected appearance had led them to mistake us for two beggars.

Our favorite pastime consisted of visiting deserted villas and slipping inside them. Our extreme thinness allowed us to get between the bars and, after several fruitful incursions, we brought together an important booty: toys, books, and, especially, a collection of stamps from all the countries in the world; I tried to decipher their origins at home, comparing them with the colored prints in my geography book. José Agustín was becoming an expert in breaking and entering until we were spotted by a neighbor or nosey passerby who reported us and we were severely punished by my father.

I have no memories of my First Communion administered by old Mossén Rovira. On Sundays we went to the parish church with our aunt and uncle and one day the bells rang loudly and there was a long thanksgiving sermon: the war was over! The bare victory communiqué from Military Headquarters in Burgos passed from lip to lip. Lolita Soler was beside herself about Franco: Spain needed men like him! Mr. Lupiani taught us the words of "Carrasclás":

With Azaña's mustache
we'll make brooms
to sweep the barracks
of the Spanish Falange

One Sunday, in the parish church, my heart missed a beat: my mother was kneeling on the prayer cushion in one of the front benches. Her hair, profile, and head were lowered in an act of meditation. Emotion held me in suspense: should I go and suddenly appear before her? Would she recognize me after so much time? What would we say to each other? When she got up to receive Communion, the spell vanished: it was a different woman. I felt almost relieved of my fears of this unexpected meeting and since then I think I have never dreamt about her again.

ABDECA shareholders drove from Barcelona to visit my father: they brought presents for us, wore Carlist and Falange badges. Friendly countries: Italy, Germany. Enemies: France, our eternal foe. England? Yes, England as well. What about Russia? The worst of all. You shouldn't even think of mentioning Russia!

Ever since María had been fired, my father had been looking for a maid. We went to see a possible candidate, Julia, who had worked in Aunt María's house before the war and could be trusted. She had spent the last two years in a farmhouse on the outskirts of Viladrau bordering on an estate belonging to the writer Marià Manent. Julia adapted immediately to life with my father. From then on, until her death, she lived with us as part of the family, with only one condition: she had to change her name to Eulalia, since the mention of her real name was painful to the widower. Soon afterward, this woman with red hair and smooth white skin from Aragon, age indefinite, would stay in our house for a probationary period, which, as a result of the bonds that gradually linked us together, in fact lasted a quarter of a century.

Now is not the time to talk about her: the important role played by Eulalia in the lives of myself and my brothers, her complex, contradictory personality, her immense goodness and affection for us, her favorite haunts, caprices, phobias, flirtations require separate treatment. The family whose service she entered, although known to her since before the war, displayed the wounds and scars of the conflict in that spring or summer of thirty-nine: a sick, suspicious, apprehensive widower whose health, although well on the way to recovery, demanded distressing treatment; a fourteen-year-old girl and three boys brought up in a wild state, without any strict code of behavior. Her generosity, self-denial, and intuitive genius helped her to ride out the situation and overcome the obstacles. Her presence during our last few months in Viladrau was discreet and sensible. To tell the truth, I hardly remember what she was like.

Grandmother Marta reappeared that summer. She dressed in mourning as we did, but carefully avoided talking about my mother or the circumstances of her death. She would come for a walk with us on the outskirts of the village and under the chestnut trees and by the fountains we met other families belonging to the colony, dressed to the nines, as if they had not experienced the war. One gentleman would take off his Panama hat when he passed us and we would jokingly tell Grandmother that he was in love with her and wanted to be her fiancé. José Agustín had gone to Barcelona to prepare for his entrance exams for the *bachillerato*, and my father was getting ready to return as well to take charge of ABDECA. Luis and I spent a few more weeks with our grandmother in Viladrau and one day we caught the bus and the Balenyà train: the carriages were packed with people, soldiers, Falangists, heavily laden women. I was excited by the novelty of the journey and sang the verses of "Carrasclás" in chorus with a group of Flechas, the Falangist youth.

Y OUR LEZAMIAN EXCITEMENT *was coming to an end:
that desire to fan and stoke the fire of your words to make
their union more furious: the pure gleam of the coals had gradually gone out and
the last embers hardly shone from the barren ash: in spite of all, the agitation con-
tinued, invented new kinds of orgasm, filled your head with sparks: inductions and
currents, yielding and malleable, captured as purely visual images: showy struc-
tures, fleetingly displayed like spidery Bengal flares or threatening Congolese or-
chids: the maaxún *cast you out of yourself, from the tiny café near the fortress*
where you had just composed and erased your Soledades *surrounded by peaceful*
smokers of kef, nebulous domino addicts, sleepy cardplayers: with the absurd tele-
vision screen Spanishing on in the background, perfectly framed suddenly there
for all to see: you, your double, the creator of give-and-take, in the company of an
unknown giant of a man, dark-skinned with a walrus mustache, both embracing,
climbing like vines, in a splendid copulation: surprise, shock, incredulity at seeing
yourself in such an awkward spot, you continue being yourself and yet someone
else, split in two, duality, inner agony, gradually a sense of shame: on the sly you
look at your neighbors to see if they recognize you, they attack your attitude, cen-
sure the brazen joy: desire to cover the screen with a hand like an ingenuous censor
at a school cinema, to cut off the electricity, to flee in confusion into the street: to
slip off, to stride down the hill, stop an empty taxi, the square, Hammadi restau-
rant, give the driver the address on the rue Molière, gaze at the pointless movement
of people while you ride, pay for it, get out, get your key from the porter, open up,
get in the lift, your flat, the lights, corridor bedroom, collapse on your bed: to the
Arab cemetery or ghost that will be the scenario for the longest night in your life:
the punctual date with the dead you left behind, the conclave of ghosts: a succes-
sion of family settings in which they, the absentees, attend to their business dressed

as they dressed before, patiently waiting for their turn, for the explanation that is continuously deferred: your father, Alfredo, Grandfather, Eulalia: the garden in Pablo Alcover, the lemon tree beneath which Father used to rest, the kitchen, the dark austere passageway, the horse chestnut tree: or else Torrentbó, the verandah, eucalyptus trees, terrace, Father reading, Grandfather's creased suit, Alfredo with his hoe over his shoulder, Eulalia's weak, unmistakable voice: meeting, recognition, appearance foreseen for some time, your relationship with Monique cleared up, while you wandered and got lost in your search for maaxún or hashish, en route to that elusive tribunal of the dead whose decrepitude you did not witness and of which, as they crouched in the shade, they did not fail to remind you: confrontations, mutual recriminations, insidious guiltiness: real people, an oneiric topography, present alternating with sudden leaps backward.

The only significant exceptions already cleared from your subconscious: the woman who died in the bombing and the hated village of Viladrau.

You can now evoke the time at the beginning of the sixties, when you interviewed for L'Express one of the political prisoners freed by Franco thanks to the international campaign for amnesty. Twenty and a bit years in the Burgos jail, with no horizon beyond the distant square of sky and the close, too close walls of his cell. After getting out, problems of adapting his vision to intervening spaces: dizziness, sickness, headaches behind the eyes. An even worse lack of adaptation to the new reality not assimilated in his subconscious. During the first months in prison, he had dreamt regularly of open spaces: his house, the village, people and places he knew as a free man. Then, surreptitiously, this ozone layer had rarefied until it disappeared: he stopped recalling the world outside the prison when he slept. If he dreamt about his mother, his mother was in prison. If he imagined his village, it was a village behind bars. The prison had penetrated his inner being and allowed him no escape whatsoever. The girls he had known in his youth, heroines of his nocturnal libido, always performed in a prison setting. The military tribunal's punishment thus won after many years an absolute victory: not only a prison for the body, but likewise for mind, imagination, and fantasy.

The destructive power of reality over his dreams still haunted him retrospectively after sixteen months of free movement. The new girlfriends he went to bed with were invariably prisoners in the murky, elusive world of his nightmares. The prisons where he had rotted—bars, walls, courtyards, warders—maintained a cruel force. A hermetic, unassailable camp with no possibility of escape, his inner world remained anchored in prison.

Only by ceasing to dream in this prison, after weeks, months, or years, would our man reach the end of his torture: the opening up of the oppressive space, dilution of stubborn images, the incorporation of new experiences. At the end—a misty mirage—the wonderful promise of freedom.

Strategies common to dream, memory, and oblivion. The decisive importance of time in their development. Wasting activity, insidious erosion finally transformed into devastating routine.

Like the obscene, persistent image that, by dint of masturbating thereupon, gradually loses its power to provoke, the impression of the painful act or the bitter memory fades away without our realizing in an empty atmosphere of boredom and insensitivity. The last taunts of frustration, the brief dull pain, will be the well-known reminder of our enormous fagocytic capacity: patches of history dominated by dream or nightmare and progressively replaced in dreams by new areas of reality.

Nevertheless a mysterious spread of light and shade: the arc light that arbitrarily bathes scenes in your life and leaves others in a discreet darkness from which you cannot rescue them.

Viladrau, to which you have not returned nor will you ever, expelled forever from the fantasy of your dreams and, in spite of that, clear in your memory, reconstructed in your imagination while you write, square inch by square inch, house by house. Beyond dream, memory, oblivion: a simple page in this book that— once printed, torn from you—will not enter your thoughts again.

W HEN I GOT back to Pablo Alcover, the house seemed smaller and was full of people. Once again we lived on the left side of the ground floor and, now that the Russian volunteers had disappeared, Miss Esther, owner of the property, established herself on the top floor with her half-caste servant. The reds had cut down the cypress hedges that divided the garden and in their place had built a two-roomed hut in the back that we used as a lumber-room, store, and playroom. Our grandparents and Eulalia lived with us and the house was also a meeting place for a number of people more or less linked to the family, whom we had lost sight of during the war: Paquita the dressmaker; Ciscu the buggy driver; Luis's Galician maid with her husband and daughter; the mother of Matías, the ABDECA chauffeur. From the start of term in October, José Agustín and I went to the Jesuit school in Sarriá and Marta to the one run by the nuns of the Sacred Heart. But my real life, with its coming and going, its reading, hiding places, haunts, would continue to be the house.

At times, with the help of the very few photos of the period, I have tried to reconstruct our busy day-to-day existence in those first squalid postwar months. My brothers and I unfailingly appear badly dressed—I'm always wearing castoffs—with my hair cut almost to nothing, dirty knees, holes in my shoes, a strange mixture of orphan and street urchin. Our social status was confusing because of its ambiguous, imprecise character: we were surrounded by pupils from bourgeois families but the experience, manners, and clothing of the rest were clearly different from ours. The Viladrau period— with the rather wild freedom we had got used to, a precocious fondness for reading, a liking for solitary life, self-taught habits—separated and would always separate me from the rest of my friends. Although the school life we were entering tended toward uniformity and discipline, the centrifugal attraction of our tribal existence was more forceful and won out in the end.

No doubt my father got by with the wage he earned from the factory but, whether because of the general poverty of the time, or the gap left by my mother in the running of the household, or a combination of the two, we did not live comfortably. The food distributed through the official ration cards was meagre and of poor quality. Matías, the chauffeur, sometimes took us to Torrentbó and we would come back loaded with sacks of potatoes or yams. On schooldays, Eulalia would fill our thermoses with bread soaked in milk or flour mixed with milk. I remember that we used to go to the dairy with her and if the owner had used up his stocks, we had to be satisfied with a tasteless, deceptively white liquid. Sugar disappeared and had to be replaced with saccharine. During that year, bread got worse: the bread sold in bakeries was small, heavy, as hard as stone. To get your teeth into it, you had to soak it. Chocolate tasted of carob beans and it was impossible to buy coffee.

Given the lack of chickens and rabbits, which were confiscated at checkpoints on the roads into the city, my father had decided to raise guinea pigs. In the garden, between the garage and the shed, he laid out wire fencing behind which the rodents began to propagate. Every day we ran to catch them and hand them over to Eulalia. Cooked in cornmeal, they were our daily diet for some time: Matías, his mother, the housekeeper, and the dressmaker enthusiastically joined in the feast.

The inhuman poverty that oppressed the country affected even the upper classes. We were warned at school against a typhoid epidemic and classes were suspended for a few days. As Luis and I spent a long time every day playing with the guinea pigs, we were soon infested with parasites. Eulalia and Matías's mother oiled our hair and carefully cleaned out the fleas and nits. The day after, my father took us to the hairdresser who clipped the three of us like sheep with a lot of good-natured joking.

This period of plagues, repression, and poverty was dressed for the outside world in fake tinsel and elation: the end of the struggle, the victory of the "good guys" were depicted at home and school in almost mystic terms.

Uncle Ignacio had brought a record of the caudillo's voice: after winding up the old gramophone, we listened to it at dusk, vaguely uplifted. World war had broken out and our visitors talked about it endlessly. In general, German victories were greeted enthusiastically; only Uncle Luis and Uncle Leopoldo expressed reservations. I had got used to reading the newspapers and I excitedly followed the incidents in the conflict: the Danzig Corridor, Poland, the Maginot Line, the Siegfried Line. I plotted the movement of troops on my maps, I found the battle zones, put markers on the ports that sheltered the rival armadas. A great passion for history was gradually added to my initial interest in geography. From then on they would be my favorite subjects until the much later discovery of literature.

Franco, José Antonio, the Martyrs, the rich, drunken beat of the "Bridegroom of Death." At the school of St. Ignatius, before breaking ranks in the playground, we hummed a song of which I remember only one verse and its strident chorus:

> War against the fatal sickle
> and the destructive hammer
> long live our caudillo
> and Imperial Spain!

One day, dressed in blue shirts and red berets, we walked down from the top of Sarriá to the center of Barcelona: Count Ciano had arrived! Under the fathers' energetic batons we shouted until we were hoarse, waiting for him to appear in an open car: thousands of arms raised, children's mouths opened, flags, music, emblems, a theatrical apotheosis. The recipient of so much fervor walked slowly before us, bellicose, hardened, erect, apparently indifferent to the cheers and applause: exemplary standard bearer, Roman consul, and gladiator, herald of the new Holy Empire. Immersed in the crowd, the boy with the shaved head was unaware of his outstanding record of service, the punishing skill of his rapid aeronauts. He also greeted, automatically, his pose as a Great Man, a titanic Forger of the Future while the loudspeakers broadcast the "Cara al sol" and those present applauded, went on applauding the processional chariot of heroes, as it became tiny, diminished in the distance.

The experience of the three war-years created a distance between me and my classmates that was difficult to bridge. There was no common ground where my interests, worries, tastes could mesh with theirs. While the majority of them had lived through the conflict within the national territory and proudly showed off their appearance and good manners, I had already felt the true harshness of life: their childishness, sociability, affected ways were totally incompatible with my love of solitude and reading contracted in Viladrau. Except for geography and history, in which I immediately shone to the point of correcting my teachers, at least mentally, my marks were usually average. At recess, I would retreat to some corner or hidden spot with a novel or an illustrated geography book. Efforts to make me play football always failed miserably. In the annual psychopedagogical reports they made to parents, the fathers would anxiously emphasize my isolation, lack of enthusiasm for games, disinterest in my classmates, my furtive reading. My odd appearance, reserved character, and surliness did not help to integrate me into the class. Referring to the excessively long sleeves of a jacket that was already quite old, one of these elegant, refined boys had remarked sarcastically: "You're so young, are you already inheriting?" This comment left me with a feeling of humiliation and helplessness and intensified my misanthropy. The childish hobbies of my schoolmates, their social code, which I did not share, brought me back to my personal world: the house in Pablo Alcover, playing with Luis, talking to Eulalia, reading the newspapers, a voracious hunger for the facts, photographs, and prints in my encyclopedia. About that time, I heard a friend of my father, to whom I shall refer later on, relate a dramatic family incident that happened in Canada some years before: his three daughters lived through the war in a luxury boardinghouse—a kind of Gothic castle with turrets and battlements—and the youngest and most beautiful of the sisters was killed in a fire. When I left school, walking down Anglí Street, I would repeat the exotic details of the drama to pupils from the neighborhood, attributing them to my own family. A precocious, obviously compensatory mania for storytelling thus became one of the main features of my character for some time. The desire to shock, to be admired, to exalt myself before my companions would then force me to write my own stories, taking advantage of the summer holidays in Torrentbó. Meanwhile, a victim of my own timid, antisocial ways, I ingenuously sought out opportunities to astonish others with sudden demonstrations of largesse or daring. My grandmother used to leave her purse in her room while we were eating, and I would use any pretext to leave the table and casually pinch her money: first, five peseta notes; then, twenty-five peseta notes—a big amount in those days. With the fruit of my thefts, I used to walk up High Street in Sarriá and go to the sweetshop that still belongs, I believe, to the Catalan poet I most admire today, the surrealist J. V. Foix. There, my grandmother's notes were exchanged for big bags of sweets, which, once at school, I gave out condescendingly to my peers. This lavish generosity—highlighted by the fact that my own lack of pleasure in sweets kept me, scornfully, on the edge of the subsequent scramble—earned me interest and friends and flattered my feelings of vanity and revenge. I remember the day one of the fathers, seeing the floor covered with candy wrappers, asked whom they came from: I got up from my seat and invented a birthday party for a member of the family. The priest accepted the explanation and, with a lordly gesture, typical of those times, ordered the cleaner—a pupil of humble origins who did not pay his matriculation and was responsible for cleaning the classrooms—to sweep them up in front of all of us before the start of the lesson. The boy obeyed without blushing and I fear that nobody in the room blushed on his behalf.

This same eagerness to make myself stand out before my peers in spite of my secretive, introspective nature involved me later on in a distressing episode that would make me hate the school forever. The math teacher, Mercader, left the room for a few minutes and when he came back an informer told him that the rule of silence had been broken; Mercader insisted on knowing who caused the din. A few students in the first rows raised their hands and, anxious to put on airs in front of the others, I raised my arm without noticing that I was the only one to do so in that part of the room. Mercader asked me whom I had talked to: as my action was pure bravado and I hadn't exchanged a word with anybody, I sat there with my lips sealed. My rebelliousness caused amazement and I was punished by having to stand during recess with my face to the wall on the right of the blackboard. The incident seemed to be forgotten when somebody—perhaps the teacher himself—noticed the word *Mercado* written on the wall followed by a swear word. Annoyed, looking serious, he tried to find out who the guilty person was and, seeing that nobody was forthcoming, he suspended break until further notice. Somebody was suspected—a pupil named Masnou—whom Mercader had told off a few days before; but the boy denied that he had written the words. As I had sympathized with him when we were leaving the classroom, he deduced, wrongly, that I was doing so out of remorse, and to shift the blame from himself, he accused me. Next day the priest who was Director of Studies called me to his office and asked me to write the word *Mercado* on a sheet of paper. Although I denied any involvement in the matter, he referred to my incredible refusal to reveal the name of the pupil I talked to, my punishment of facing the wall just where the graffiti appeared, how ugly and hateful in God's eyes was stubbornness in deception. Stupidly trapped in my own game, I entrenched myself in a pitiful silence. There was no way to prove anything and, consequently, I received no punishment. But from then I felt some teachers bore a grudge against me and my reaction was to lose interest in my studies. Reports on my behavior and my examination scores suffered the effects at once. When, a year later, my brother José Agustín had a personal quarrel with the tutor of his class, my father, very sensibly, decided that the place was not for us and enrolled both of us in the school run by the Christian Doctrine Brothers in the Bonanova district.

The injustice I had suffered, provoked by a chain of events for which I was partly responsible—the manly deed of raising my hand for the gallery although I had not been making a din; my silence and apparent guilt; my inopportune feeling for the boy accused of the graffiti revealed to me the close relation that can exist between our acts and their consequences that, once set in motion by them, turn us into sorcerer's apprentices. Hurt by the suspicions of which I was the object and mortified by my own stupidity, I decided to be more cautious and controlled in the future. Although I had learned from the experience, the distress it caused did not disappear. Being accused of something I had not done—a theft, lie, crime—would henceforth become a repeated, obsessive motif of my nightmares. Even today, I am still haunted by dreams of persecution from time to time: I am in the hands of Franco's police or of the KGB. I don't know whether this adult mental script goes back to the spontaneous childish gesture of raising my hand or is the product of a later insidious feeling of guilt. Whatever its source, the many-episoded, monotonous tale of the nightly trial began early in my life and, like those eternal television serials consecrated by public success, forty years later, does not seem to be coming to an end.

At the beginning of July, after the examinations, we moved to Torrentbó. Immediately after the war my father had bought the undivided parts of the estate allotted to his brothers and from then on he was the owner of the entire farmhouse and its land. The changes suffered during the period it gave shelter to President Aguirre after the fall of the Basque country were not serious: although scattered about, dusty, full of cobwebs, most of the furniture and belongings were recovered. The extreme penury of the period and the abundance of a cheap, passive labor force, inspired in my father the idea of setting up a modest farm with some livestock. After drawing up new contracts for grape-picking with the wine producers and organizing the collection and sale of the cork from the cork oak woods, he concentrated on two objectives: the breeding of cows, pigs, rabbits, and chickens and the cultivation of all the agricultural produce that was scarce in Barcelona and commanded very high prices on the black market. Alternating irrigated and dry land; cultivating each properly; clearing hills, mines, and streams; planting fruit trees; fertilizing, sowing, and harvesting; selecting, buying, and caring for animals; all needed the presence of a factotum expert in such matters. In our first postwar summer holidays in Torrentbó, the hardworking, wise, responsible, versatile man prepared to shoulder the enormous task of establishing the model farm was named don Angel, and on our arrival he was introduced as a paragon of virtue. A veterinarian, a traditionalist, and a Catholic, the new overseer held all the cards necessary to seduce my father. He too had suffered the drama and persecutions of the red period and his wife, seriously ill as a result, was recovering from her illness near Badalona. In his small portable library—which, on his departure, remained mysteriously left behind—books of religious devotion and books dedicated to the Carlist struggle rubbed shoulders with dog-eared manuals from his years of college study and works on the feeding and care of cattle, pigs, and horses. At my father's suggestion, he had also bought dozens of rabbits and hens to feed the family every day and, not satisfied with putting them in the coops and barns, he put some in rooms on the floor where we were going to live. When we arrived, don Angel moved their lordships to the lower floor where the laborers slept, and the landing and rooms next to the chapel had to be cleaned out. But neither his nor my father's enthusiasm were dampened as a result: sitting in the garden, together they planned new improvements and developments before burying themselves in the revision of the voluminous book of accounts.

I can remember don Angel in his role of the perpetually busy man, walking across the terrace with some tool, giving the laborers their orders, putting right some botched job. He had an enormous range of responsibilities and had to be constantly vigilant: unblocking pipes, changing the cows' straw, swilling out the pigsties, watering the rows of potatoes, getting the buggy ready, harnessing the mule, giving the rabbits their grass. To satisfy my father, he had planted a number of prickly pears in the wood next to the house and used the fertilizers he had suggested for both dry and wet lands. Despite this determination, when their carefully made plans were put into practice they met with a worrying succession of obstacles and unforeseen problems. There was a myxomatosis epidemic that suddenly wiped out the rabbits; several cows stopped producing milk; the vegetables and greens did not respond as they should have to the use of new chemical products. These setbacks—and the hesitations they provoked—seem now from a distance very similar to those that overwhelmed Bouvard and Pécuchet and put an end to their ambitious plans. The distance between don Angel's plans and their meagre results became a subject of conversation in the family. Eulalia, with her innate suspicion and solid peasant instincts, had elaborated almost scornfully a series of comments on him that gradually damaged his prestige. Hardworking? A lazybones! The interest and diligence he displayed in the presence of my father disappeared as soon as my father's back was turned.

Forewarned by her, my brothers and I would catch don Angel stretched out enjoying a peaceful siesta under some tree. In the fields his incompetence was notorious and the laborers did not seem to feel much appreciation for his tiresome exaltation of Carlist ideals. Such useless idleness finally disabused my father and as, to cap it all, the accounts didn't square and the supposed profits were inexplicably transformed into new expenses, the fantasy reign of don Angel came to an abrupt conclusion. My father decided to get rid of him and entrust the running of the farm to a true family of smallholders.

The manager of one of the adjacent properties wanted to work for us and my father reached an agreement with him. Although indelibly stained by a discreet red past, he had, however, looked after his master's estate during the war and this respect of his for other people's property, added to the fact that his only daughter was the fiancée of a hardworking, right-wing Catholic lad, gave him an aura of respectability. The Rat—this was the nickname by which he was known in the village, in spite of his reddish drinker's complexion and considerable paunch—at once displayed his skill and diligence: the farm's general appearance improved; the crops prospered. Things might have continued on the right track with him and his son-in-law, but the restlessness and itching for experimentation that always niggled away at my father fatally predisposed him toward new adventures.

After he had resolved our immediate problem, our lack of fats and protein, with the domestic breeding of guinea pigs, his anxious mind sought other spheres to conquer. The first stage was his discovery of a dye from juice extracted from walnut shells. He intended to market it commercially, baptized it "walnut paint," and daubed it on the walls of several rooms until, convinced of their ugliness, he gave up on it. Later on, his great liking for prickly pear cacti and their fruits, which he had taught us to pick with pliers at daybreak, led him to concoct a hair cream with a vegetable substance from their leaves. After the typhoid outbreak and the plague of fleas, we once more wore our hair short as was the fashion then and, like all other boys, we used to stick it down every day with dabs of Lucky Strike. After concocting some suspicious looking mixtures and brews, my father decided not to try them out on somebody else's head, but to experiment first upon himself: his

already greying hair immediately acquired a gentle greenish hue. But he was
not a man to lose heart over such trivialities. He assured us that his mixture
strengthened the roots of the hair, stopped it from falling out, and made it
look natural. Fortified by his own experiment, he insisted on extending it to
the family: one morning, despite my tears and protests, he decided to grease
my hair with his product. I had to give in, weeping, and at school the strange
color of my hair immediately roused my companions' curiosity. The butt of
their jokes, I shut myself in the toilet in a rage and furiously soaped my hair
until all trace of the wretched invention was gone. Unfortunately my father—gradually hemmed in by his shareholders in the management of AB-
DECA and eager to prove his business acumen to himself and everyone
else—did not always come up with such simple, cheap schemes. All it took
was a catalyst to bring out his secret desire to emulate the spectacular economic successes of Great-grandfather. Two or three years after the end of
the war, a scientist with ideas and interests similar to my father's began to
come to our house. I shall call him Dr. Roset. Bald, bespectacled, untidily
dressed, also beset by digestive problems, he belonged to a well-known family and had lived for several years in Canada: there he had separated from his
wife, and now he lived with his two twenty-year-old daughters. They were
fair-haired and exceptionally beautiful and their visits with us to the Caldetas beach had the effect of a tidal wave on the bathers. Dr. Roset was a fa-
natical anti-Communist, and already at that date he had predicted the man-
ufacture of destructive weapons capable of annihilating once and for all the
Bolshevik system in Russia. His political ideology and firm religious beliefs
naturally inclined my father very much in his favor. As a result, his ambitious
plans in the field of plant bacteriology—a new method of inoculating plants
aimed at stimulating growth and greatly increasing the number of fruit—
were immediately greeted with great enthusiasm. With my father's money,
he rented a dilapidated house on the Santa Eulalia Avenue in Sarriá and set
up the bacteriological laboratory where he carried out his experiments. His
youngest daughter, my sister, and two of our cousins worked there, in their
white coats inoculating soy plants with the contents of his little tubes. As a
layman in matters of chemistry and natural sciences, I cannot judge whether

the enterprise had any rational basis. In the opinion of some close observers who are better informed than I am, neither my father nor Dr. Roset were on the wrong lines in the practical application of their analyses. However, between the analysis and commercial viability stretched a hazardous path that was very difficult to follow given the austere, precarious state of the market. Since the capital necessary for large-scale promotion was lacking, my father's laboratory could never be anything more than an amusing but costly family toy. After the first tests in the garden in Sarriá, Dr. Roset and my father extended their experiments to the fields and furrows of Torrentbó. Ignoring the fear and suspicions of the farm-manager they sowed enormous amounts of soy on dry lands: some had been inoculated, some hadn't. Marta, my cousins, and the doctor's daughter had been photographed in their white coats holding up a plant pot in each hand. Just like the advertisements for a miraculous hair lotion in which the first image of a horrible, decrepit bald head is followed by another image of the same person, smiling, hairy, amazingly handsome, the half-dead plant on the right was contrasted with the healthy, tall, leafy plant on the left, all attributed naturally to the wonderful virtues of inoculation. But the indisputable results in Sarriá were less impressive in Torrentbó. The differences between plants in height, thickness, and number of seed-bearing pods were often nil. In some cases, to the consternation and dismay of Dr. Roset and my father, the inoculated plants were clearly inferior. This disturbing mystery, welcomed by the impassive farmer with a slightly ironical look, was clarified for me by his son-in-law Alfredo, many years later. Upset by the conceit and apparent omniscience of Dr. Roset—who was naturally contemptuous toward the traditional peasant methods of cultivation—the Rat had amused himself by maliciously changing some of the labels and tags, putting the inoculated sign on the plants that hadn't been inoculated and vice versa. I am not sure whether this cruel trick did or did not precipitate the end of the enterprise. Faced with the impossibility of expanding the market beyond the boundaries of Torrentbó, the bacteriological laboratory had become a hindrance, and after several lethargic years and considerable financial losses, my father decided sensibly to shut it.

My description of my father's obsession with eccentric, even preposterous, undertakings has perhaps inevitably been ironic. I have not done justice to his creative intuitions, to the interest he always showed in the harmonious development of nature's resources, to his real, if modest, contribution to our knowledge and defense of the natural habitat. My father often wrote for the scientific magazine of the Jesuit fathers of Barcelona and, as I was told later by an expert in these matters, his articles, apparently influenced by Teilhard de Chardin, were stimulating and innovative in the context of this mediocre period. From childhood, he strove to bring us up with a respect for a certain ecological balance threatened, he would say, by mechanization and progress. His hatred for artificial ingredients, preservatives, and the manipulatory strategies of the food industry put him in the vanguard of the present movements toward natural foods and natural living. What my adolescence took for manias—his linking of tobacco and cancer, his hostility to prolonged sunbathing, and the pernicious effect of additives and coloring—were eventually proved to be undeniable facts. My father had also, in his way, the misfortune to live in an adverse family climate. His tastes and enthusiasms, unshared by his children, condemned him in turn to a distressing isolation. My personal world, given over passionately to books, the rather petulant fifteen-year-old decision to become a novelist, must have been as strange and alien to him as his failed ventures and scientific disquisitions were to me. These differences of vocation and interests, combined with some traits of character completely opposed to mine, did not favor our mutual understanding. His lack of insight, his blindness in relation to his children met with our parallel blindness and lack of sympathy. My father sincerely believed that by giving up ideas of remarriage and trying to give us a brilliant future, he was sacrificing himself for us. This future—projected by him toward science or business—responded, of course, to his aspirations, not to ours. Although he modified his attitude as time passed—when forced to accept my role as a writer, he dreamt I would at least have a brilliant, successful career—the impossibility of making him accept the true nature of my life doomed from the outset any pretense of dialogue. Our short, infrequent encounters in his last years teetered along under the pious cover of deceit. As we could not discuss crucial matters, our conversation was reduced to a string of commonplaces. Any revelation of my religious agnosticism, Marxist ideas, sexual behavior would have been an unbearable blow to him. It would have been gratuitously cruel to lead the conversation around to any of these topics. Condemned to dissimulation, I remained emotionally distanced from him, not worrying too much about his sad, frustrated life, mentally prepared for the time when he would disappear completely. Only after he was dead, after the unexpected meeting with him, alive, real, almost flesh and blood, the night I was delirious after taking too much *maaxún*, could I judge him more objectively and even experience an outburst of unsuspected tenderness for him.

Before we left Viladrau, our grandparents put Aunt Consuelo back in the nursing home where she had previously been cared for, and they moved in with us on the ground floor on Pablo Alcover. Their presence was scarcely felt in that average-size badly arranged house, which already contained six people counting adults and children. Grandmother Marta had not yet shown the first signs of absentmindedness, and she fulfilled the usual functions of the Catalan *yaya*. She used to take Luis to the infants' school at the top of Anglí Street and, at home, she read him, with inexhaustible patience, the little books in the *Marujita* collection that we both consumed so voraciously. Grandfather Ricardo entertained himself with the help of the daily papers and, weather permitting, used to sit and rest at the end of the garden. Both lodged in the room at the front of the house next to the office: a room filled by a huge plate-glass wardrobe in front of which my parents had their photo taken on their wedding day, a matching double bed, and a bureau in the top drawer of which she put her purse. I could not say if my first raids on the latter began then or after we returned from our second summer in Torrentbó. I probably filched something every once in a while and my regular extractions—once or twice a week—began at a later date.

I slept alone in the library-office, on a divan squashed between the wall and a piece of furniture: after going to bed I could see my grandparents slip into their room and listen to their chatter and prayers until they put out the light. One night, when the whole house was in darkness, I had a visitor. Grandfather, wearing his long white nightshirt, came up to the head of my bed and made himself comfortable on the edge. In a voice that was almost a whisper, he said he was going to tell me a story, but began straightaway to tickle me and cover me with kisses. I was surprised by this sudden apparition and above all by its furtive character. "Let's play," Grandfather would say and, after putting out the bedside lamp by which I sometimes read before falling asleep, and which I had switched on upon hearing his footsteps, he stretched out by my side on the bed and gently slipped his hand down my pajamas until he touched my penis. His touch was upsetting but I was paralyzed by fear and confusion. I felt Grandfather leaning over my lap, first his fingers and then his lips, the viscous trickle of his saliva. When after several unending minutes he seemed to calm down and sat down again on the edge of the bed, my heart beat rapidly. What was the meaning of all this playing around? Why did he make a kind of groaning sound after fingering me? I had no answers and while the unwelcome visitor tiptoed back to the adjacent room where Grandmother was sleeping, I lay there for a while sunk in a state of anxious confusion.

Grandfather Ricardo asked me to keep it a secret and during the day nothing in his behavior would allow one to guess that that peaceful old man sitting with his newspaper in the shade of the chestnut tree was the same person who the night before had got into my bed, all sniggers and tickles. At night, he walked through my room with Grandmother. But, half an hour later—just long enough for her to fall asleep and for the house lights to go out—he repeated the previous night's visit. Unable to react to the new situation he was imposing on me, I pretended to fall into a kind of trance while he masturbated me with his hand and lips: this time he had switched on the light and the idea of seeing him kneeling next to my bed was more than I could take. I don't know how often Grandfather came back to paw me on the warm June nights that preceded the summer and our trip to Torrentbó. Five, ten times? I adopted the ingenious strategy of sleep and so avoided the spectacle of his repeated, annoying fingerings.

Weeks later, in a small grove of carob trees next to the gardens in Tor-rentbó, I told José Agustín what had happened. We had been discussing Grandfather's character in general terms—his meticulous hygiene, reserve, and stinginess—when the desire to tell him about my recent, embarrassing experience overcame my instinctive shyness. When I finished the story, fear-ing the likely complications if it was spread further, I begged my brother not to repeat a word of it. If Grandfather resumed his tricks when we returned to Barcelona, I added, I would contrive by myself to disappoint him.

With this in mind I piled a stack of books up by my bed on the night of our return. My grandparents went through my room as usual and, when the lights went out, I remained awake, crouching down, several encyclopedia volumes within reach of my hand, ready to throw at the intruder as soon as he showed up. But Grandfather gave no sign of life and, greatly relieved, I finally went to sleep with my small and now useless throwable library. The next day, after school, José Agustín said that Father wanted to speak to me. I went up to the small terrace above the garage where Eulalia used to hang out the washing. My father sat on a wicker armchair looking serious and forbid-ding and he asked me at once whether the incident with Grandfather was true. I said it was and his cold, gaunt, hawk-nosed features sharpened and stood out even more like those of a bird of prey. He did not attempt to hide the hatred he felt for his father-in-law, and he explained that this nasty vice of his was a crime against nature and had already ruined his promising ca-reer. As I found out then, my grandfather had held an important position in provincial government before the war, until he was caught touching a young lad and relative in a changing-room at the spa in San Sebastián near Barce-lona. People wanted to lynch him, my father said approvingly. They took him in handcuffs to prison, like a criminal, and when we went to see him with Grandmother and your mother, they cried tears of shame while he was silent and didn't even try to apologize. More and more excited, my father re-lated in detail the disgrace and stigmas the guilty man had brought upon himself and his family: early retirement from the Town Hall; public dis-honor; a perpetual stain on the good name of the family. Out of respect for my mother, he had had to swallow his disgust at that effeminate behavior and lack of virility; but this latest exploit was more than he could endure and his punishment should really teach him a lesson.

I don't know what was said in the interview between the two men, which no doubt took place on the same day I talked to my father. That afternoon, my grandparents packed up their personal belongings and, under the righteous, reproving gaze of their son-in-law, went to live in a small sublet villa about three blocks from home. Their departure, humiliating for both of them, coincided, I think, with the sudden worsening of Grandmother's health. From then on, they both ate lunch and dinner with us, but returned to their new house after rosary and evening prayers. Without taking into account the effect his behavior might have on his mother-in-law, my father did not bother to hide the aversion he felt for the guilty man, the greatest cross he had to bear, he would say sighing deeply. This systematic, persistent, small-minded persecution would continue over twenty years until they both died almost simultaneously. Conscious that he held all the cards, my father came up with a thousand ways to humiliate him. Forced to tolerate him for material reasons—ever since his forced departure from his job with ABDECA and the failed experiment with the bacteriology laboratory, most of our family's income came from the pension and savings of his father-in-law—he made him pay for that fact with an anger that rightly infuriated Eulalia and was often counterproductive. In 1951 when he flung himself into his last and most disastrous adventure with the latest Nazi boy wonder, he did so by coercing Grandfather, almost blackmailing him, into selling a boarding-house he owned. Instead of elevating us to the heights of opulence, as he trustingly believed, the proceeds from the sale disappeared, as if by magic, into the bottomless pocket of a certain Calvet, who was persecuted by the Belgian police because of his shady dealings with the Germans.

The tension provoked by this fact and, in general, the incessant harrassment that preceded it have been described by Luis in his novel *Antagonía* and I won't linger on it. Like many old married couples, my grandfather and father had created for themselves a small private hell whose routine allowed them to survive. The constant bitterness of the one and the cowed resignation of the other were the daily bread of life in Barcelona: a distressing ele-ment, whose intolerable repetition was a decisive factor in my hatred of the place. To move away from home, the district, the city: all my brand-new stu-dent plans centered on the idea of escape. The day I finally broke loose, I already lived outside mentally. When you go away it is because you have already left.

The incident with grandfather and the reaction it aroused in the family certainly had a traumatic effect upon me. My father's visceral hatred of homosexuals—Grandfather provided the nearest loathsome example—sometimes reached morbid extremes. He once related with great satisfac-tion to José Agustín—who wasted no time in repeating to me—that Mus-solini ordered the summary execution of "all queers." Although at that time I had not the slightest idea about my future sexuality, the news, rather than exciting me, filled me with unease. Of course, I thought that Grandfather's behavior toward me was reprehensible; but his punishment, cheerfully trumpeted around the house, awoke my sense of injustice and earned my condemnation. Mussolini's crude therapy must have been mentioned by my father, just as a simple piece of information, in the presence of my grand-father, who accepted it without protest—as usual. His submission to other people's judgments, his passive acceptance of his pariah state as natural, his inability to react against the attacks he continuously suffered much later pro-voked in me tremendous pity for him. His compulsive pederasty, shamefully hidden for decades, had been lived out as a secret tragedy: a vice condemned by the religion he believed in and the society that surrounded him. Since he did not have the moral temper necessary to control it, he had no choice but to offer his head to the executioner's axe each time he had the misfortune to give in to it and was then exposed to public pillorying. The memory of this self-contempt resulting from the scorn of others, of the shame that was ac-cepted and transmuted into inner guilt, weighed very heavily in my decision to affirm my destiny whatever the cost, and to set everything out clearly for myself and others. When Monique published her first novel, entitled *Les poissons-chats*—a work that describes the love of the heroine for a homosex-ual—Grandfather Ricardo read it, two or three years before he died, and was terribly shocked. Luis told me how he had explained in tears that the passions explored in the book were a hateful sin, that he had suffered from them throughout his life, and that whenever he yielded to them he had most deeply offended God. The idea that I might follow in his tracks, that I too might resign myself to a miserable, broken existence was the best antidote for my doubts and hesitations when, not entirely surprisingly, I found myself in the contradictory position of enjoying an intense emotional relationship with Monique and discovering the physical happiness I had not felt till then with a Moroccan construction worker living temporarily in France. With wise timing death saved my father from this final cruel blow: the realization that his secret fears, perhaps his darkest forebodings, had finally been expressed in me.

My grandmother began to suffer from loss of memory around the time I started to steal regularly from her purse. She was constantly forgetting where she had left things, she looked for them time and time again even in the most unlikely places and, if after turning the whole house upside down, the object that had gone astray did not appear, she would rush from one end of the passage to another like a madwoman, saying that she had gone out of her mind and mumbling like a spell the prayer to Saint Anthony:

> If you seek miracles, look:
> death and horror banished,
> poverty and the devil fled,
> the leprous and the sick healthy . . .

Her disturbed state got worse after our return from our second summer in Torrentbó, and I felt partly responsible. The twenty-five peseta notes that vanished mysteriously from her purse kept tormenting her. But it was here; I left it here with the keys only this morning . . . Grandfather would listen to her patiently, and, much to my relief, diverted any suspicions about theft into possible mishaps in the street, when she took Luis to school or came back from her meditations in church. These scenes, which followed the rhythm of my stealing, did not make me excessively remorseful. From the start, I had latched onto the precious immunity her absentmindedness provided me and used it in the most brazen manner. While Grandmother searched the house with her black oilskin bag under her arm, trying to recall where she had put the blessed note, I calmly stroked it in my pocket, thinking about the packet of sweets with which I would amaze my fellow pupils after the almost daily call at the wonderful Foix sweetshop. Grandmother no doubt suspected me as the probable thief; but rather than accuse me and show me up, she preferred to heap the blame on herself and put the losses down to her disorder and forgetfulness. Sometimes she asked me to recite the supposedly miraculous prayer along with her and I did so without any hesitation, proud of my lack of vulnerability. This shocking lack of any moral sense, almost certainly a fruit of our precocious experience of war, was to affect collectively each of the four children: we would all have, at one moment or another in our life, to struggle fiercely against it, to impose a norm of personal honesty, in a long, exhausting conflict whose outcome was unsure. As far as I am concerned, I did not forge my own code of strict integrity in fits and starts, but much later: far from home and in opposition to the values of our milieu, from the day I began to take an interest in politics where I also discovered a particular kind of trickery and deception. But I find my own unexpected lack of compassion much more surprising than our early amoral attitudes. My grandmother's infinite goodness, her self-denial for us, her boundless patience, the succession of tragedies that marked her life were not considered at all from the moment I decided to swipe from her purse. I can remember with a retrospective sense of shame the day that, no doubt fearing one of the forays I liked to carry out during lunch, excusing myself from the table on the pretext of going to the toilet, she sat down with her oilskin bag, and I was furious at seeing my plans foiled and insisted that she take it out as a matter of good manners and respect for the other guests. Grandmother obeyed me with tears in her eyes and as she left to put her purse in the usual place, she muttered in her distress, "Just as you wish, love, just as you wish."

Aunt Consuelo's death in the nursing home, the conflict between my father and her husband, the rushed move to the new abode far from the rest of the family, were certainly the main causes of Grandmother's mental disturbance. But her knowledge of the facts, of the reasons for their expulsion from our house is and always will be a mystery to me. Did my father or grandfather tell her what happened? Or else, as I sometimes think, had she noticed herself when Grandfather deserted their bed on those nights and slipped into the room next door with intentions that could be no secret to her after his previous arrest and imprisonment? Did she have to resign herself to her husband's final, painful act of madness, perhaps suffering in silence his kissing and sniggers in their grandson's bed? In its turn, had her more or less certain awareness of all this set off the defense mechanisms of her own madness? What is certain is that she soon added a mania to her absentmindedness, her real or supposed waywardness, and her loss of sense of direction. When I discovered it, I was really perplexed. She collected and rummaged through the garbage. At home she had begun, much to the consternation of Eulalia, to collect the skins of fruit and other leftovers, hoarding them carefully in her bag. She would walk to and fro in the garden loaded down with rubbish, aimlessly, until my father or grandfather told her to sit down. We children spied on her while she stirred up the garbage can and once when she was caught starting to hide some scraps, she lifted a piece of orange peel to her face and explained, as if playing a joke on me: "Look, I've got a mask!" But the initial, ambiguous excitement we felt as we stalked her soon changed to dismay when Grandmother extended the radius of her activity and began to poke furtively into the trash of the whole neighborhood. She had been so neat and tidy in her black hat and suit and obsessed by the idea of washing her feet before leaving the house—she would say that death might catch her in the street, like a woman she once met, with dirty ankles. Now she walked around in a terribly slovenly state: her hair was dirty and dishevelled, her stockings sagged, and her slippers were full of holes. When I spotted her one day in the distance crouching over a garbage can, my heart gave a turn: she looked like a beggar. Grandfather and Eulalia would nag at her affectionately, but in vain: she should look after herself better and leave the trash in peace. What would the neighbors think of her? Grandmother was silent or she would laugh: she was teetering on the brink. When we went to Torrentbó in the summer she stayed in Barcelona with her husband. One day she caught the train to Caldetas to come and see us. Although she knew the route perfectly well, she got lost when she left the station on the way to the *riera* and reached home flushed, out of breath, without money or purse, accompanied by some strangers who had taken pity on her when they saw her lost and alone. She had to be escorted back to Barcelona like a naughty girl who had run away. She spoke incoherently and seemed ridiculously scared that Grandfather Ricardo would scold her.

On our return to Pablo Alcover at the start of term we suddenly discovered her absence. Without us knowing, my father and grandfather had taken the difficult but inevitable decision to intern her in the nursing home where Aunt Consuelo had been. The death of her two daughters and the family tension created by her husband's behavior had swept away the last traces of her sanity, suddenly and indiscriminately removing all her memories. She had eternally sacrificed herself to the good of others and was incapable of thinking of herself. The successive blows that had rained down on her left her unprotected, with nothing to cling to. Although I don't discount the natural inclination to madness present on my mother's side of the family, hers was instead the product of an exceptionally bitter destiny and her almost total inability to fight back: she left the stage on tiptoe, with "shush" on her lips, so that we could enjoy the party peacefully without her.

The unhappiness common to almost all the women in my family and their patient acceptance of their lot show, with astonishing clarity, the truth of the arguments and positions of the feminist movement. Why were they always cast in the role of victims? A passiveness inherent in the supposed "feminine condition" or rather, as they themselves would say on acceding to the use of words, the necessary consequence of the pressures of society? Our grandparents Marta and Ricardo had lived in parallel form through a mutually oppressive situation without being able to help each other: traditional, Catholic, Spanish morality would finally crush both of them.

I only saw Grandmother once more, months later, on the day Eulalia and I went to visit her in the suburban nursing home where they looked after her. The description of this melancholy encounter in *Señas de identidad* spares me the painful task of recalling it in detail here. For those who haven't read the work, I shall just note that grandmother didn't recognize me and that, after exchanging a few polite phrases with Eulalia and myself, she returned to the opaque world that protected her from her unhappiness, where, mistress of a vast void, she undoubtedly lived a better life.

Since the disappearance of don Angel, our summers in Torrentbó had assumed a regular scenario: the same curtains, the same dialogue, the same actors, the same ritual. Aunt Catalina, my father's eldest sister, moved with her two daughters into the bedrooms next to the chapel and with the help of an old Navarrese servant, La Genara, her family cooked and ate, separate from us, in the dormer rooms on the top floor. Widowed quite some time ago by a husband she never mentioned—as if shrouding him in a cloud of unrelenting, implicit disapproval—she devoted all her time and energy to two main preoccupations: her prayers and the persnickety care of her delicate health. Forced to divide her day between her medicines and her worship, she followed a timetable that was as necessary, absorbing, and exact as those usually imposed in barracks or boarding schools in order to stiffen the resolve of the recruits or pupils. The range and antithetical character of her pains demanded the regular consumption of a series of medicines each of which was usually aimed at overcoming the damaging effect of the previous medicine: the potion she took for her liver apparently had a negative impact on her stomach, which needed as a result a brew that, unhappily, damaged her kidneys for which she then needed a special pill, which in turn . . . In between her brews and concoctions, syrups and drugs, Aunt Catalina fitted a tight schedule of prayers and pious acts that were sometimes part of the daily routine and sometimes linked to the calendar of saints' days: rosaries, hymns to the Trinity, novenas, prayers for indulgences, and a litany of lesser prayers to the blessed and saintly she particularly worshipped. Fermín de Urmeneta's journalistic contributions to the *Diario de Barcelona* similarly filled her with ecstasy. Don Fermín, a man with a powerful imagination, had specialized, in a manner of speaking, in the subject of the Holy Spirit and, with enviable fertility, assembled new facts, data, and refinements on the object of his ethereal passion. "What a wise man!" she would say in awe, "Have you read his latest article on the Paraclete?" Although she was assisted by her servant and eldest daughter from bedroom to terrace, from dining room to verandah, Aunt would end every day in a state of exhaustion, deprived of a pleasing, well-deserved solace from her innumerable duties and aches and pains. Stretched out on the chaise longue, with her eternal rosary of black beads in her hand, she remained absorbed in the computation of her prayers and pills while Genara and Eulalia discussed their affairs, podding beans or peas into a basket in the shade of the eucalyptus trees in the garden.

Uncle Leopoldo's visits were equally regular but much shorter: the Rat or Alfredo would pick him up at the station in Caldetas and he would come up the *riera* in the buggy with the bag where he kept his books as well as the tobacco, sausage, and olive oil reserved for his own personal consumption. My father's impulse in offering the house to his brothers and sisters would have been really selfless and praiseworthy if he hadn't spoiled it, as was often the case with him, by imposing mean restrictions and petty reminders on his generous largesse. In order to avoid getting a reputation as a sponger, Uncle would arrive in Torrentbó with samples of slightly rancid, "off" sausages, which he would dress himself in the kitchen, under Eulalia's severe and disapproving gaze. His rather cynical, bachelor spirit of independence, his original, outlandish ways, his lack of respect for convention and ignorance of good manners made him a pleasant, attractive person. He was a fixed star in our summers and his delight in evoking his childhood or displaying his knowledge of geography and astronomy, his skill in dishing out gossipy anecdotes, which, but for him, would have remained in oblivion, granted him a leading role in our family's imaginary world. Under a variety of names and disguises, he would appear in one of my novels and in my brother Luis's trilogy, fixed forever in the heart of a literary enterprise whose existence he would be unaware of.

The passion we shared for geography soon took shape in long, interesting conversations about places and territories that neither of us had ever seen. He was selfish, comfort-loving, and sedentary but, although he detested anything new that required an effort on his part and had hardly set foot outside Catalonia, Uncle Leopoldo spoke excitedly, with a dazzling display of detail,

about the Peruvian altiplano and the Argentinian pampa, the climate of
Zanzibar and the subsoil of Angola. Following his advice, I acquired a voluminous picture atlas, illustrated with plates and photographs, which was
my favorite reading matter for two or three years. Thanks to this, I soon
memorized the size, population, capital, main cities, legal status, and natural
riches of every country in the world. Our chats would range from the oro-
graphic makeup of the Caucasus to the French colonial settlements in India
or the South Pacific. Uncle spoke about Numea or Pondicherry as if they
were well-known spots where he used to spend his weekends. Convinced
that Europe would end up in ruins, whatever the result of the war, he tried
to shape my destiny by encouraging me to live far away from the continent.
Each of the territories or states described in the book received its share of his
attention. Nigeria and the Congo offered the European colonizer a vast pan-
oply of natural riches, but the heat and humidity dominating their weather
should discourage me from living there; Brazil had obvious advantages:
large stretches of uncultivated land, a cheap, diligent labor force, a language
that could easily be learned, the welcoming, open nature of the inhabitants;
in Cuba and Argentina our relatives could help me get started after I had arrived. But a trip along the Niger River, with its vast plantations of cotton,
groundnuts, sorghum, and rice, outdid in appeal every place already considered: the hippopotami, canoes, oleaginous palms, pictures of the native
women collecting coconuts aroused my uncle's enthusiasm. "Did you see
their breasts?" he smiled mischievously. "They look like real melons!" But
the imaginary journeys with which he compensated his becalmed state of
inertia had brought him a few problems and headaches before I was born.
Uncle Leopoldo had inherited a fair amount of money on the death of
Grandfather Antonio and, allowing himself to be swept up by his nomadic
fantasies, he had invested part of it in shares in exotic companies from which
he never recovered a cent. But misfortune, far from restraining him, had increased his theoretical interest and thirst for knowledge about distant countries and locations. As he was unable to embark on adventures because of his
age, he said, he wanted to pass on to his nephews his frustrated vocation as a

migrant: "Did you read the report on the Ecuadorian volcanoes? Pichincha, Chimborazo, Cotopaxi. Oh, if only I were your age!"

His knowledge of astronomy was equally remarkable. Under the August night sky, when the stars shone like embers gently stirred by the freshening breeze, Uncle would examine the firmament as if he owned it and would patiently teach us to decipher the constellations. As I looked up, Archer, the Two Bears, Cassiopeia, the Valley of the Lyre gradually stood out, clear and bright, in the midst of the confused flickering of the galaxies. Thanks to my uncle, I discovered the infinitude of the cosmos and our tiny presence within it. When I was assailed by my first religious doubts a few years later this awareness of the ridiculous smallness of the earth played a vital part in them: did the inhabitants of a lowly, secondary star really deserve such a lot of attention from their Maker? What absurd idea had led the Latter to sacrifice Himself so gratuitously for them? Was his ridiculous choice from that dense, sparkling swarm pure chance or caprice? Why just us and not the rest?

Together with this seductive penchant for geography and astronomy, Uncle Leopoldo also had opinions and characteristics that distinguished him from the rest of his brothers and sisters. He was an Anglophile, didn't believe in the Germans' victory, and when he defended his ideas against my father and Uncle Ignacio, all three would end up in a temper, insulting and reproaching each other. In our conversations after lunch or in the evenings on the verandah, he would bring out and show off the family's skeletons, much to my father's annoyance. Fixing his glasses on his enormous Basque nose, he would describe the uselessness and extravagance of the Taltavulls, Grandfather Antonio's pompous views, the pigeon-brain of one of our cousins. His sister's piety was often a target for his shafts and darts. Did she really think that a Hail Mary, mumbled mechanically, half asleep, would redeem the blessed souls in purgatory from millions of years of suffering? The emphasis he gave to his words and his sarcastic expression had the virtue of riling our aunt: her face, which was usually bloodless and pale, suddenly went beet red.

On Sundays and public holidays we took the buggy to the church in Torrentbó. Aunt Catalina and my father always made themselves comfortable
in the front pews, next to the four or five well-to-do people from the set-
tlement, while my brothers and I, next to the peasants in the back pews, listened to the timeworn sermons on modesty in female dress and the immoral
spectacle on the beaches. Mossén Luis spoke with his eyes half-closed, but
watched his parishioners' behavior out of the corner of his eye; once he called
our neighbor's daughter to task for partially baring her elbow, and he demanded she leave the House of God immediately. After the service, the
young people usually walked back while my father and aunt exchanged obsequious greetings with the wealthy widow of a banking family and her escort of noble ladies. On Fridays, the priest would come to our house and celebrate Mass in the chapel: afterwards there was breakfast with the altar boys,
at which Mossén blessed the food, and we waited with our heads lowered for
the cue to throw ourselves at the toast.

With our cousins María and Carmen we went to the beaches in Caldetas
and Arenys de Mar or else, equally loaded down with picnic baskets, we
hiked to the top of the nearby mountains or walked through the woods as far
as the Corredó well and hermitage. On the way, we picked fruit from the
fields and were often insulted by the peasants. Apart from these weekly excursions we remained within the boundaries of the farm; depending on the
season we looked for almonds, cherries, figs, or grapes to break the monotony of our daily diet. Now that he was no longer managing ABDECA, my
father didn't have the use of the company car and our journeys with him or
our uncle or aunt were in the buggy. This was usually driven by the Rat but
after his daughter had married Alfredo, his son-in-law would often replace
him. He was a strong, handsome young man and would later become a good
friend.

At home, we read, played mah-jongg or croquet, bathed in the pond,
chased after our dogs. José Agustín and I had frequent quarrels and, since he
had age on his side, I tended to seek protection from the grown-ups and
adopt the nasty role of tattletale. His unfortunate position as the firstborn—
and always unfavorably compared by my father to the brother who had dis-

appeared prematurely—throws enough light on the psychological difficulties he would meet later in life. In that period, his misbehavior was typical of
his age and our fights always ended quickly without any grudges or enmity.
Luis preferred to play with the children of the neighboring peasant-farmers,
and Marta and my cousins talked about movie stars and had written a fan-
letter to one of them asking for an autographed photo.

The summer holidays followed an unchanging rhythm, the only new developments occurring a few years later: my scribbling excitedly in notebooks
in the naive belief that I was writing novels and my equally frenetic and assiduous masturbating on the eruption of puberty.

The content of my reading matter had been changing during my years at
school: my liking for the little books in the *Marujita* series was followed by
the discovery of Elena Fortuny's characters—Uncle Rodrigo, Celia, Cuchi-
fritín—and then straight on to *Emil and the Detectives* and, especially, the
illustrated series of the *Adventures of William*, certainly the best of its kind.
My interest in Jules Verne and Salgari came rather later: it was a direct result
of my visits to the local cinemas where they showed adventure films and, in
any case, did not last very long. At the age of fourteen, on the advice of my
Uncle Luis, I had begun to get absorbed in the study of history books: biographies of Queen Victoria and Marie Antoinette, the enormous bound
volumes of Lafuente's *History of Spain*, a *History of the Girondins* translated
from French, Spengler's *Decline of the West*. In the summer, I lingered over
the marvellously engraved pages of the old *Spanish and South American Illustrated Magazine* and alternated these samples of a world that fascinated
me—of emperors and czars, assassinations, colonial activities, and royal
weddings—with a careful survey of books and chronicles referring to the
last war, generally written by Spanish correspondents who witnessed it. Uncle Luis was cut off from all communication because of his deafness. To
speak to him, you had to roll up a magazine like a tube and shout through it
into his outer ear. He was an avid reader of autobiographies and memoirs,
copies of which were arranged in neat rows in the living room of the bach-
elors' flat he shared with Leopoldo. As I gradually lost my penchant for ge-

ography and my affection for exotic journeys, I sought out books and magazines that corresponded to this new direction my curiosity took. Thanks to
Uncle Luis, I acquired in the space of two or three years a vast, heterogeneous, disjointed knowledge of areas of European history. The endless lists
of capitals, rivers, mountains, cities, and natural produce of the entire world
that had amazed my geography teachers were now replaced by lists of dy-
nasties, linked conflicts, wars, battles, defeats recited by me at the first opportunity with all the timing and aplomb of a parrot. My prodigious memory and an absurd appeal to my vanity changed me for some time into one of
those intolerable know-it-alls rightly hated by masters and pupils alike.
When by some trick of memory I go back to that time, the very temporary,
ephemeral confusion of our identities leaves me really confused. This life as
an insincere poseur started at the age of fourteen or fifteen and lasted beyond
adolescence. My facility for storytelling as one way of compensating for family traumas soon expanded into an adjacent area: during the long summer
holidays, I would pour these more or less imitative dreams and fantasies onto
paper to form a string of historical and adventuresome nonsense.

My fertility in this vein was extraordinary. Seated at the desk in the up-
stairs verandah in Torrentbó I composed without any corrections in a state
of delirious enthusiasm. The dual influence of films and my knowledge of
geography can clearly be seen in one of my manuscripts that was recovered
years later and now resides in a private collection at Boston University. My
sister used to buy the film magazines of the time and to avoid the tiresome,
annoying business of describing characters, I got the idea of cutting out photos from them and sticking them on the pages of my exercise book with simple captions indicating their identities. This trick—the discovery and use of
which would no doubt have modified the novelistic art of such conscientious
and detailed authors as Balzac and Galdós—allowed me to get on with the
ins-and-outs of the exploration of the Amazon, which I was describing,
without worrying about useless character sketches or tedious particulars. I
was a most precocious author of photo-novels and was also pioneering a way
into that soon-to-be-fashionable world of behaviorist narrative. No commentaries or digressions—straight to the point! With a similar facility and

enthusiasm, I wrote a sentimental novel about Joan of Arc and introduced some anachronisms into it. I am unsure if they were unconscious or not but they would now be greeted by the most prominent critics as examples of a daring, outspoken desire for change: rather than die on Bishop Cauchon's bonfire, she died on Robespierre's guillotine after a dramatic confrontation with him. I have a much vaguer memory of my other fifteen-year-old creations: I think there was one about the French Resistance to the Nazis, another with new scenes in the life of Kit Carson, in an episode of my own making. The films shown in the two Sarriá cinemas that I visited regularly with Luis were a source of second-rate ideas, characters, and settings for the proliferation of plots. Fortunately any notion of originality and plagiarism was not yet part of my personal literary baggage.

Once the work was completed, with a rapidity worthy of Corín Tellado, I implacably subjected my cousins to the reading test. I did not realize what torture I was inflicting on them until the evening of a special free dinner for the residents of Our Lady of Guadalupe College in Madrid University. After dinner we were led into the lounge where I believed, in my innocence, that there would be a brief speech from the writer-star of the unexpected banquet while we had coffee, but once the doors were discreetly closed at a perverse signal from the director, the brief speech turned into the interminable declamation of a drama the end of which could have belonged to that marvellous Chekhov tale: the hurling of a paperweight or similar weighty object that smashes with exquisite precision on the magpie head of the dramatist-novelist and interrupts forever the wonderfully soporific development of the third act. Wary now as a result of my own experience, I never again erred into this horrific abuse so common among literary people of deliberately imprisoning a captive audience. The practical application of the rule of "If you read me, I'll read you" is such an important advance for the Republic of Letters that I think it should appear, as a mandatory precept, in the first article of its Constitution.

Not one of my teachers or masters played a role in the development of the literary tastes I have just mentioned. My reading evolved exclusively within the family, without the slightest connection with what they taught or tried to teach us at school. The idea of giving us texts of the classics to read rather than stuffing our heads with dates of births and deaths and the titles of their many works had not yet even penetrated the brains of the ignorant, small-minded priests in charge of our literature classes. The only book that deserved the honor of being read in class throughout my secondary school life was a volume of Father Coloma's stories, in my last year with the Jesuits. We didn't even get that at the Bonanova school: the good brothers of the Christian Doctrine referred body and soul to the learned critical judgments and proven knowledge in the subject of Guillermo Díaz Plaja. Considering the educational system we suffered, it is not surprising that my love and interest in literature derived from other sources: first, Uncle Luis's advice and then my mother's library. Self-taught like almost all the men and women of my generation, my culture, which was tentatively shaped, would for a long time retain the mark of the prejudices, gaps, and insufficiencies of a barren, sun-baked Spain choked by the censorship and rigors of an oppressive regime. It is very significant that the books I would soon rush upon would be almost without exception by foreign authors. I read the novels that I devoured between eighteen and twenty-five either in French or in the second-rate translations that were smuggled in from Buenos Aires. The teaching handed out at school not only made me hate our literature—which was transformed into a collection of pedantic glosses and banal analyses—but also convinced me that there was nothing there worth getting to know. While consuming works by Proust, Gide, Malraux, Dos Passos, or Faulkner, I maintained an Olympian ignorance of our Renaissance or Golden Age. I even thought that Cervantes' universal reputation was suspect: flattered and praised to the skies by the school textbooks, the *Quixote* had to be a boring, tedious book. Intoxicated by Voltaire or Laclos, I felt no interest in the madness of the old *hidalgo* from La Mancha. I was twenty-six and living in France when I decided to look at the book and was thrown off my saddle, like Saul on the road to Damascus: those execrable school manuals were right. With a mixture of passion and anger I then threw myself at the work of our classical authors—anxious to regain the time wasted by my false educators. My amorous relationship with some of them was established immediately but, as I realized at once with rage, at the wrong time: like a youth who tastes the ineffable delight of intercourse after a long virginity, I had through my own fault been deprived of the most intense enjoyment. My exaggerated youthful prejudice against anything Spanish led me astray in this area as in so many others. I find this mistake the most difficult to forgive of the mistakes I made as a result of my narrow school training.

After my father changed our school in the autumn of forty-three I stayed in the one in Bonanova until the end of my secondary schooling. Five years whose monotony and lack of significance are expressed as much in the sparse memories as in the very slight traces they left in me. Unlike the period from the death of my mother to the senility and internment of my grandmother—a stretch of about four years from which I have very exact reminiscences and to which my memory often returns—what came afterwards seems superficial and distant, a simple change of skin abandoned by someone else on the edge of the road. Nothing that was said or happened in the classrooms influenced my life directly or indirectly. That life continued developing on its own, anchored in the family circle, essentially self-taught. When I began to masturbate at the onset of puberty, the incredible new pleasure casually discovered on a summer's day became one of the centers, if not the epicenter, of my life. This potential for enjoyment sited in my body overwhelmed at once, with raw strength, the religious or moral speeches that stigmatized it. In bed, in the bath, at Torrentbó, I regularly surrendered to respect for a material law that, for the space of a few seconds, confirmed me in my isolated, private existence, my irreducible separation from the rest of the world. However, I do not mean that traditional Catholic doctrine on sex, which was drummed into us in classrooms, confessionals, pulpits, religious manuals, made no impression on me. The idea of sin—of mortal sin with its hair-raising consequences—tortured me for several years. Dozens of times, kneeling opposite one of the local parish or church priests, I confessed my guilt and tried to reform myself. I knew full well that hours or days later that vital source of energy bursting out of me would impose its law and would imperiously destroy the fragile framework of precepts that con-

demned it in vain. Aware of this I escaped the reproaches of the same con-
fessor or spiritual director by regularly changing my church and confes-
sional in a kind of hide-and-seek, the absurdity of which was only too
obvious. Although my expressions of piety were forced and my religious beliefs were fragile and lukewarm, the fear of the torture and punishments of
hell besieged me for some time. Threats based on the sixth commandment,
from preachers and printed in pamphlets like those by Monsignor Tihamer
Toth, had a potentially traumatic effect on adolescents in the heat of puberty
who listened to or read about the supposed physical and moral ravages of the
impure act, a mere foretaste of the eternal, subtle, and most refined tortures
awaiting them in life after death. Like all Catholic boys of my and many previous generations I was subject to the harsh test of Saint Ignatius's Spiritual
Exercises in the famous refuges belonging to the order, in my case, the ones
in Manresa and Sarriá. The precise, detailed, exact description of these by
James Joyce—and before him the descriptions by Blanco White of the ones
carried out in a cave in Seville by Father Vega, who was clearly imbued with
the techniques of manipulation favored by disciples of the Loyola order, at
that time temporarily abolished—spares me the task of expounding them
to my readers. In *Portrait of the Artist as a Young Man* and Blanco's *Auto-
biography*, which I translated in part into his native language, my readers will
find point by point, trick by trick, example after example of the theatrical development and dramatic stage-managing repeated decades afterwards for
me and my companions, with the same inertia with which companies lacking a new repertoire routinely embrace the eternal, profitable revival of *Te-
norio* each year as All Souls' Day approaches. The ridiculous excesses of one
of the orators had a counterproductive effect on me. In spite of the hysterically issued terrestrial and extraterrestrial threats, the secret, enjoyable, absorbing masturbations continued with almost daily refinement.

The grotesque nature of that impossible-to-observe rule—aimed, as in
the case of ecclesiastical celibacy, at forming a guilty conscience readily sub-
missive and yielding to the higher or worldly interests of the Church in
Rome—was soon proved to me the night or morning I experienced my first
nocturnal pollution after abstaining from masturbation for several days after

a distressing confession. My awakening, with an erect penis and a sticky patch on my pajama trousers, filled me with terror. What had happened? Had I touched myself without noticing while I slept? Or had someone slipped into my bedroom and repeated Grandfather's nasty antics? Confused and not knowing where to turn, I decided the next night to sleep behind a locked door and with my tight swimsuit on to avoid any direct contact with my hand. But the heat of the night, combined with the unsatisfied lust of my body and the pressure of the material, again provoked the predictable leakage, to my amazement. The conviction that it was a natural act and hence outside the morbid scrutiny of my confessors gradually dawned on me. Together with the panic that the discovery of penicillin aroused among the guardians of Catholic morality—expressed by the brothers of the Christian Doctrine in a desperate affirmation of the existence of varieties of germs of venereal origin that were *resistant to penicillin*—this conviction soon rid me entirely of guilt and gave their sermons on youthful chastity a necessarily ridiculous aura.

As I said, my real life was still centered at home: my reading, novelettish stories, daydreaming, masturbations. School—its courses, studies, breaks, classmates, teachers—was merely a parenthesis in my experience that was closed as soon as I crossed over the leafy garden presided over by the order's founder and reached the Bonanova Avenue. My relationship with the brothers and teachers responsible for teaching the different disciplines was always distant and impersonal. While I write, they reappear before me faded by oblivion and the passage of time: the rather harrowing executioner's face of Brother Vicente, whose horrible expression and gesticulations as he described the inevitability of death convinced me that he suffered, as rumor had it, from epileptic fits or some nervous disorder; the smiling face of "Clémens," slight yet and energetic, with a small Hitler-style forelock or toupée, a lovely person although he worshipped the Nazis whose salute he forced on the class to the cry of *Heil Hitler*—he cried like a child on the day of his hero's suicide in the bunker; Brother Pedro's face, fussy and maternal like a broody hen—he had the arduous task of rebuffing on cyclostyled sheets almost the whole of world philosophy—sometimes with strange ad hominem arguments, whether it was Rousseau's effeminacy, or Nietzsche's madness—in the name of the principles, as solid as they were eternal, of the doctrine elaborated by Aristotle and St. Thomas of Aquinas.

The memory of the grey, blurred mass of my fellow pupils is even more amorphous. With one or two exceptions I didn't see them again after leaving school and, to tell the truth, I never took too much interest in them. Around the age of fifteen or sixteen, I became increasingly aware of the economic decline of our family because of my father's unfortunate business enterprises and the gap between our domestic straits and social pretensions. This decadence, symbolized not only by the gradual worsening of our style of life but also by the air of wear, decay, and age that fell over people and things in the Pablo Alcover house, led me for the first and only time in my life to try to make friends, although I knew we had very little in common, with two boys whose social position was much higher than mine, with the illusory hope of being integrated into a society I imagined to be seductive and brilliant. For one or two years, a pathetic, hypocritical boy by the name of Juan Goytisolo tried to imitate the elegance of dress, adopt the distinguished manners, and copy the affected mannerisms and accent characteristic of that fauna so typical of Barcelona—the "playboys of the Diagonal." Pretending to be a member of the set, he attended one or two society gatherings at which his timidity and lack of social graces showed him in his true colors: he couldn't dance, court the well-to-do girls, talk about luxury cars, or even move his body with youthful self-confidence or affected indolence. The feeling of failure and inability to adapt to that milieu left him confused and depressed. But the bitterness didn't last long: the hollow petulance of the two fellow pupils whom he had taken as models in a desire for social success convinced him at once of his mistake. The life of this copycat, snobbish double was fortunately short and its reproduction in the odd photo in grown-up clothes—stiff, awkward, and serious—provokes in me today when I look at it mixed feelings of pity and sarcasm.

Having abandoned my frivolous illusions I returned to the secrets, anguish, and conflicts of the family orbit. I continued to be an uneven pupil, well-endowed, according to my teachers, for the study of history, grammar, and languages, and, on the other hand, weak if not hopeless in science and mathematics. My ineptitude and lack of interest in the latter were total and absolute and convince me of the truth of the old saying that when all is said and done, intelligence is a matter of taste. Luckily for me, a friend in my year with whom I often talked in the playground and on the walk home confronted the same problem from the opposite direction. Highly intelligent and able in the areas of physics and mathematics, he reacted with indifference to the subjects that appealed to my curiosity. A friendship that was very beneficial for both of us developed from the mutual revelation of our respective qualities and deficiencies. While I wrote my friend José Vilarasau's essays, he gave me a generous helping hand in the subjects I hated. By helping each other, we managed to finish our crippled *bachillerato* without too many mishaps.

Vilarasau was also the first person in whom I dared confide my religious doubts. We had gradually exchanged some thoughts on the subject and outside the classroom Brother Pedro's supposed philosophical disquisitions were the target of our jokes and ridicule. Both of us thought the Creator's goodness and omnipotence somewhat problematic and contradictory. When we formulated some of our objections to an anonymous list of questions set by the brother to facilitate moral consultations, he suspected we were the authors and began to keep an eye on us. But my school years were coming to an end and the artificial, second-rate, petty world where my wretched tutors had tried to imprison me would soon vanish without a trace. *Time which passed, pricked them like bubbles over the surface of the water/ breaking their miserable tyranny*, wrote Luis Cernuda. Like him, I remember them today, as I write, *smiling in my sorrow*.

Final snapshots of Pablo Alcover: cypress hedges, wild rose-trees, bougainvillea in flower, langorous honeysuckle, a horse chestnut tree, an old man reading or nodding off under the shadow of the lemon tree. Territories patiently acquired through usurpation: my father's, Eulalia's, Grandfather's.

A steady process of deterioration: a carless garage, a defunct heating system, new, unrepairable faults. The inside got darker and darker: anemic light bulbs, penny-pinching illumination, furtive shadows wandering along the ghostly corridor. My father, in his slippers and white coat, preparing his strange potions, stirring the yogurt with a spoon. Grandfather, in his corner, reading the newspaper, always trying to pass unnoticed, occupying the least space possible. Eulalia, sitting in the dark in the kitchen in order to save electricity, listening to the ever-weaker heartbeats of the house, sounding out its decay, fatigue, asthenia, the ominous signs of its decrepitude: my father's endless warfare against Grandfather, griping, manias, mumbled rosary beads, the stifling enclosure of petty passions, senility, gradual deterioration. Equally there were changes in the young people that ruined and aged it: Marta, a woman, ready to get married; José Agustín, a university student and about to leave us to follow his studies away from home; Luis and I, still tied to school, but ready also to take flight, as it sadly felt, to flee from that house that was falling down around us, partition by partition, wall by wall, ceiling by ceiling. The poor Aragonese servant, made pregnant by the master of the house where she served, unmarried mother of a boy who was always introduced as a nephew, forced to emigrate to Catalonia, to experience changing houses and getting the sack, putting up with the shortages and difficulties of the war, Julia forever transformed into Eulalia, the jealous custodian of three boys whom she would get to love like her own children, ignorant, wise, pathetic, generous, turned, as a result of circumstances, from the central position her strength of will and character gave her among us, into a lucid, fatalistic witness of the decrepitude of things and people: worried at seeing us disappear one after the other, left alone, with two old men, in a ruined, broken-down house, on the lookout for the illness that was silently destroying her, forerunner of the Sphinx to which she euphemistically alluded when there was some misfortune in the family. Leaks, flaking paint, voracious mice, hungry wood-worm, coughing, spitting, decadence, decline: the images, sounds, impressions of my last years in Pablo Alcover, Barcelona, and Spain, ready to leave for wherever, my foot in the stirrup of an as yet imaginary horse. It was a wait punctuated by sudden evasions until the grace or blessing of my final departure. The memory of what I abandoned ceased to belong to me a good long time before I really left: the end of the story, the three deaths, would be beautifully integrated by Luis, with the passage of time, in the literary space of *Antagonía*.

I T ALL HAPPENED *as you had predicted: like an ephemeral, unstable house of cards, the collapse of one would bring* down the rest.

There was Luis's phone call bringing the bad news you had feared: Grand-father was dying, just a matter of hours according to the doctor, you should catch the first plane if you wanted to be at the funeral. Forty-eight busy, intense hours,* in a country where your name already figured on the black list, sidelong glances from the border police, an unwelcome, inopportune guest, attacked in print by the pack, a discreet watch kept on you, behind you a persistent shadow whose discor-dant movements clearly indicated that it didn't belong to you. Yours had stayed be-hind when you left for Spain where you returned like a ghost, an individual with a profession, civilian status, residence, place and date of birth fixed in his passport, but deprived by decree of a real identity: the possibility of writing, publishing, ex-pressing yourself in public, meeting friends without fear of compromising them. An unearthly, shadowless, shrunken Hoffmannesque character.

In spite of all you arrived in time to witness Grandfather's Catholic death, for-tified, as the death notice read, by spiritual support and apostolic blessing: his confession with a young priest whose dialogue with the moribund man, audible in the next room because of the latter's deafness, seemed like a short farce or comic sketch. Well, don Ricardo, you are very old and you must start getting ready. Get-ting ready? Why? How old are you, eighty? Oh, a lot older! And then Grand-father's pleasure as he received the holy oils, convinced as he was that he was being treated with a new, efficient remedy for the eczema that tormented him. Good, the pomade! Brothers and sister sat in the next room while Eulalia and Father, hidden,

*The entry and departure days stamped on your passport 4 March 1964 and 6 March 1964.

silent, scared, conscious that the Sphinx she evoked had finally arrived, waited for the denouement in their respective corners with a touching helplessness.

Five months later, on August eighth, it was Father's turn, on his deathbed, looking at you but already not recognizing you, eaten up, wasted to the bones by the illness's implacable advance. Eulalia in her room surrounded by the presents sent to her by Monique, enclosed in her distress, replying in monosyllables to your digressions and questions. Still you could read the silent question that pursues her and that she cannot put into words: what would she do now if the old ones left her?; and especially what would happen to her in that empty, condemned house? The Sphinx already knew the address: just when it was least expected, whenever she felt like it, she might prowl through the district and repeat the visit.

At midnight, the nurse whispered to you to come to the bedroom: your father lay with his eyes open, death rattles and gasps alternated more and more slowly, his lips hardly opened. The spongy unreality of moments without emotion, a feeling of being split in two. You went to the ceremony of the washing and preparation of the corpse to be handed over to the funeral undertakers: the lids were lowered over the fixed, seemingly dazzled gaze of the dead man; Marta's precise, rapid gesture as she removed the gold ring before the hand became rigid. The ridiculous ceremony in the Sarriá parish church, solemn farewell to the mourners, procession of black cars toward the cemetery, stopping in front of the luxurious pantheon where your family's remains rot. Feelings of horror at that mausoleum, your place reserved in it: a firm decision not to allow yourself to be buried there. Visitors with their condolences, an anxious conversation about the state of Eulalia, the intolerable oppression of the decaying scene of your childhood, desires to flee, catch the plane, get to the Prat airport, departure stamped by suspicious police, verification of the assertion of the Pueblo slanderers of a name with more popularity in police stations than in bookshops.

Regular news, through Luis, of Eulalia's cancer, first in Paris, then in Saint-Tropez, finally in Morocco. The selfish, cowardly resolve to continue your wanderings, even though the end is near and definite: the unbearable idea of confronting the terrified, defenseless woman, being forced to hide the reality of her pain, laughing to cheer her up, looking pleased, making up a rosy, happy future for her, lying to remove the grimace that doesn't make it to a smile and sticks in a motionless, stiff, desperate grin. Tetuan, Xauen, Al Hoceima, Meknes, scrutinizing the postes restantes *expecting a letter until the plain telegram, opened with trembling fingers, that was waiting for you in Fez. A sudden break in your journey as a confused fugitive from yourself: you return immediately to Tangier, find momentary refuge at home, digest the crushing news, drown your resilient feelings of guilt and go up to the comforting shade of the citadel in search of hashish or* maaxún.

From the moment you slump on your bed till the difficult, frequently delayed decision to get up painfully from the mess of topsy-turvy sheets, you lose all sense of time. No light filters through the half-closed shutter and when you look at your watch, it is almost eight o'clock. In the morning? The lights of the port and the nearby buildings dispel any doubts: it is dusk and your neighbors are gradually retiring to their rooms. What have you done during the day? A need to drink water, lots of water, to urinate, take a couple of aspirins. You will leave solving the riddle for later.

Twenty hours stretched out in bed, recreated gradually in the street taking deep breaths of the reviving breeze. Your head is still thick and aching but capable of reflection. Sitting on a terrace on Spain Avenue, the job of exhuming the incidents, encounters, visions, impulses, seizures of the longest night in your life: rescuing them carefully, like an archaeologist, from the depths into which they have subsided, dense strata of oblivion, shapeless masses, mists, opaqueness. Scrawling on the empty Gitanes packet the key words: pebbles, landmarks, signs that will lead you backward to the searing memory of what had happened.

Agile, light, delicate, perhaps momentary suspension of the universal imperative of gravity. You hover gently, no dizzy feeling, just above the ground, swift, tenuous, weightless, swaying or levitating in calm, wavering rhythm: a persistent dream ever since, strangely incorporated in the future into your usual modest repertoire. You are in Torrentbó: Father sitting in an armchair, probably dressed in white, with that natural, rather picturesque elegance that old age bestowed upon him during his final years. He's dead and you both know. However, you greet each other and exchange a few words. No pain on your part, no remorse. His presence is pleasing, gentle: he radiates a soothing impression of quiet, sweetness, peace. You say good-bye with mutual expressions of affection and you rise up again, garden, terrace, fountain of the frogs, somebody with a hoe over his shoulder (Alfredo?) smiles, waves from afar. A new decor, horse chestnut tree, wild plants, lemon tree and, in its shade, real Grandfather, in flesh and blood, his newspaper in his hands, looks at you for several seconds, he's old, very old, without interrupting his reading, there's nothing to say to you, absorbed in the news, world war has probably broken out.

Relapse into oblivion, spongy unreality, gradual distress, apprehension at the reunion that is being forged so tentatively, possible attempts to get up, piss, finish off the bottle of Sidi Harazm, peace that had vanished forever, anxiety, torture, tossing and turning in bed, black, everything black, your overburdened breast, head on fire, shooting pains, ominous premonitions, frustrated desire to escape, symptoms of panic, involuntary dampness, insistent palpitating of your heart, paralyzed limbs, imminence of the face you fear, the figure of Eulalia invoked by the excess of your own fear, already visible in the shadows, clearer and clearer, hair, skin, eyes, lips, cheeks, absolutely exact, shy, distant, silent, a bitter, reproachful gesture, image, presence, corporeality that overwhelms you, improvised, useless repentance, confused memory of pleas that went unheard, tardy declarations of love, an endless day in the dirty, stained bed, as if you were rooted there, spilling out everywhere, untrammeled, all you kept inside yourself, ghosts, mistakes, disloyalties, acts of cowardice, fears, a complete course of Freudian therapy for the price of a glass of maaxún.

Fertile, germinative consideration of transmigration by the light of poetry: the easy flight of the soul from one body to another body, similar or identical to the one it sustained in life: moving from the hard times of this life to another that appears freer and more flexible, clothed with the respect for a belief that consecrates it and raises it to the heights of an ideal throne: sheltered by Islam's warm shadow, the crouching old man calls you silently: his hand is thin, stiff, emaciated: his jellaba's hood half-covers his face but allows you to see the lean face, skin stretched tightly over his bones, his curved nose and bloodless lips: looking at you as if you are transparent, he quietly repeats, perhaps to himself, fi sabili Allah *and another tradi-*

tional call to the faithful, with the resigned calm of that other moribund fellow, Alonso Quijano on the edge of his grave, when you tiptoed into his room as soon as you arrived from the airport: your father, the succession of incarnations of your father in the squares and alleys of Fez or Marrakesh, crouching down, dignified, begging, chance or methodically planned encounters generating the spark, the arc light that was never lit in life: itinerant ritual, maze evoking the sadness of a non-meeting that nevertheless recalls him to your memory and affectionately brings him to life.

P A R T 2

"... et existe autant de différence de nous à
nous-mêmes que de nous à l'autrui."

MONTAIGNE

A T THE BEGINNING *of 1963, during your second visit to Cuba, a guest on this occasion of the Institute of Cinema Arts and Trades, you were invited by the poet Manuel Navarro Luna to accompany him to a meeting that was to be held in an education center for women conscripts on the outskirts of Havana. The old writer, whom you had met a year before on your visit to his native city, Manzanillo, was a convinced Communist, dedicated body and soul to the cause of the Revolution: he lived very modestly in a small hotel a few blocks from yours and was introduced to you by friends you had in common, who worked with him on the weekly magazine* Verde Olivo. *On his advice, the army magazine had published extracts from your report* Pueblo en marcha *and when lengthy sections of it appeared in the illustrated supplement to the daily* Revolución, *Navarro Luna warmly supported you in the polemic aroused by your phonetic transcription of popular Cuban speech. His great personal nobility and political integrity—the complete opposite of the revolutionary opportunism of so many other writers who had wretchedly compromised with the Batista dictatorship—together with his considerable devotion to Republican Spain, had swept aside the obstacles of his unconditional attachment to the USSR and, what was more serious for you, to the cultivation and defense of arthritic literary forms. At a time when the* arrivisme *of some of your first friends was beginning to show its true colors, his honest record, free of any ambition or desire for power, seemed a pleasant, comforting contrast. Several writers of your generation, like Heberto Padilla, shared your appreciation of the old poet whom they saw, not without reason, as the antimodel to a Nicolás Guillén, another lifelong Communist, but already complacent and proud of his privileges and official glory. Generous, selfless, exemplary, Navarro Luna embodied a moral strength not to be scorned in those agitated times of change and confusion.*

He picked you up at the Free Havana hotel along with an exiled Spanish Communist and the three of you went to the suburb where, he told you, he was going to preside over the closing stages of a political education course for several hundred girl volunteers. When you reached your destination it was already nighttime and the audience was waiting. One of the teachers of the course quickly told you about the day's activities: two lesbian girls caught en flagrante *in one of the school dormitories or showers had been submitted to public censure in an assembly and their final expulsion from the school had been unanimously decided. Your companions supported the decision without a flicker of doubt and, feeling vaguely ill at ease with a stifled sense of disgust, you followed them to the platform erected in the school's main playground, from which Navarro Luna was to deliver his speech. You can remember the violent glare of the floodlights, the ritual greetings, the disciplined rhythm of the applause: your friend, the poet, had introduced you to those present with affectionate hyperbole, as "a young revolutionary intellectual from Spain" and the uniformed adolescents had stood up and clapped interminably in honor of that courageous, heroic representative of a people in struggle, a worthy descendent of the heroes of Guadalajara and Brunete, messenger from muted workers, avenging fist of the exploited who hand in hand with Navarro Luna and the school's spiritual director responded to their greetings with a gentle swaying of raised arms, repeated their slogans and calls with a fleeting, blurred smile, integrated into a kind of choral* sardana *or slave dance, you, I, that juan goytisolo suddenly ashamed of his role, of the unbridgeable abyss opened at a stroke between reality and words, overwhelmed by the tumultuous applause for the imposter who had usurped his name, that ghost imposed on his real self like a double, or an unwanted guest, as expressed by one of Cavafy's most beautiful poems: astonished and incredulous at the grotesque contrast between his hagiography and the opaque reality, totally alien to the puppet or robot whose voice had ceased to represent him, and on the contrary represented his oppressors: the pretender perched on the stage where the anomalous behavior of the accused girls had just been judged, the cowardly, silent legislator of a sentence directed in the end against himself, against his real unprotected crouching self: abandon the catacombs, come out, breathe, spit in the other's face, the double, the ghost, treacherous enemy of your intimate feelings, sad despoiler of your individual traits and coordinates, loathing, only loathing at his presence, strong desires to throw off the mask and be exposed to public scorn, to confront the destiny of the accused, anything but imitate the laughable, mechanical movements, the rhythmic shaking of raised arms, empty ritual, painful feeling of being rent asunder, deceit, schizophrenia, gagged.*

But the other, the ghost, stayed on the platform at the education center for militia women with their syncopated gestures and empty smiles, outwardly adapted to his contemptible fiction, a complete imposter, not one sign of cracking, waving and swaying to right and left like some rag doll, retrospectively the object of horror and hatred on the part of the spectator split in two and suddenly silent on the journey back to the hotel, impatient to be alone with himself, to settle accounts with the ventriloquist, rescue his voice before it was too late and the other, the intruder, imposed the correct tribal norms, stifled your surging rebellion, disguised the truth, changed you into a zombie.

Seminal value of an experience that, by putting you on guard against lies, would cut off the path to the precipice: things did not happen at the hectic pace of your narrative but more gently; yet what was felt in a confused way then would gradually become clear after a few months until its blinding evidence won out: fear had established a growing margin of alienation between you and your persona, and, as you can verify now, when describing the lasting consequences of the fissure, a sudden, overpowering desire for authenticity.

A CROSSING OF THE ways: few times in my life have I had the feeling I had that summer of walking on shifting ground from which my existence could branch off and take different routes. In spite of my absolute incompetence in mathematics and science, I had just passed the awesome state examination and, throughout what would be my penultimate holidays in Torrentbó, I contemplated the options opening up before me with a feverish mixture of excitement and apprehension. I knew that I was leaving forever my previous comfortable refuge—the family shell and its natural extension, school—and the instinctive fear of the leap into the void of my future independence often clouded my joyful anticipation of the latter. Indecision about the path I should take, awareness of the need to earn my keep because of family straits, tormented me through sleepless nights. As I struggled to get to sleep, I felt the desire to retreat, to shelter in the cheerful irresponsibility of childhood, hide my head under my wing, be protected by the maternal cloister. These brief, intermittent attacks lost their strength as summer progressed and the desired but dreaded date of my start at university approached. Gradually, the pleasing certainty of loosening family ties, of finally distancing myself from my father and the oppressive world of Pablo Alcover brushed aside those worries. The drive to flee from the past weighed more heavily than any uncertainty about the future. There were only a few days left before matriculation began and I was still hesitating about my choice of courses. I preferred the humanities, especially history and literature, but the ways in which they were taught, which I had already experienced at school, warned me to act cautiously. In contrast, my father's gentle pressure in the direction of profit-making studies and my elder brother's example suggested law as the right choice. After carefully considering the pros and the cons, I sat on the fence and enrolled in both departments. I thought that time and circumstances would provide an opportune solution to the problem.

There was a crucial factor behind my rather compliant decision to qualify as a lawyer: my stubborn obsession with travel, seeing the world, getting out of Spain, had led me to conceive the silly, inept idea of becoming a diplomat. At a time when the possession of a passport and the subsequent opportunity to leave the peninsula were jealously reserved for a privileged few, diplomacy appeared like a miraculous panacea, the open sesame that would one day allow me to live in another nation, different from mine, to know other customs and lands, in a word to visit those places and panoramas evoked in my conversations with Uncle Leopoldo or by the illustrated pages of my ever-loyal picture atlas I thought any country was better than the one I had lived in till then and, unknowingly repeating Blanco White's experience a century and a half before, I sensed darkly that far from being a punishment for me, exile from my country would be a blessing. Although my present character and temperament are at the opposite extreme to the supple moderation required by diplomats, the underlying desire that dictated this choice was clear enough. I had proudly declared to all around me the irrevocable pattern of my future: I would become a kind of elegant, cultured Paul Morand, a brilliant polyglot, able to unify his personal literary inclinations with the pleasant tasks imposed by his career. The fact that I did not know any other languages beyond my impoverished Spanish did not even enter the arena of my preoccupations: I would study them. Armed with the conceit of my adolescence I felt ready to embrace a vast series of disciplines without sacrificing in any way my inveterate addiction to literature.

When I first entered the classrooms and courtyards of the old university building, I had no friends: the few companions I had been close to at school had enrolled in other departments and the handful who were studying law with me seemed either indifferent or alien. I had not found one familiar face in literature and arts lectures. This initial isolation favored my intention to concentrate entirely on my studies. My double matriculation, however, with its timetable clashes, presented me with a dilemma: as it was impossible to attend all the lectures, I decided to give priority to the law classes and restrict my commitment to the other courses as an "undeclared" student. This early choice had naturally been brought about by the routine, dull focus of the literature professors: this was my deepest, most vital interest and I feared, quite rightly, that a wretched time in the lecture theatres might make me hate what I was made for, the precious field of my future vocation and inclinations. I thought it was better to concentrate on boring, harmless subjects, with the prospect of one day entering, thanks to them, the Diplomatic School, rather than wasting valuable time on a counterproductive apprenticeship and throwing away my eventual talents as a writer. With the exception of Vicens Vives's and one or two other lecturers in areas remote from my interests, the arts faculty of the time could offer me no intellectual or moral sustenance. The civil war and its devastating aftermath had reduced university teaching to the lowest level: nine years after the end of the war, the majority of the chairs were still in the hands of mediocre, conformist teachers, chosen less for their knowledge or competence than by virtue of their faithfulness to the glorious principles of the Movement or the degree of their servility in the bending of their spines. The same desolate panorama, with the exceptions I shall later note, awaited students enrolled in law, but I personally didn't care. What I heard or might hear in classes flowed over me, I felt it was distant and alien. Having opted for a marriage of convenience instead of a passion that might be thwarted, I enjoyed the advantage of seeing things from the sidelines, with a generous margin of impassive detachment.

It is almost impossible for those who did not have the sad privilege of knowing Spanish universities at the end of the forties to imagine the soporific state of destitution in which they vegetated. After the hopes aroused by the Allied victory had vanished, student agitation reached its lowest ebb. The struggles to rebuild the University Student Federation were only a vague, distant memory: its members repeatedly fell into the hands of the police and this gradually destroyed the ranks of the organization until it was swept away altogether. When I ventured into the law faculty in 1948, nobody showed, not even privately, the slightest interest in politics except for the odd Don Juan supporter like Senillosa and a small band of rowdy Falangists who spoke openly about José Antonio and his supposedly betrayed revolution. The Opus Dei actively recruited supporters and followers: a few old acquaintances, including my Aunt Rosario's eldest son, had yielded to their assiduous attentions and then proceeded to eye fearfully those, like myself, who frankly rejected their proselytizing. A mere admission of religious agnosticism was enough to cause a furor: as I would later discover to my dismay, not one of my fellow students had had the courage to make one. Apparently unanimous attitudes of conformism in matters of religion, morals, and politics viewed any expression of dissidence as a challenge or as lunatic behavior worthy of punishment or contempt. The silent opponents whom I would detect later—including almost all those in the ranks of Catalan nationalism—shared sometimes, in other areas, the majority criteria: I can remember clearly the day when, because I had allowed myself a joke at the expense of the saccharine figure of Pope Pacelli, I only just avoided Albert Manent's hysterical kick at my innocent testicles. The politically and intellectually aware students of years previous to mine, people like Castellet, Marsal, Reventós, or Manuel Sacristán, had already finished their arts or law studies or were about to do so. Gil de Biedma was taking his first literary steps and was preparing to complete his studies in Madrid with a view to entering the diplomatic corps. Carlos Barral, not yet wrapped up in one of those showy cloaks that would later change him into the ideal protagonist of *Don Mendo's Revenge*, was already getting drunk and writing poetry. I would only hear of Gabriel and Juan Ferraté years later. My year and the ones that followed were probably the dullest and most mutilated in our wretched postwar period: the last embers of resistance had died out in the smoke and ash of a deceitful peace and the first sparks of youthful rebellion had yet to fly. The miserable experience of my school years was thus repeated at university: no teachers, no guides, often without the books I desperately needed—inaccessible because of censorship or my cruel ignorance of other languages—my intellectual and moral education was going to proceed by chance, falteringly, at the mercy of casual encounters, reading, conversations outside the lecture halls. Circumstances made me an autodidact and by myself I would forge a disorganized, capricious culture the effects of which would drag on into my thirties and from which I would not be free until the day when, definitively distanced from the atmosphere of Spain and Barcelona, I began my own revision of the values and norms that had ruled my life till then without the blinkers or prejudices inherent in all ideologies and systems.

WHEN RECENTLY, as a result of a public reading of *Makbara*, I walked once more through the classrooms, corridors, and inner galleries of the arts courtyard, my memory tried painfully to rescue from a confused magma a few details and snapshots to corroborate the presence in this milieu of that anxious, vulnerable, frenetic youth whose ironic condescension toward his peers, really aimed at hiding his profound timidity, led him to use and abuse a show of knowledge and paradox with pedantic satisfaction. Strangely I have no photograph of him, as if my present alienation from the period and my unconscious desire to throw off everything I did or thought then had induced me to destroy the proofs of our embarrassing identity. Well, the youth in whom I recognize myself only with difficulty was nevertheless me, and the image he projected in those years, perhaps retained by those whom I afterwards lost touch with, had followed a path separate from mine, as the gifts and powers of miracle workers are sometimes carried on from inertia long after the perplexed creator has lost faith in their existence.

Shoes: black. Suit: beige or light grey. A well-tailored overcoat and gloves the same color as the suit in the style of a future diplomat. The boy stationed under the courtyard arches, withdrawn and indifferent to the noise and bustle of his companions, is carrying a briefcase full of books in which course books and notes are mixed up with novels and plays printed in Buenos Aires. Since leaving school he has become a feverish reader. His favorite authors are still Unamuno and Wilde. The first taught him to ask questions that would nourish his naive philosophical anxieties; the second, the art of witty, disrespectful contradiction, the caustic timing of the *causeur*. Catholicism, morality, ecclesiastical hierarchy are the preferred targets of his lances. His irreverence causes a scandal and wins him some appreciation and a number of enemies. Significantly, it encourages his conceited propensity to stand out, to surpass the rest in originality and intelligence. He studies assiduously and is soon one of the top students. He has arrogantly revealed to his colleagues that he is writing novels and, in his spare time, begins to learn French.

Generally, he is bored by the teaching of the first-year topics in the law school, but will overcome the tedium with stubborn persistence. The university rector forces them to memorize with an undaunted smile twenty Latin definitions of natural justice and this youth submits unflinchingly to the loathsome test. Roman law appears more bearable inasmuch as it blends in with his reading at home: from the first Caesars to Justinian, its compilers emerge with a halo of long-standing familiarity. He is interested in political economy: his studies will help him to understand the relationships that exist between society and ideology, their mutual dependence and interweaving. Luis G. de Valdeavellano's classes surprise him with their clarity and rigor: the slanderers brand him as a Republican and the description, far from lowering him in his eyes, confers upon him the prestige inherent in the unusual. This is a rara avis in the university of the day.

The contacts and exchange of ideas with his companions are more encouraging. Bypassing untalented, boring grinds, he will soon discover links and affinities with three students as fond of reading as he is: the first of them, Juan Eugenio Morera, is an ex-seminarist who is striving to make up for the time wasted at a Jesuit school by taking on with ruthless self-discipline both the law and arts degrees; the second, Mariano Castells, offspring of a well-known Barcelona family whose brilliant, disorganized character, together with a passion for books only comparable to his own, seduces and attracts him. Although the third, Enrique Boada, does not reveal any great enthusiasm for his studies, the dandyism and ironic indifference he displays in class arouse his attention and interest. Thanks to Morera, who is older and so gains a degree of moral authority over Mariano and himself, the latter attend Lucas Beltrán's economics seminar for a few months where Keynes's and Schumpeter's theories are discussed in a heavy atmosphere of pipe smoke and American cigarettes: as participation in the discussions is unavoidable, our would-be diplomat and budding dilettante plays with the strange idea of focusing one of them on the untypical Wilde essay, *The Soul of Man under Socialism*. Lucas Beltrán cautiously sets out the different economic options in modern society and Marx's name will appear for the first time in our student's conversations without any of the insulting epithets that usually disfigure it. The publications of the Fondo de Cultura, introduced more or less clandestinely from Mexico, circulate by hand and the supposed brilliant contender for embassies acquires a good number of them in the name of his future studies. At the same time, Morera has put them in touch with an ambitious, mordant assistant lecturer who within a few years would scale the peaks of the university hierarchy: Fabian Estapé still lives with his parents in an old flat on the Paseo de San Juan, does not hide his atheism and hatred of the church, and supplements his meagre income as a lecturer by giving private lessons in political economy. The trio of friends agrees to join them and every week meets him in Mariano's grandmother's flat, where Balmes crosses over the Gran Vía. Through Estapé's influence our young man discovers Anatole France and devours at a stroke his *Complete Works* published by Aguilar, the distribution of which had been forbidden by the censor. The economics classes often give way to religious or metaphysical discussions that confront Estapé and himself with Juan Eugenio Morera, who, in spite of having given up the novitiate, retains intact his faith in Christianity. Mariano hesitates, but finally opts for theories of agnosticism, much to Morera's annoyance. The varied diet of economics, law, history, and literature soon extends gradually to some philosophical works: Ortega, Croce, Jaspers, Bergson, Kierkegaard. The desire for knowledge, to accumulate the greatest erudition in the subject, nourishes a childish rivalry between Mariano and himself, in which intellectual progress will sometimes be confused with a desire to purchase more books, especially those that, being rare or inaccessible, convert their discovery into a sought-after, prestigious title of nobility. His small band—to which Enrique Boada does not belong because of his indolent individualism—tends to clam up spontaneously and welcome any intrusion by strangers with reserve or distrust. The latter will be the target of their satire and, when they realize this, some companions who initially wished to ingratiate themselves will wisely opt to keep their distance. From time to time the trio and a few occasional guests celebrate a kind of assembly aimed at showing off their wisdom and learning to the outside world: our young man has prepared a long, pompous dissertation on French foreign policy, whether "from Talleyrand to Louis Philippe" or "from the Commune to Fashoda" and, with the same dauntless spirit that aimed the products of his wit at his cousins, he would now direct them pitilessly at his indulgent friends. Less fortunate than our student, an Argentinian outside the clan, the author of a huge tome on the Spanish spirit in the conquest of America, probably inspired by the ideas of Maeztú, Morente, and Menéndez Pidal—whom Mariano rapidly assigned to the thankless category of bore—conceived the unhappy idea of reading to them with great emphasis and enthusiasm the beginning and a few later chapters of his work. In his ecstasy he did not notice the exchanged glances, arching of eyebrows, grimaces, and chuckles of the genial trio until the deep, threatening silence after one of his pauses convinced him of the need to interrupt his reading and seek his audience's opinions: in turn, his implacable judges overwhelm him with sarcastic commentaries on the style, composition, opinions, and general aim of the book, leaving him sunk in a state of complete confusion and despondency. In a desperate attempt to break the siege, seeing a pack of cards on the table in the office where they are, the victim proposes a pause in the round of criticism: let's play a game of bank. The goat's always climbing up the bank, Mariano comments ironically. The Argentinian takes the blow courageously while our hero and his friends take delight in their cruel victory. Belief in their own superiority in their eyes legitimizes this harshness and bullying. The elitist philosophy, shot through with contempt for those judged to be on a lower level, gave them the right to adopt, for reasons of self-interest, a sycophantic, opportunistic attitude toward their teachers: private visits or consultations with professors on the pretext of broadening their studies, the organization of a celebratory lunch in the name of a group of "distinguished pupils." It is true that this example of *arrivisme* is ennobled by references to Machiavelli: Mariano and our man are at the time devoted admirers of *The Prince*. Such a cynical, cold strategy, together with the serious efforts devoted to their studies, will get its reward at the end of the year: when the exams arrive, Morera, Mariano, and himself will be awarded first-class passes in almost all their subjects.

The brief description of my homonym's first steps in the university thirty-five years ago creates in me an impression of amazement similar to that I imagine would be felt by a learned professor specializing in Calderón or the pre-Socratics if, as he walked along the corridors in the metro nearest to home, he were to come across a string of posters with a youthful portrait of himself advertising, all smiles and mustache, a natural, protein-filled shampoo or a snow-white, gentle, almost caressing shaving soap. Sleep-walking? Blindness? Nightmare? Instead call it incredulity tinged with sadness at the way this character totally contradicts your later reality. A nagging doubt about your identity after your childhood and the real existence of that absurd period would insidiously escort your steps to the main lecture hall where minutes later you were to begin your reading.

I S IT A FUNCTION *of involuntary memory to preserve the hidden impressions destroyed by the mechanics of remembering? doesn't the Freudian hypothesis, attributing to the latter a cannibalistic, predatory action over the traces of a buried past, perhaps condemn your naive attempt at recovery, since the possible results may be opposed to the end you pursue? the slow sedimentation through the years, every stratum vegetating in fertile semi-oblivion, would in this case be subject to an organized raid, the structuring force of which would not compensate—quite the contrary—for the devastating manipulation: confronted by the harshness of the theory you have no choice but to accept the contagious suspicion: the task you so trustingly undertook, that sudden decision not to allow your life, experience, emotions, what you are and have been, to disappear with you has gradually been transformed into territory plagued with traps and snares forcing you to advance cautiously, to look backward, question the precision of your accounts, submit them to verification by other witnesses, have recourse to written documents that in some way correct or change their laborious reconstruction: like dreams recounted at the moment of waking so they do not fade from memory, change at once and lose their aroma, the fidelity of the impression you describe requires a prudent injection of disbelief: your changeable personality in those years, with its often antithetical features, tempts you to grant it a later coherence that, despite its teleological truth, will be a subtle form of betrayal.*

H APPILY, I DO not think all the aspects and features
of the youth I was are today distant or alien. My intense passion for books and firm twenty-year-old decision to doubt the
norms and values of the social milieu in which I was brought up contained
the seed of my later break with that milieu and a still confused reaching for
new, more authentic forms of existence. Shut up in my room in Pablo Alcover, I often stayed awake until the early morning scrupulously reading
through the French books in my mother's library or devouring hundreds of
pages of Dostoyevski, Poe, Conrad, Pirandello, or Bernard Shaw. The
choice of these authors was in my case, as with Mariano, a product of chance.
Using the last penny at our disposal, we would search through the second-
hand bookshops in Aribau Street looking for a possible bargain or a rare,
fabulous copy. Books printed before the war, especially in the years of the Republic, were the continuous object of our searches: paperbacks published by
Cenit, worm-eaten translations of D'Annunzio, Maeterlinck, or Andreyev.
When the source of strange, extraordinary books seemed about to dry up,
Mariano would take advantage of his family connections and enable me to
penetrate the back rooms of two or three bookshops where prohibited
books were kept. There, trembling with excitement, my friend and I scru-
tinized the shelves and heaps where these books were either lined or piled
up, dazzled by the incredible plethora of authors and titles that we only
knew from hearsay yet whose assimilation we sensed as indispensable to our
correct intellectual development: Proust, Kafka, Malraux, Gide, Camus,
Sartre. To meet my growing bookshop expenses, I had to have recourse to
the pious strategy of convincing my father that they were legal reference

works, vital to the success of my study. At home, I hid my purchases in different and often ingenious hiding places, fearing my sister would discover them and reproach me for possessing and reading works included on the index of forbidden books: at the time, I continued to maintain the fiction of a surface Catholicism and on Sundays, soon to be accompanied by Luis, I would walk around the district pretending to abide by the rule of attending Mass. The enforced furtive nature of my explorations—the enjoyable awareness of entering forbidden areas—infused my reading with a thrill of excitement and stimulation that can only really be understood by those who have tasted the same waters. The results of this precocious discovery would have a beneficial influence on my life: the idea of pleasure, associated in my inner self with notions of transgression and clandestine activity, would later open the way to the gradual, reticent, laborious acceptance of other more hidden, intimate impulses.

The relative tolerance of the Francoist authorities toward authors deemed "less dangerous" allowed them to turn a blind eye to the clandestine circulation of their works: although the performance of Lorca's dramas was prohibited, the Losada editions had begun to appear on discreet shelves in some bookshops; Ortega and Baroja were harshly censored in church circles but it was possible to read them. Other more hostile writers remained, on the other hand, on the regime's black lists and direct access to their writings was nigh impossible. During my first year at university, a companion fond of poetry had handed me typewritten copies of Alberti's poems: that kind of samizdat did not reproduce, as a reader today might imagine, the committed poetry of *Entre el clavel y la rosa* or some angry war poem, but innocent compositions like *Marinero en tierra* and *Sobre los ángeles*. The difficulty of approaching the work of intellectuals who had taken sides against Franco transformed the act of reading into an amazing adventure. Italo Calvino's paradoxical statement that repressive, authoritarian regimes are the only ones that take literature seriously by granting it subversive power that it unfortunately does not have and by trying naively to prevent it being read contains in my view a great deal of truth. The best readers of a work, yesterday in Spain, today in the USSR and Soviet bloc countries, have been, will be, the surreptitious ones: those who take a huge risk to get at the work and yet accept the challenge and gradually exorcise their fear. Compared to an experience of this order, the facilities enjoyed by readers in open societies inevitably lower the intensity of the lived feeling: it is in no way the same thing to creep furtively into a religious or pagan harem excited by the idea of a plot hedged with dangers as to choose without any kind of pressure from among the dozens of consenting wards in a brothel. At the cost of upsetting someone, I maintain and have always maintained that my most intense, fertile reads belong to my youth, either due to the vague sense of engaging in a criminal act, or the certain enjoyment of disturbing desecration. I am obviously not talking about the level or quality of the works but about the emotions that enriched my reading quite independently of the works themselves. While the purchase of books I wanted involved me in a series of sacrifices and hurdles—both from the prohibitive price at which they were sold and the difficulty in finding them—I collected them lovingly until I had a modest but worthy library. When, as a result of settling down in Paris, I could get all the books I wanted thanks to the position held by Monique Lange in Gallimard, there was a mysterious decline in the value I attached to knowing them and I renounced my collector's conceit, lost interest in owning them, and didn't hesitate to get rid of them or give them away with a detachment inconceivable only a few years before. This waning of my property instinct toward cultural goods—books, records, engravings, and artistic-style objects—from then on would become a lasting feature of my character. I haven't reached Genet's monastic asceticism but I find life easier and more comfortable without the showy cultural robes that surround the majority of writers I know. It is only the content of books that attracts me, they are an object for immediate consumption: once read they get in my way and I'm happy to get rid of them provided I can buy them again whenever I may need them.

In the Spain of my youth it was the exclusive privilege of a handful to purchase the works of Orwell or Bernanos, Vallejo or Neruda: as with today's refined drugs, whoever wanted to read them needed simultaneously money, connections, and patience. When one of us managed to lay hands on some precious volume, after it was read, it would circulate at once within our group of friends. Although the trio of Mariano, Morera, and myself did not allow intruders into its more private discussions, we sometimes met in a café on the Ronda de la Universidad to exchange opinions on books and authors with a dozen or so students. These gatherings were informal and any participant could speak. I remember the evening one of the members gave a summary of his recent reading of *Le deuxième sexe* and the rest, led by Morera, rushed in with rather pedestrian arguments against the then novel and bold exposition of feminist theories. Enrique Boada, although eyed suspiciously by Mariano, would come to these encounters and supported me in my arguments with the others over a totally hedonist conception of life: aesthetics, we claimed, was above, and not answerable to, ethics. The reading of Thomas De Quincey, discovered by Mariano, brought new, efficient, and sometimes unusual arguments to my passionate defense of Art for Art's sake. Although no one at that stage upheld the doctrine of the social value of literature—not one of us had heard of Lukács or Politzer's gloomy creed— our extremist positions collided head-on with Morera and his justification of moral values. At other times the gathering was the arena for strange incidents that enlivened the monotony of some discussions with an unexpected touch of color. One night a student in a higher year, whom I knew by sight from Jesuit school, read a very suggestive, well-written text on the presence of *magic* in Andalusian poetry. His contribution was welcomed and everybody congratulated him. However, a few days later I leafed through the latest Lorca volume to arrive from Buenos Aires with Mariano, and we discovered first to our amazement and then with a degree of perverse excitement that the passage we liked so much was right there. Wishing to avenge our gullibility and punish the deceit, we invited the guilty plagiarist to our next meeting and exposed him to public humiliation. The episode and the violence it generated among us put an end to our gatherings for a time. The approaching exams and consequent shortage of time I believe also led to the break.

The most serious literary discussions were held in Mariano's house. There, next to the beautiful, spacious, well-appointed library in his room, the books—the fruit of our *razzias*—were read, discussed, and commented on passionately and at length. My friend was not forced as I was to hide works judged to be immoral or anti-Catholic. His parents were extremely tolerant and, as I later discovered, his mother, although a strong supporter of the social order installed by the regime, shared our attitude toward religion. In her eyes, the latter fulfilled a useful, moderating function: it kept the lower classes in their place with the promise of wonderful rewards in the future. Because of that she accompanied her husband to Mass although deep down she felt the ceremony was hollow and without substance. She had the foresight and intelligence to grant her only son a broad measure of freedom trusting that he could use it sensibly to develop his understanding and culture in a society that she herself considered sterile and mediocre.

The front balconies of Mariano's house faced directly onto the Borne market: the area had lost its residential character decades ago but the traffic of commercial life gave it intense life and bustle night and day. His flat, stuffed with furniture and objets d'art that had been carefully preserved, was a stark contrast with the image of ruin and destitution in the house on Pablo Alcover. The presence of a woman, his mother, cruelly emphasized the gap left by the disappearance of ours. Mariano moved with natural modesty around his territory. Although his social position was superior to mine, he had the elegance not to make me feel this. It was in his house that I tasted for the first time since the war one of those Vienna rolls that my mother gave me for breakfast as a child: I was used to the heavy substance we still consumed at home and the difference made me ashamed. His grandfather was a famous art collector: he lived on the lower floors of my friend's house in a kind of museum that I visited more than once. Romanesque statues and carvings stood there side by side with numerous pictures by Catalan painters of the Quatre Gats period: one small drawing room was entirely decorated by Nonell murals. The cultural, artistic milieu where my friend was brought up favored the development of his sensitivity and had been a decisive factor in his early but determined resolution to be a writer.

Mariano had shared his secret with me from the beginning of our friendship and this mutual confidence had sealed a solemn pact between us: our law studies were but a means to gain time with our families, a kind of temporary screen to conceal our true vocation. We had just discovered *Metamorphosis* and *Nausea* and, in full existential, metaphysical rebellion, we perceived no other outlet for our doubts and anguish than through creation. We were both going to be great novelists, with the range and depth of those we so admired. To reach the level of our models, we needed total dedication to the enterprise, to channel all our energies into the completion of our future work. Intoxicated by our reading of De Quincey, Baudelaire, and Huysmans, we aspired to live by only one rule in life, the search for sensations and experiences favorable to literary and artistic genesis. Our schooling would be alcohol, drugs, and the most refined, exquisite vices. Cure the soul through the senses and the senses through the soul, advised Wilde. But while we repeated the formula like a magic spell, we remained entirely chaste and sober. Our defense of every vice and perversion, proclaimed from the rooftops, was only theoretical. Maldoror's cruel exploits, diametrically opposed to the insipid morality of Christianity, swept us along. We wanted to be pitiless, malign, extravagant, and adopt a morbid, scandalous life-style. However, apart from the ironic, contemptuous attitude we displayed to most students, we were very careful not to put our ideas into practice. Neither Mariano nor myself had ever stepped inside a brothel, let alone got drunk. Possessed by literary fever, we calmly hovered on the frontiers of our kingdom, in a delightful state of dreamy fervor.

As a result of this focus and consequent change in priorities, my zeal for study declined. The unbearable tedium of the second-year law topics depressed me and gradually I began to put them to one side. I didn't give them the final brush-off in order not to upset my father, but I ceased to be the model student I had been months before, both opportunistic and servile toward my teachers. Even the idea of entering the diplomatic corps lost its attraction: as time passed, and I became more convinced I would one day rival Gide and Baudelaire, I reached the healthy conclusion that that life was not for me. This change was not sudden and thanks to the knowledge gained and the prestige earned in my first year I was able to save face and keep out of any trouble. It had the advantage of giving me a year's breathing space:

the time, on the pretext of continuing my legal studies, to complete the great literary work that would provide a posteriori justification.

My gradual movement away from the lecture halls had the unexpected effect of bringing me close to two students I had not previously been very friendly with on account of my devotion to my studies and my professor-worship: Enrique Boada whom I've already mentioned and Carlos Cortés. The former had followed my brilliant but short-lived career as a collector of first-class awards with indulgence and without comment: naturally endowed with aristocratic indolence, I readily accepted Mariano's criticisms when, perhaps jealous of my esteem for him, he branded him as capricious and unreliable. Boada's artistic tastes were much broader than mine: they ranged over music, dance, painting, and avant-garde events and activities. He accompanied his parents to the opera and occasionally succeeded in dragging me to the rare studio theatre performances tolerated by the censors. Just like Mariano and myself, he was confronting a problem of identity whose crises and sudden jolts would soon fill me with alarm. At that time, he was happy to stay awake nights listening to music and to go out at dawn driving fast through the city's deserted streets. Carlos Cortés only made the odd appearance in the arts faculty courtyard and I was introduced to him by a common friend before I totally rejected my dedication to my studies: he was an eccentric nonconformist dressed in a red bow tie that emphasized his bohemian looks, pleasantly different from the rest. He was a hardened reader like me and, to subsidize his addiction, he spent his time, like today's junkies, buying and selling literary works. He placed in my hands, for the first time, Blake's poetry in a prewar Catalan translation and encouraged me to read *Demian* and *Les caves du Vatican*. His passion for Gide and Hermann Hesse was contagious and as a result I wasn't satisfied until I had all their works. Cortés didn't come from a well-off family like the rest of my friends: his domestic straits and refusal to follow studies that were profitable forced him to live from day to day on the difficult, chancy book trade. He frequented the Barceloneta and Barrio Chino brothels, came drunk to the arts faculty, and displayed a gut aversion to the future lawmongers. In a rather provocative tone, he informed me that he was Jewish—his father's family belonged in fact to the *chueta* community of Majorca—and his contempt for social taboos and conventions made a deep impression on me. From the start he tried to initiate me into the mysteries of a life that Morera described as dissolute: those *leprous evenings*, as Cortés himself baptized them, dedicated to alcohol and whores. I was totally unaware of Barcelona life outside the conventional bourgeois circles in which I moved, but cautious pusillanimous habits that I would take some time to get rid of made me resist and so waste what I now consider to be precious time. This fear—which I could not then articulate—of putting my senses to the test, together with the simple-minded idea of preserving my strength to execute the masterpiece with which I would amaze the world one day, killed off that first opportunity to match actions with words and cast aside the rigid corset of inner censorship that, despite my external display of liberated, experienced youth, oppressed and paralyzed me. Only two years later, in Madrid—and consequently safe from the inhibitions created by a close circle of eye witnesses—would I have the courage to confront the adult experience I stupidly rejected then: the sudden discovery of alcohol, brothels, red-light districts, bars open in the early hours, and alongside, in the cottony depths of the new, persistent reality, aspirin and bitter coffee to combat hangovers.

WITH TIME MY conversations with Mariano had centered on a single, almost obsessional topic: the creation of our work, of that future work the light from which would immediately project us to the pinnacles of fame, if not of immortality. We both declared we were engaged in the task and it was certainly true in my case: in that autumn of 1950 I had rekindled my old passion for writing novels and once more I was filling dozens of pages with scribble strongly influenced by the gods of the moment, Gide and Hermann Hesse. I wrote in my room in the afternoon and furtively hid the manuscript behind a pile of law books: from time to time my father would look eagle-eyed through the door to see if I was studying hard and the enthusiasm and concentration he discovered dispelled his doubts and soothed his mind. Civil law must be very interesting, mustn't it, boy? he mumbled before disappearing; and I would pretend to emerge from deep involvement with the minutiae and requirements of emphyteutic domain and affirmed that indeed it was. My novel was advancing at a good rate, but the very facility with which I was writing, a product of unconscious, insidious imitation, at times filled me with anxiety. I knew that my Barcelona Spanish was impoverished and lacked precision and, forced to consult the dictionary continually, I fell into that rather stiff, bookish, stilted style that would to a greater or lesser degree affect the prose of my first novels. Neither was I convinced by the main theme: the moral, physical, and material decadence of a family as viewed through a refined, perverse adolescent was too transparent a result of my reading. However, fear of submitting myself to the criticism of others and confronting their negative opinions encouraged me to carry on to the end and avoid the temptation of discarding it halfway. Mariano was my only confidant and I often discussed the content of the book with him. Our rivalry had made us mutually demanding. My work had to be equal to those we most admired—*Les nourritures terrestres*, *Steppenwolf*—or be thrown into the wastepaper basket. Convinced as we were that one day we would achieve literary fame and glory, we could not endanger our objective by overhaste nor risk failure or mediocrity. Mariano was more radical than I and aspired to create a unique work that would be so absolutely perfect that to avoid its profanation by the gaze of others it would have to be eradicated once it was finished: a sublime act of destruction through love, he added, that a more responsible, conscious Creator than ours would have reserved for the universe rather than leaving us the wretched product he had cobbled together. As the months went by, my friend spoke with growing excitement about this work he had so severely, so implacably predestined to the flames. He composed by night, after drinking a few glasses to get in the mood: his writing then flowed automatically with no need for corrections or crossing out. Of course, I felt a great curiosity about the work; but Mariano was in no hurry to read to me from the closely written pages where he condensed his emotions, feelings, and ideas. There was probably a touch of coquettish apprehension in his reticence: a desire to keep my interest alive and at the same time a fear of disappointing me. One day when I confessed my lack of enthusiasm for my own novel—spoilt by awkward expressions, immature scenes, badly drawn characters, and influences that had not been at all assimilated—I succeeded in getting him to read a page of his: a text, written in the first person, which took on the voice of the *Maja desnuda*, but I was appalled by the childish clumsiness of the writing. Mariano immediately broke off reading as if he had read my thoughts and did not ask my opinion. Neither did I dare to express mine and, although the episode seemed to fall into oblivion, as I later noticed, it opened a breach for the first time in our friendship. Mariano never mentioned his work to me again and ceased to be interested in the outline and development of mine. We went on talking about literature and the books that impressed us: however, the previous certainty about our exceptional, luminous talent vanished.

While our doubts about the value of what we were doing put an end to our frenetic duet, we began to feel the need to establish relations with other new writers, to exchange ideas with them and get to know their works. It was impossible to find anyone in our class who could meet our exacting standards so we decided to look around previous classes. We knew from Estapé—whom we still saw in spite of our abandonment of the lecture halls—that Alberto Oliart had written a novel entitled *Gales* with which he hoped to win the Nadal prize. Estapé made out he had flipped through it and didn't spare us his sarcastic comments. He advised us to get to know Jaime Gil de Biedma, the author of a poem that earned the future rector's praises; the latter, playfully indiscreet, didn't hesitate to describe the amorous nature of the poem: read it slowly and you will understand, he said with a smile. But Gil de Biedma excused himself, invoking his end-of-course studies, and we could not associate him with our project. Fortunately, Luis Carandell and Mario Lacruz, two students in José Agustín's year whom I had met through him before my brother decided to take his law degree in Madrid, shared our interests and enthusiasms and were also looking for a platform from which to get themselves known. They welcomed the idea of meeting from time to time to read and discuss our work publicly; other people were also keen. Someone suggested the desirability of also inviting writers who were successful or at least had some published work in order to give our meetings more prominence. Advised, I think, by Carandell and Estapé, we worked out the list of eventual participants and got in touch with them.

Until then, the only flesh-and-blood writers I had come across were Sebastián Juan Arbó and Ana María Matute. The former lived nearby in the Tres Torres district and used to work in the cafés: in the morning in the defunct Rhinegold and in the afternoon in another café that has disappeared from the corner of Aragón and Paseo de Gracia. Arbó was a pleasant, modest, middle-aged man whose rather awkward manners revealed his peasant background, an image that was completely out of line with my idea of a writer. I imagined the latter to be aristocratic and distant, haughty and slightly perverted, brilliant modern combinations of Des Esseintes and Dorian Gray. I often bumped into Arbó on the Sarriá underground and he was always kind and attentive toward me but his common ways, country accent, and the unfortunate story of his recent visit to the Mexico College in the University City of Paris with his naive fascination for the show of freedom displayed by French women students and the faunlike behavior of his fellow countryman, Palau Fabre, forced me to arrogantly dismiss him with severe contempt. I was convinced that the true writer's genius must be deduced not only from his work but from his dress and appearance and I wondered rather anxiously if I myself would one day achieve the exquisite dandy-cum-bohemian alloy that would unveil my inner greatness to the world. It is pointless to state that I am now truly repelled by this narcissistic, provincial belief in the glorious, unmistakable aura of the poet that is still common in Spain. When I wrote years later "a genius and character right up to the grave: the more genius, the more character: the more character, the more genius," the Julianesque irony was not only aimed at the obstinate confusion of a great number of colleagues but at myself as a youthful would-be writer with pretensions. The continuous desire to perform, be in the limelight, play at being important, really converts the Hispanic literary tribe into a bunch of overdressed street performers: necklaces, cats, walking-stick handles, silvery slippers, admiral's hats, learned poses, old sea-dogs' beards, and cultivators of amphibious prose. If I compare the mimicry, showiness, and gauche manners of the baritones and tenors of the day with the simplicity, modesty, and reserve of Genet and other writers whom I had the opportunity to meet or know simply by sight, the contrast fills me with shame and strengthens my decision to keep myself on the edge of the dominant exhibitionism: I shall be that withdrawn, furtive Arab in Paris, dedicated to the tenacious exercise of his unspeakable manias. I must add in self-defense that, in spite of my ideas then about an artist's manner and appearance, I issued the invitation to Arbó: but he declined it, alleging overwork and scant liking for nocturnal activity, and perhaps he mistrusted the young amateur who disguised his condescension with the opportunist's obsequious manner.

My relationship with Ana María Matute was different right from the start. I also knew her from the Sarriá metro and two of her brothers had studied with me in the Jesuit college: I can remember them clearly, dressed as acolytes, in shiny red silk cloaks, edged in imitation mink. Ana María was at that time a very young, beautiful woman: she had already published a novel and was writing others that, according to gossip, posed serious problems for the censor. I maintained silent admiration for her, not daring to speak to her, until a mutual friend introduced us. Her warm, sweet voice, her openness and modest ways, immediately won my sympathy and affection. When I explained to her our plans for a literary circle, she gave her generous support: she knew and appreciated Mario Lacruz and promised to come to our discussions.

The initial nucleus that launched the Turia gathering soon counted on new patrons: the most enthusiastic of these was undoubtedly a theatrical author and director of some renown, full of plans for cultural developments and with more experience than we in organizational matters. It would be impossible for me to state now who introduced him to us and how he won our confidence. The dramatist—a lean, nervous man, in his forties—was pleasant company and showed us friendship and sympathy. He was branded as a homosexual in theatrical circles but Carandell and Lacruz were convinced that it was merely an artistic pose: the innocent pygmalionism of someone anxious to bring about the spiritual development of the young and in turn be enriched by their refreshing, exuberant company. In any case, our new friend revealed genuine interest in our first hesitant steps in the world of adult writing; he read, censored, corrected, and encouraged us; he returned the pages that we timidly submitted to his scrutiny with comments and notes that were often critical, I seem to recall, of our intellectualism and lack of tenderness. With general agreement, we had decided to adorn our gathering of budding and almost unknown authors with the prestigious, classical name of Mediterranean, which we all liked. We had invitation cards printed for the inaugural session, but the illustration that should have figured on them was a source of problems: our new friend suggested an athlete by Phidias while Mario Lacruz and Carandell insisted on it being a Venus, symbol of fertility. After a series of erudite discussions, the latter got their way and the card with the engraving of Venus was posted to a hundred friends, writers, or simply lovers of literature.

I do not propose to trace the ephemeral history of our circle nor to describe the presence there of people as different as Barral, Oliart, Díaz Plaja, and Salvador Espriu. We paid an unusual homage to André Gide on the occasion of his death and there was a competition for short stories, read by their authors, which I entered with two short texts and which was won on a show-of-hands vote by Ana María Matute. The latter's story and my tale, "El ladrón," would be published months later in a literary magazine subsidized by a devotee of the circle, a sailor-poet who wrote gloomy poetry on the human condition in the solitary refuge of his boat, which apparently was moored along the quayside of the Seine. This first entry into print, rather than flattering my vanity, depressed me: suddenly faced by the weakness and poverty of my creative powers, I realized that I was very far from the imaginative genius I aspired to and that I naively believed I had within me as a result of my conversations with Mariano.

During those weeks—February, March 1951—the dramatist had tightened his links with us: out of curiosity not without other motives—the desire to put to the test the purity of his intentions toward the group—my brother José Agustín and myself spent a weekend with him in a pension in Llafranc. But, either through cautiousness or lack of desire to confess his position, our friend kept up his guard, avoiding the verbal traps José Agustín cunningly set for him. His role as the open, refined educator, a kind of chaste Tiresias, admirer of noble, youthful beauty, had begun to establish credit with us all when an incident occurred that not only destroyed the image but also precipitated the end of our brand-new literary circle.

One night, Mariano turned up at home in a state of great excitement. He had gone out by himself for a walk with the dramatist in the Montjuich gardens: they had a friendly conversation on life and literature until his companion, with the mistaken belief that he had cleared the ground by quoting Plato and referring to Gide, tried to Mariano's horror and surprise to put words into action. Mariano's innocence in the matter and his desire to be admired as an expert in the field of art and literature had of course played an important role in the unfortunate slip: my friend needed someone to believe wholeheartedly in the genius of the work he was planning and, disillusioned with me because of my cold reaction, he thought he had found a substitute in the person of our mentor. The scene could have been comic had it not been for Mariano's rage: he was absolutely incensed by the act and demanded that the whole group ostracize the guilty party. Although I thought his reaction was exaggerated and tried to underplay the event's importance, the news spread. The circle's other patrons joined in Mariano's furious attacks: as I had already seen from what happened in my family, the insulting term of queer continued to be the *monstrum horrendum, informe, ingens*, a stigma or reproach that allowed no excuses or pity. Luis Carandell was given the task of telling the reprobate of his expulsion without it ever occurring to the latter to rebel or protest. Society's sacrificial lamb, he bowed his head like Grandfather and respected the oppressive, iniquitous law: having internalized the discourse of condemnation, there was no other way out but silence, shame, and humiliation.

Although my sexual inclination was in no way resolved at this time, I was disgusted by the prophylactic measures of my friends. Enrique Boada felt as upset as I did, and we agreed, behind the backs of the others, to make an embarrassed visit to the outcast, assuring him of our cowardly esteem and friendship. But the following gathering took place without him in an atmosphere rarified by rumors about what had happened. Given the lack of an organizer capable of coordinating our activities and the studied movement away by some members, Lacruz, Carandell, Mariano, and myself decided to make a clean break with the public announcement at the end of our fifth or sixth meeting of the definitive close to our literary gatherings.

M Y DECEITFUL BEHAVIOR in the contemptible episode I have just related was of course the reflec-
tion of an embarrassing uncertainty about myself. At twenty years of age,
my identity, not only as far as my character and moral standards were concerned but also the pleasures and phantoms that would later shape my life,
remained shrouded in a mist that I could not clear away. I had noticed with
anxiety and surprise from adolescence that, unlike my friends and companions, I was not at all aroused by being close to women physically or emotionally. The neighborhood girls I passed in the street did not make my heart
beat more quickly nor was I filled with a desire to go out with them: no falling in love, no sudden passion but alienation and introspection while in
sharp contrast to me José Agustín went from flirtation to flirtation and Luis,
with remarkable precocity, began to get telephone calls from his admirers
and friends. This indifference to the opposite sex extended equally to my
own: the close friendships I maintained with some friends did not involve
any elements of ambiguity. My male friendships were always straightforward and have continued to be so to the extent that they have not gone beyond the limits of my social class and the aseptic milieu of my culture. My
coolness and indifference toward the girls and boys my age and, in general,
to all the men and women integrated in the daily texture of my life did not,
however, exclude the insistent pursuit of my instincts. As in previous years I
continued to masturbate with monotonous regularity. The mental images
that assaulted me at such critical moments invariably introduced ingredients of force and even violence: I remember the day when a gypsy savagely
beat his mule in front of our house and that scene, far from arousing feelings
of mercy, excited me so much that I came in the middle of the street. The

external paraphernalia of exuberant, exotic, overwhelming virility—the photographs of Sikhs in military training, of two strongmen locked in the sinuous, oiled embrace of Turkish wrestling—similarly provoked and stimulated my fantasies. But these sudden, repeated sensations did not mesh with the rest of my daily experience: they remained isolated and beyond assimilation, totally outside the events of my real life. As I still had not gone beyond the frontiers of the bourgeois world and urban space in which I lived, my mental representations and the figures in my dreams had no possibility of taking on real shape: they were merely persistent shadows, condemned in the circumstances to wither in a hidden, latent state. In my maturity, I have often thought of the absolute lack of connection in those years between my libido and the objective world and I have reached the conclusion that if I had then lived in a heterogeneous or less closed environment— or, even better, under the favorable cover of *sotadism**—things would have been different. But, immersed in a limbo or a void worthy of a bell jar, the lashes that sometimes pained me did not provide any lead or key to an eventual way out: the pure civilian territory entirely occupied by my peers excluded a priori any possible temptation. Since nobody around me attracted me physically, I didn't even pose the question of whether I was homosexual or not. Consequently, I experienced a feeling of anxiety and astonishment the day Mariano—months before the incident with the dramatist—confided that someone I had met by chance days before had gone to him scandalmongering that I was a pansy. The accuser—the representative of a famous Argentinian publishing house—earned a living selling books as a door-to-door salesman: I had ordered some books from him and, if my memory does not deceive me, he asked me pointedly when he delivered them why I was interested in Wilde and André Gide. Incredulous and angry I persuaded Mariano to invite him to his house and to rebuff his slander with some energy. My friend did just that, while I listened to their conversation hidden behind a half-closed door to the sitting room. The book-trader— from a well-off family who would be arrested months later for his involvement in an armed robbery—had to confess that he had no proof, but insisted

*See "Sir Richard Burton, peregrino y sexólogo," *Crónicas sarracinas*, 170–71.

on the assumptions he based on my literary tastes. Before bidding farewell he mentioned various acquaintances who were also homosexuals and fans of Gide according to him. Although soon forgotten, the incident nevertheless left me with a bitter taste. The idea of being taken for a member of that guild, an object of universal contempt and hatred, filled me with anguish and fear. My father's pathological horror, daily exacerbated by enforced co-existence with Grandfather, had left a deep impression on me. All my friends, with one or two exceptions, professed equally virulent disgust toward "perverts." Eager to escape possible suspicion, I began to show a simulated interest in the girlfriends of Mariano and Juan Eugenio Morera. But these attempts to forge a "normal" image for myself immediately struck the impenetrable obstacle of my reserve and distance from girls. Since there was no ground for common understanding—a love of reading, personal likes—their company bored me and I soon left them. In the months after the end of the Turia gatherings, my previous warmth toward Mariano went cold. While he seemed to consider the period of his literary ambitions closed and was preparing to engage in stormy intrigue and adventures with women as I would have the opportunity to testify a year later in Madrid, I had sought refuge in writing and tried unsuccessfully to rewrite my novel. Among the people we saw during our failed cultural initiative, there was a poet and art critic from Santander whom Enrique Boada and I visited in his home. Fernando Gutiérrez was a man in his forties, simple, warm, and honest: he welcomed us straightaway with open arms and from that first encounter his house was a real home to me for just over a year. His wife and daughters were friendly toward me and my life with them became a regular habit. The gloom, decay, and old age that dominated Pablo Alcover suffocated me: forced to hide from my father the fact that I had abandoned my studies, I wrote in hiding, in a state of anxiety and oppression that clearly influenced the predictable collapse of the novel. I needed to escape, to flee from that intolerable climate and begin my work from a new base. Fernando Gutiérrez understood this and gave me invaluable support. After piously promising my father that he would help me review my law subjects, he managed to get me away from home regularly without arousing his fears. Established in his

flat on Bailén Street, packed with books and paintings, I helped him correct
his translations, sought his advice on the difficulties and snares of my novel,
and enjoyed the comforts and advantages of family life, away from home
but as if I were at home. I possessed an instinctive fear of stepping out of my
sterile, anesthetized world into other territories where I felt in an uncertain,
intuitive way that life existed; a fear of leaping into the void and discovering
what I really was kept me wrapped in a chrysalis for a year—no temptations,
no desires whatsoever. Neither the sudden explosion of the tram strike that
shook Barcelona out of its stupor nor the showy, shocking celebration of the
Eucharistic Congress, with its cohort of grotesque ceremonies, succeeded in
taking me out of my soft covering. My exclusive interest was the novel. Fernando Gutiérrez had soon noticed the defects and gaps in my Spanish and
encouraged me to overcome them. Although through my shortcomings he
could not then share his love for the poetry of our classics, he did manage to
extend and improve the content of my reading, limited at that time to
French books and confused translations from Buenos Aires. His patience
and generosity toward me led him to support my entry for the Prize for
Young Literature created by the publisher Janés, for which he was secretary.
In spite of the many corrections, my novel was clearly clumsy and immature:
the shadows of Gide and Hermann Hesse were visibly present and situations and characters suffered from melodrama and lack of realism. Nevertheless, the affectionate, prejudiced vote of my friend and his absolute confidence in the value of my work persuaded the publisher to award me the
prize, incredible in my eyes, of a check for ten thousand pesetas. Fortunately,
El mundo de los espejos was never published: Janés himself, when he received
me, had very tactfully let me know that his prize was only a stimulus to continue along the path to become a real writer one day. In the company of Fernando Gutiérrez and his family, I feasted my sudden riches on oysters and
champagne. His wife, who maintained intense passionate relationships
with his friends, also encouraged me to continue my apprenticeship with
them and even dreamt of seeing me marry one of her daughters. One of her
letters had fallen into my father's hands and its excited tone made him mistakenly alarmed about the nature of her feelings. I disillusioned him im-

mediately, but with the not-totally-erroneous idea that my friendship with
Fernando Gutiérrez was visibly taking me away from my law studies to
bring me close to literature, he began to make frequent lengthy visits difficult. The fiction of my legal studies poisoned my daily life and was each day
more difficult to sustain. I didn't know how to tackle the dilemma I faced
when chance decided for me. My father's miraculous business with one
of these half-Nazi half–professional swindler characters who inevitably
crossed his path had taken a disturbing turn during 1950 until it became an
unmitigated catastrophe threatening to ruin us. José Agustín had carried
through the necessary deals in Madrid, avoiding the firm's bankruptcy with
money from the sale of one of Grandfather's properties, but, when he was
forced to join the army after finishing his legal studies, salvaging whatever
from the shipwreck fell to me. That blow had finally sunk my father and the
atmosphere in Pablo Alcover could not have been gloomier. After bidding
farewell to Fernando Gutiérrez and the few friends I still saw, lighthearted
and greatly relieved in spite of the gravity of the circumstances, I took the
plane to Madrid.

F ACES APPEARED ONE *morning nobody knew from where:* *ghosts from beyond the city wall, perhaps from the execu-tioner's wall where they had been shot to pieces: righteously anonymous, their symbiosis in a common grave, a forgotten bed of hollyhocks: with us once more, despite that great clear-out, the seed of some deep, unbearable nightmare: an empty gesture to rub your eyes, wake up all at once, smile at a life that remains unchanged, at the civilian horizon of peace won through arms: still coming across them, rough, dark, frowning, with cold determination: an image aroused of times of whispered exchanges, a nervous start at the ring of the bell, a furtive, withered hand drawing a lace curtain, steps muffled by the carpet in the passage, prayers muttered under the breath, fear, lots of fear: they're advancing in tight-knit groups from the crowded side streets, worn-out shoes, threadbare clothes, external signs of poverty unseemingly displayed: a beslippered, middle-aged woman giving out leaflets to the curious: hoarse, incomprehensible cries from a small, lean individual wearing glasses: dozens, hundreds spring up from the urban asphalt at the bottom of the Ramblas like mushrooms after a shower, chanting slogans next to the smashed glass from the trams, general transport strike, a city completely paralyzed: the authorities rendered powerless, overtaken by the breadth of the protest, the sudden collective fiesta atmosphere, removal of the fear that kept lips sealed, the passersby's timid smiles, amorphous camaraderie, clumsy relearning of words and gestures that had been eliminated. Fleeting images, scraps of sentences, Father's anxious conversations, Eulalia's sighs in the kitchen, waiting expectantly, the crushing official response, the resonant voice on the radio, bold type in all the news-papers, foreign agents, revolutionary groups, hostile elements, actions skilfully co-ordinated from abroad, the traditional enemies of our values, dark conspiracy, hatred, ancient anti-Spanish hatred.*

Gradual preparation of the ground: machinery carefully arranged in the weeks preceding the great event: a general cleanup of the city, erection of crosses, podia, Eucharistic emblems, proliferation of shields marked with the symbol, setting up of loudspeakers on the main roads in the center: obsessive propaganda over the radio, entire editions of newspapers devoted to the event, Pastor Angelicus's ubiquitous photograph, expectation raised to the point of paroxysm: first motley experience of mass tourism: enthusiastic pilgrimages, flags, banners, oriflammes, greetings written in Latin: priests, nuns, monks, prelates, chaplains, deacons, curates, protonotaries, bishops in residence and in partibus dressed up in their corresponding clothes, habits, ankle-length suits, birettas, bonnets, chasubles, mitres, rain capes: far-sighted construction of walls to hide the wretchedness of the areas close to the processional route: peremptory expulsion of hundreds of slumdwellers, rapid removal of prostitutes and undesirables: enormous nighttime purges of our traditionally welcoming, hospitable city today held in check by an emotion impossible to put into words while it awaits the arrival of the Nuncio and his impressive retinue of military, civilian, and religious leaders: ever-present, hateful voices of an aggressive, dominating state Church that would pursue you for days, wherever you went, with tenacious persistence: to return home after an investigative wander through the devastated shacks and find your father kneeling opposite the radio set that is broadcasting at that moment the solemn blessing of the Pope.

Those who expected their liberating fleet to disembark in forty-five, just after the Allied victory and the four-sided Potsdam agreements, were probably not the same ones who came to welcome them on that luminous morning along the breakwater: men, women, children, the elderly, drawn by curiosity, a novelty soon to become routine: the Sixth Fleet's aircraft carriers and vessels anchored on the horizon on their first friendship visit: smaller boats brought the sailors on leave to the quayside of Peace: tall, strong, cheerful, friendly, dressed like in the films, they waved to the pleasure-boat travelers, gave cigarettes to the boys, willingly gave themselves over to the touts and pimps, went off with the boldest early risers amongst the prostitutes: admired on all sides they went up the Ramblas surprised by the gleeful disposition of the women, the incredibly cheap prices, the broken English of guides and waiters, the atmosphere of expectation, as if there were a fiesta in all the lower part of the city: society was changing, politics were changing, the world was changing, and the Americans were there, in their immaculate uniforms and hats, just like in Gene Kelly's musical comedy, walking across the Plaza de Cataluña, through the pigeons, happy, arm in arm: street photographers and amateur snap-shooters captured the scene from Singin' in the Rain *in the sun, without the tap dancing, although it was being played, as someone gloomily remarked, after a delay of seven bastard years.*

Duhring the time I lived under the friendly shadow of Fernando Gutiérrez and his family, my links with my university friends were loosened. In some cases, as with Morera and Mariano, the branching out was mutual; in others, it was due to outside circumstances that unexpectedly broke off our relationship: Enrique Boada had suffered a crisis of conscience—the first of what was later to be a rapid succession of them—and, for a period of a year, he took refuge in the diocesan seminary in Balmes Street. I visited him there two or three times in his ridiculous disguise as a novitiate, just before he set his habits on one side, obviously disenchanted with the boredom and routine of his experience. After completing his military service on a RIF air base, he entered the White Fathers community and disappeared for a time in the mirages and illusions of Algeria. Although it happened after my journey to Madrid, the break with Cortés was even more sudden: I knew of his hatred for the regime and his Catalan nationalist sympathies, but I was totally taken aback the day I found out that he had been imprisoned. Apparently he had been caught in a police roundup of a clandestine organization of the socialist movement then led by Pallach and he remained under arrest, awaiting trial, in the military fortress of Montjuich.

I left Barcelona certain that I was beginning a new stage in my life: the city where I was born and had grown up was hardly visible in outline, already lost in the mist, and I was moving away, as a poet wrote, "without grief or nostalgia." Madrid was still not the free land where, sleeping or waking, I stubbornly sought asylum; but the degree of movement it allowed me, without the ties or restrictions imposed by proximity to my father nor my overwhelming distress at the family scene in Pablo Alcover, seemed broad enough to make a paradise out of the capital that was still hungry, provincial, mediocre, and savagely punished by war. For the first time, I didn't have to tell anyone about what I was or was not doing. Although I had promised my father that I would continue studying to be a lawyer and would matriculate in the new Faculty of Political Sciences, I did not intend to waste my time on subjects I hated and I freely used my time to explore a world that, because of timidity or inhibitions, I had not even approached, without neglecting my plans and ambitions as a writer. My duties concerning my father's unsuccessful business venture were lighter than I supposed. My first cousin, Juan Berchmans Vallet, my Aunt María's elder son, had been given a post as notary in the capital two or three years before and, with a true family spirit and affection that I would have occasion to experience later on, he gave me valuable directions to steer through the legal labyrinth of the case to which we were committed to try to rescue what could still be rescued. My cousin Juan was a traditionalist, Catholic father of a large family, and had a virtue unheard of in the Spain of those times: respect for the ideas of others. Although he knew that mine and my brothers' were a thousand miles from his own beliefs, he courageously intervened first during the imprisonment of Luis and later in the campaign unleashed against me by the regime as a result of what happened during the presentation in Milan of *Campos de Níjar*, to stem the torrent of insults poured out by the press and to reestablish the truth.

When José Agustín was in Madrid finishing his law degree, he had stayed in the university residence hall, Our Lady of Guadalupe, then situated on Donoso Cortés Street, in the Argüelles district. This hall was originally created for young Latin American students pursuing their studies in Spain but some Spaniards from the provinces also stayed there. The political characteristics of an authoritarian government like Franco's had naturally attracted a handful of intellectuals and university students who were sympathetic toward them; some even enjoyed official scholarships and set themselves up as defenders of nebulous Falangist ideals: poets like Ernesto Cardenal and Pablo Antonio Cuadra worshipped the unblemished figure of José Antonio, before undergoing religious conversion as the first did to revolutionary ideals and yielding to the spell of charismatic leaders like Castro and Guevara. Others, like fellow Nicaraguan Mejía Sánchez and the Colombian Eduardo Cote, prudently stayed outside politics. When I arrived in Madrid, future poets or novelists like José Angel Valente and Julio Ramón Ribeyro had left the college or were about to do so, but two enthusiastic lovers of literary life still lodged there: Hernando Valencia Goelkel and Rafael Gutiérrez Girardot.

In the rush to organize the journey, my family had forgotten to reserve a room: when I appeared, they were all let. But Argüelles was then a residential student area and there was no problem in finding a sublet room. I settled down in one, hardly two blocks away from the college, in a family lodging-house, where they served both breakfast and lunch. Although I knew no one when I moved into the area, José Agustín's numerous friends immediately appeared on all sides. Besides, winning the Janés literary prize gave me a little fame and the poets and writers who gravitated around the Guadalupe wanted to get in touch with me and cultivate my friendship. Thanks to Eduardo Cote and Hernando Valencia I discovered the North American novel, alas, through very poor Argentinian translations: from Dos Passos to Hemingway, Madrid was just one moveable feast. It was the year of the publication of *The Old Man and the Sea* and Hernando Valencia was preparing a critical study of the work. I can remember that it was Hernando who showed me the first copy of the novel *Other Voices, Other Rooms*, by the then very youthful Truman Capote, which I read at one sitting as enthusiastically as he had. However, the author I found most fruitful during those months was William Faulkner. I was engulfed by his novels, captured by a tension and fascination that were new to me and, paralyzed by the sumptuous violence of the universe that closed around me, I stopped writing for the moment. I was helped along by this pause in my obsessive addiction to writing: freed from the burden of having to scribble futilely on sheet after sheet, I could at last devote myself to simpler, more pleasant activities. The Argüelles bars and cafés were the assiduous haunt of my new friends and, with a rapidity that surprised me, they initiated me into the attractions of leisure, lounging, and alcohol.

As I write these lines I can picture mentally every small detail of the tiny bar where we used to meet: the owner, Honorio, jovial, bald, friendly, preparing coffee or washing spoons, cups, and plates, always chatting to his customers; the vaguely academic barmaid, with her glasses and apron, who shared the confidences and worries of the Latin Americans who frequented the place, one of whom she would finally marry; the line of tables and benches parallel to the bar at which students, youths, or scholarship-holders and the less young but unemployed drank, smoked, discussed, played dominoes or cards throughout the day; at the back the gloomy lavatory to which the beer-drinkers regularly retired and where for the first time in my life I was sick from pure inebriation. Honorio's regulars were older and more experienced than I: on the whole they were lifelong drinkers who had generally neglected their studies and vegetated in Madrid thanks to opportune help from their governments or the monthly checks from their families. Some of them owned real individual stashes of wine or museums of alcohol catalogued under "literatures" according to their peculiar terminology: English, Russian, or French depending on whether it was gin, vodka, or cognac. Their cheerful lack of occupation and abundance of money made relations easy with girls and women in the area: their standard of living, much higher than the contemporary Spaniard's, turned them into real potentates and they peacefully enjoyed life untroubled by conscience. Their world, manners, behavior, accent, idiomatic expressions were new to me. I was accepted into their midst as the younger brother of José Agustín and their immediate friendliness helped me overcome my natural shyness.

The first day I stepped into Honorio's bar I met a couple of Colombians whose strangeness and fondness for drink attracted my attention. One of them, Lucho P. B., was a strapping man almost in his thirties, dark-skinned, with a face that seemed to have been carved in a violent fit of vision, endowed with extraordinary strength, vitality, and magnetism; he was finishing his medical studies but used to spend most of his time in the local bars. The other one was related on his father's side to the populist leader Jorge Eliecer Gaitán, murdered in Bogotá a few years before; young Pedro Antonio Gaitán looked more like a flamenco singer or a temporarily unemployed tango dancer whose company had gone bankrupt. With a lively gift of gab he com-

bined the odd check from his disappointed family with efficient, elegant recourse to the art of borrowing: as I later discovered, he was not following any
studies and strove to prolong his stay in Spain with every kind of argument
or excuse. Pedro Antonio had boundless admiration for Lucho: he followed
him like a shadow, sang his praises, encouraged his alcoholic leanings, and
when he succeeded in getting him drunk, would chastise him till he was beside himself and then let Lucho's insults rain down on him.

The group of Colombians addicted to Honorio's bar also included three
students who more or less successfully alternated their attendance at lectures
with a hectic nightlife that swept beyond the familiar boundaries of Argüelles and reached the bars in the center and the San Marcos brothels: Ramón, Herman, Jorge Eliecer would turn up at dusk when their two fellow
countrymen had already drunk a lively mix of rum, beer, and cognac and
were enmeshed in one of their interminable arguments. Pedro Antonio—
with that drooping mop of black hair which, like a monk's cowl in a hygro-
meter, forecast an impending storm—would run off when it was time to
pay, and his financial irresponsibility would provoke a thunderous down-
pour of insults from his irritable although faithful benefactor. At other times
Lucho, possessed with the dark aura of a giant gladiator, responded to the
curiosity or doubt of some passerby with one of his wonderful shows of
strength. He theatrically wrapped a handkerchief around his left hand,
seized an uncorked bottle full of water by the neck, and with his other hand
dealt it a confident crisp blow, shattering the bottom of the bottle. The group
of friends was then possessed by a powerful external force and suddenly
swept out of the bar.

Barely two weeks after my arrival in Madrid, I was already part of that
select band of drinkers. Conscious of dealing with a novice, my new companions took every care in my education: the airs I gave myself as a serious,
shy, wilful young man with a promising career as a writer before him were
soon scattered in that happy den where fortune or misfortune had guided
me. I began to mix wine, manzanilla, and cognac: I remember clearly my innocent surprise at the heavy blanket cast over my mind and the clumsiness
of my movements as I got up to urinate. Honorio's bar became my canteen

and my support system immediately: after lunch, I settled down there with some novel recommended by Cote or Hernando Valencia and read and waited for the noisy arrival of my friends. At night I followed them to the bars or cafés in the area or I went on a bar-crawl with them to the farthest dives of Carretas or the drinking houses on Echegaray.

The promiscuity, dirt, and harshness of the areas through which we flitted naturally affected my moral sensibility; but the fascination and stimulus they exercised over me were more powerful than my feelings of pity or condemnation. At the age of twenty-one I thus discovered what would then be a constant in my life. My dislike and even horror of urban areas or zones that are open, clean, symmetrical, and despairingly empty, with their beautiful, well-planned streets, fenced-off spaces, rapid traffic, and dreamlike existence: inhabitants entrenched in their houses, gardens, fences, external signs of unshared wealth, frigidity, egoism, anesthetized vitality. My passion, on the other hand, for street chaos, the brutal transparency of social relations, the confusion of public and private, the insidious flood of merchandise, precarious lives, improvised, packed tightly in a merciless struggle for survival, fertile barter, a mysterious magnetic pull. A bipolarity that would be intensified with the passing of time to the extreme of dividing up the urban landscape and my feelings for it into two opposed, irreconcilable camps: an irreversible hatred for the monuments and symbols of an ever-cynical, cruel history, for those severe, threatening, official districts whose false grandeur and solemnity hide the original sin of their construction at the expense of humiliations, sufferings, and blood; an attraction toward those areas where life is spontaneous, dark, dense, and proliferating, in which the creative act can take root and nourish its juices. My subsequent obsessive movements whether in Paris, Istanbul, New York, or Marrakesh—the instinctive seer's guesses guiding my steps toward territories neither sterilized nor subject to rigorous planning or control—perhaps originated thirty years ago during my hazardous forays through Madrid with my group of Colombian friends. The picaresque movement of beggars, aggressively displaying their poverty and servile respect for an authority that was no less terrible and suffocating for being distant or discreet, distinguished that postwar capital—no longer heroic but enthralled—which, with its sores and violent convulsions, would be my entry to the present metropolitan centers threatened by the subtle, avenging infiltration of the formerly colonized, the marginalized, and the victims.

My nightly excursions with Lucho, Pedro Antonio, and his compatriots went on pleasantly for several weeks: I experienced the problems and inconveniences of hangovers, thick heads the morning after, the confused impression of unreality. My brand-new incarnation as a drinker appeared from under the skin of my old life and made me realize how unstable and false that was. As on other occasions during those years of apprenticeship, I could identify surprising discontinuities in my biography: the existence of breaks or ruptures in habits and norms of behavior that I thought had deep roots. The curious, extroverted young man who had put his writing aside and expectantly savored the friendly immediacy of his companions in Honorio's bar seemed at first glance to be setting out on a carefree, untroubled phase in life when an inopportune event upset his hopes and brought him back to earth.

On one of my now daily alcoholic evenings, I accompanied Lucho and his friends through the different bars in the area; whether because I had drunk more than usual that day, or because Lucho insisted on putting my resistance to the test, what is sure is that we were both left at 2:00 A.M. in a café on Gaztambide near the college, having left our fellow adventurers behind on the curbside like lost possessions swept from a carriage by a furious wind. Slumped over the table next to the last round of empty glasses we exchanged the usual drunkards' confidences and I think, although I am unsure of the murky chloroformed images filtered by memory, we embraced and I caressed him under the waiter's impassive gaze. I don't know how we managed to leave the place given our state nor how I dragged Lucho to the bedroom in my *pensión* where he collapsed on one of the beds as soon as we arrived and his violent snoring prevented me from sleeping on the other one. When we got up the day after, neither of us remembered anything: we went down to Honorio's bar for a coffee and said a cheerful good-bye. However, some hours later, Lucho appeared in the *pensión* with a worried look on his face. He told me in an even tone, unreproachfully, that he had been seen the night before in a local bar as drunk as a newt and an unspecified friend had been acting in a *strange* way toward him. Although Lucho didn't spell out what this strangeness consisted of, he asked me to go out with him and, rather anxiously, I followed him to the café where we had both collapsed the night before. My friend exchanged a few quiet words with the waiter and left again with me. That fellow says that my companion touched me up, the whole works, Lucho commented laconically. His words terrified me; but Lucho interrupted the conversation: he insisted on inviting me to dinner and without mentioning the incident or my behavior, he embraced me as usual when we said good night.

That moral setback sank me into a state of humiliation and disarray that is difficult to express: what I had darkly and instinctively felt since I ceased to be a child had happened with an alarming sense of timing. I felt naked, vulnerable, defenseless, exposed without reason or guilt to insult and condemnation. What most upset and offended me was that the episode happened without any intervention of my will: simply and inevitably, it was an absurd punishment or cruel trick of destiny. Someone lurking within me and taking advantage of my temporary incapacity had become involved in improper behavior that I myself, when in control of my faculties and lucidity, condemned without qualification. But who was that malevolent, mocking intruder who, with alcoholic courage, identified me with pariahs, as an object of general repulsion, and was within an ace of discrediting me with my friends? My fear and horror for this undesirable Mr. Hyde, of whose stealthy reality I was suddenly aware, forced me to rekindle my vigilance toward myself: to avoid in the future, if I wanted to restore my damaged image, whatever circumstances might favor his reappearance. But the evil was done and, overwhelmed with gratuitous remorse, I nevertheless rebelled with all my might against the verdict of my distant, elusive tribunal.

In the light of my later experience it would be very convenient to endow what happened with some prophetic sense and establish a perfect chain of causes and effects from then on. But that is not my aim: I intend to narrate events as I perceived them when they happened. My helplessness and inability to interpret things exactly encouraged the vague, derisory hope I could disregard the truth. One way or another, the episode had its impact: with ill-concealed envy, Pedro Antonio referred to it maliciously. Forced to confront this disaster in my biography, I redoubled my efforts to bury it in oblivion. Fortunately, Lucho did not show any resentment: curiously, he had increased his display of friendship toward me. With a delicacy that was hardly in harmony with his brusque, direct manner, he never mentioned the matter nor allowed anyone else to in front of him. Perhaps enjoying his secret power over me, taking me affectionately by the arm, he insisted on my joining his group of friends in their customary forays in the carefree quarters of the city.

On one of these evenings, seven or eight of us settled down in the private room of a bar with two prostitutes. One, called Mely, was slim and well proportioned, with her hair dyed blonde; the other one, Fernandita, looked robust and healthy and acted like a peasant. Wine flowed freely, unleashing nostalgia and tongues, and my friends came dangerously near to an out-and-out declaration of their deep patriotic feelings: from "When you have departed, the shadows will consume me" to "Look they are looking at us looking at each other" the chorus of Colombian songs uttered in alcoholic tones resounded more and more enthusiastically in the private room while Lucho, embracing the two women, made them take turns sitting on his knee, proudly displayed his muscles, drank mouth to mouth with them from the same glass and observed me with his dark, metallic, inscrutable eyes as hard as mica. I interpreted this as a silent message and, changing my seat, I settled down next to Mely. I kissed and embraced her clumsily with an audacity I didn't think I was capable of—sustained of course by alcohol and Lucho's watchful presence. She looked at me with eyes I imagine were beautiful and light and, more experienced than I, her lips separated mine and her cool, slippery tongue entered my mouth like a dart. We went on kissing for a long time, sucking each other, savoring that new, warm intimacy. Meanwhile Lucho had taken Fernandita's breasts but I noticed that he was following my progress out of the corner of his eye. His implicit approval and my desire to eradicate all memory of my past behavior encouraged me to copy his example: I leaned over Mely's breasts now freed from the black bra and caressed, kissed, and nibbled her nipples. I don't know if it was she or her friend who decided it was time to go. There was a *meublé* next door, she said, and we could conclude our respective activities there more discreetly. We paid the waiter and went into the street. I remember the drunken Colombians' songs, Mely embracing me, and Fernandita, Lucho, the sharp, dry wind, the numbing wait for the nightwatchman to open the front door. Then the night in the company of Mely, her ritual stripping, the black lace garters tied round her waist, the generous crop of pubic hair, her friendly help in achieving an erection, the disturbing touch of her nails, the syncopated, panting coming together; and my light sleep, hearing her measured breathing, as if shaken by the wind, my feeling of relief at washing away the stain, that I was the same as everybody else, I could look Lucho and his friends in the face without blushing.

Comforted by this first experience, I continued to frequent the bars and whorehouses of Echegaray and San Marcos. My inhibitions and frigidity toward "decent" girls and women had gradually given way with those whose time and services were paid for. Although since my demonstration to Lucho I no longer felt the need to justify anything, I continued my visits to the cheapest, busiest brothels, directed by some inner affinity with that harsh, sordid, irregular universe, which in my eyes had a coherence and suggestiveness that reduced the people and places in my family, school, and university by contrast to the size of a decrepit, dusty window in a bourgeois store, crammed with fans, dolls, and junk; the brutal, unadorned image of a ruined, crumbling society where the ordinary people of the capital survived with a struggle was then revealed, I intuitively felt, in those bawdy houses, combining hospice, public auction, marketplace, and hideout and seeming to await the brush of a Goya to startle us with their mocking familiarity. During that harsh winter of fifty-three, full of events and new developments, I was unexpectedly visited by Mariano in the *pensión* where I was staying. I was surprised by the way he had changed in a few months: his youthful features looked as if they had gone flabby and he spoke in confident, rounded tones entirely new to him. I was told how he had problems with his family because of the girl he was living with: she was a dark, very beautiful Andalusian girl called Argelia whom he introduced me to one night in Barcelona just before my departure. Argelia had a flat on the other side of the Retiro Park and they had decided to take refuge there for a while waiting for the storm to die down. There were spare rooms in the flat: if I was interested, he could let me have one where I could live and write in peace and quiet. Although the offer did not appeal, since I would leave behind my fiery, sparkling band of friends, I finally accepted. The meagre funds I was getting from home were rapidly disappearing on my nightly jaunts and I now had no money to pay my lodgings. On the other hand, he added to tempt me, he and his girlfriend would have to go to Barcelona on the slightest pretext: in their absence, I would be in charge of the flat and would enjoy total freedom.

Perhaps to avoid the boredom of living alone with Argelia, Mariano tried to rekindle our old discussions on literature. However, his rich, exuberant passion for the novel seemed to have waned. His points of reference hadn't changed in two years, from which I deduced he had given up reading as well as writing. Like many other youngsters smitten by a love of literature and repeatedly scorned, he had signed an individual peace treaty with literature out of exhaustion. While even I was temporarily setting to one side my plans for novels, the only virtue of his well-meaning advice was to annoy me. The timeworn discussion of Hesse or Lafcadio's gratuitous act was a muted repetition, like a scratched recording of our university arguments. I tried to communicate my recent admiration for the North American novelists of the lost generation to him, but Mariano, browsing through the mediocre translation of a Hemingway novel, proclaimed contemptuously it was the work of a village idiot.

Taking advantage of his generous hospitality, I invited my gang of friends, much to Argelia's delight. My memories of that evening are fairly confused with music, dancing, singing, and alcohol on tap. Lucho had assiduously flirted with our hostess—clearly very happy to arouse Mariano's jealousy—and ended up drunk, unable to stand up. I went with him to my room and helped him to lie on the bed. Just as I was about to leave, I heard his hoarse voice pronounce my name and invite me to stretch out beside him. Even today, after thirty years, I cannot decipher the real meaning of his words: was he suggesting real intimacy between us or else, as I then perhaps mistakenly judged, was it a final test he was putting me through to clear up the truth about my *strange* behavior? If this were the case, if his drunkenness were exaggerated or put on, couldn't he be setting a trap only later to show me up in front of the others? The magnetic attraction he held for me in my alcoholic stupor did not work that night when I had only drunk a few drops: Mr. Hyde did not reappear. With a prudent small-mindedness that later I wouldn't hesitate to reproach myself for, I acted as if I hadn't heard him and tiptoed out of the bedroom, pleased with myself, but my heart was beating loudly. My stay in Argelia's home didn't last long: the possible legal consequences of my father's ridiculous business venture were almost resolved and my presence in Madrid was no longer indispensable. I held on as best I could for a few weeks to bid my leisurely farewells to Cote, Hernando Valencia, Ernesto Mejía Sánchez, and the group of Lucho's friends. The thought of returning to Barcelona, to the decline and distress of the world of Pablo Alcover, depressed me. But I wanted to rewrite the novel in the light of my new experiences and knew that for that reason I should leave Madrid.

A WARENESS OF THE *dangers and snares of the enterprise: futile attempt to erect a bridge over the disconti-
nuity of your biography, to grant coherence after the event to a mere accumulation
of ruins: looking for the underground channel that nourishes the chronological
succession of events in some way without being sure whether it is an archaeologist's
dig or a dazzling work of engineering: not just the arbitrary omission of memories
judged to be unimportant but the embroidering and assembly of the ones chosen:
a deceitful precision of detail, unconscious anachronisms, presumptuously clear
outlines: looks and appearance of the first woman you went to bed with, means of
transport used to go to the capital: images evoked but impossible to verify, lack of
trust in your rescue work, worrying absence of proof: the impression you're building with precarious materials, transmuting uncertain reality into the faked structure of a book: clearing out what remains of your past on the treacherous subter-
fuge that you are saving it from the viscous density of oblivion: the initial impulse
to tell all, to accept metaphorically the painful goring of the bull, dissolves and
loses shape when submitted to the insidious laws of written and oral narrative: to
convert life into style would be to have the ingenuity or pretensions of an alche-
mist: your arduous, uninterrupted struggle with writing has yet to endow you
with the secret of the philosopher's stone.*

I N MY ABSENCE, things had subtly changed: Luis had finished his secondary schooling and had started on his law degree with no more conviction than I had and had begun to mix with a group of students who were intellectually aware and interested in politics; José Agustín, after completing his military service in Mahón, was working and writing a book of poetry, *The Return*, his hopes set on the Adonais prize; Marta had a rather evasive, mysterious boyfriend: his surname, of unclear origins, displeased my father, obsessed as ever by genealogies; he referred to him as "a nameless being" and didn't hide his fears about possible Jewish forebears.

But changes were not restricted to my family: they extended similarly to the cultural, university circles in which I moved. My elder brother, after getting a job as an adviser to a private water company, had reestablished contact with the writers and intellectuals gathered around the *Laye* magazine: Sacristán, Castellet, Barral, Gabriel, and Juan Ferrater. This publication theoretically depended on the Falange Propaganda Office: consequently it was not subject to censorship. Thanks to this and taking advantage of the personal friendship that linked some of its members with the man nominally responsible for the publication, our friends had infiltrated the editorial board until they had changed it into something entirely different: a space for discussion where, with the necessary precautions, one could criticize more and more clearly the stagnation, poverty, and oppression of contemporary Spanish cultural life. Studies or essays on poetic language and the narrative techniques of the North American novel rubbed shoulders with brief, incisive, shattering notes on the protégés and clowns canonized by the official press. The ferocity of some reviews added to the obvious nonconformism promoted by the editors soon aroused suspicions and created obstacles. When José Agustín and I approached the nucleus that animated *Laye*, the magazine was going through a period of conflict. Pressure from the media and people criticized in its pages to get it suspended was intensifying daily. Months later a journalist sadly famous for his attacks on writers in exile and morbid detection of "reds" would write in a Falange daily a note entitled "The crows won't peck our eyes out," which, as an official denunciation of the small flock of black sheep, achieved final closure, after a violent tussle between the editorial board and the man responsible for the Propaganda Secretariat who was indirectly implicated in his accusations. My only article in the magazine—a criticism of Guido Piovene's novels—appeared in 1954 in the very last issue. As it was impossible to explain the reasons for the closure or even mention the fact, the editors used their wiles to put on the front cover a strip of mourning black with the piquant quotation from Garcilaso, "Suffering that which I cannot mention."

But I am anticipating events. In the summer of fifty-three, the major intellectual novelty for me was the double discovery of politics and narrative objectivism as defended by Castellet. The impact of the works of Sartre and Claude Edmonde Magny in relation to the novelistic technique of Dos Passos, Hemingway, and Dashiell Hammett—evident in Castellet's essays as collected in *La hora del lector* and their direct offspring, my short articles in *Problemas de la novela*—confronted us simultaneously with the concept, or rather dilemma, of "commitment," which was apparently insurmountable. I was writing, with the incorrigible haste of my youth, the definitive version of *Juegos de manos*: although I had included in it the milieus and experiences of my stay in Madrid, the novel still revealed the influence of Gide and other French writers. The unpleasant aftertaste of intellectualism and unsuccessful attempts at poetic writing for which I would reproach myself over a period of time nevertheless prevented me from falling into the morass of some works that I then took as models. On the other hand my first theoretical steps under the umbrella of Lukács and Sartre would lead to thoughts that, rather than reflecting the fruit of my experience as a reader and writer, would reveal the same painfully undigested reading as the majority of my innovative colleagues of that era. Like all-consuming energetic boa-constrictors we gulped down the ceremonial oxen of recently discovered Marxist aesthetics and remained quiet, passive, bloated, belching over the enormous, stolid prey until they were finally swallowed. Although the results of such gymnastics were of little relevance for a foreign reader with direct access to the sources where we anxiously drank in our ideas and doctrines, the latter fulfilled the function in our closed, provincial society of spreading the good news about what was happening on the other side of Franco's protective wall. From today's point of view, what then happened to my friends and me seems inevitable. Our intellectual orphanhood and the cultural desert we inhabited encouraged us to make the mistakes of those who have nothing to cling to and yet strive to take their first steps. Terrified by the void we suddenly discovered around us we embraced a body of clear, coherent doctrine that allowed us to rapidly forge a theory explaining our backwardness: imported bit by bit from France or Germany, the defense first of "behaviorism" and then of "critical realism" would be the tribute we paid to the intellectual wastes of the postwar years in our well-meaning desire to eliminate them. As T. S. Eliot says in a quotation picked out from José Angel Valente's recent illuminating book, "to theorise you need tremendous ingenuity; not to theorise requires tremendous honesty." Cast fatally into the ranks of the ingenuous, our task of knocking down the opened doors required in Spain the application of elementary, commonsense criteria. The need for an honesty beyond simplistic dogmatism and opportunistic, Manichaean attitudes would only be clear to us many years later when the practice of politics and the mocking persistence of concrete reality would force some of us to open our eyes.

The old idea of going to Paris took firmer root as I got on with the novel: to prepare for my first timid attempt to escape, I threw myself into studying and speaking French. In the Turia discussions I had met a youth my age with a British name and French origins: in his house on nearby Ganduxer Street he used to welcome his compatriots or Frenchified Catalans with whom it was possible to talk and improve my accent and vocabulary. There I heard for the first time Brassens's repertory and numerous of Piaf's creations with that excitement that "the unexpected imposes on the imagination."* In my usual hurry to achieve what I thought to be desirable at a particular moment, I wasn't satisfied till I understood the words of the songs. After assimilating the slang in Sartre's novels and stories I felt ready to tackle the plan I had nurtured from adolescence. Such a state of mind and mental disposition may explain the fact that my first novel, magnificently translated afterwards into French by Maurice Edgard Coindreau, read much better in this language than in the original defective Spanish: when I had to revise it some years ago to be included in some pompous Complete Works the continuous difficulties I met in revising the text convinced me that the only satisfactory way to erase them would be to retranslate the novel scrupulously from the language in which it was unconsciously conceived. My physical stay in Spain, apart from two excursions to Paris, would last until fifty-six. However, my intellectual life, and not only my fantasies, began to develop outside the country. I abandoned the translations imported from Buenos Aires and read the work of Proust, Stendhal, or Laclos, as well as authors from other quarters, only in French. This filter would distance me for some years from poetry and novels written in my own language, with consequences not difficult to calculate. But literature is and will be the kingdom of the unexpected: my passion for that world, lived like a real leap into the void, would cast me one day into a mysterious enjoyment of Spanish by virtue of the same strange logic through which I would find that my identity was aggressively affirmed in sex.

*Jaime Gil de Biedma, "Elegy and Memory of the French *Chanson*."

I T WAS NOT only intellectual factors that intervened in my nascent interest in politics—understood already as a critique of the conservative, clerical, authoritarian system imposed on Spain by the victory of the military insurgents of 1936. Scorn for my social class, the decadence and precarious state of which I saw reflected in the decline of my own family, had grown as I bitterly witnessed the robbery and lack of scruples in that collection of virtuous bourgeois Catholics behind the swindling of my father. It immediately became a moral imperative for me to put an end to that hypocritical society, a real cradle for the worst instincts of theft and plunder. When someone placed in my hands a Marxist primer bound in hardback with the title of Ignacio Agustí's novel, *Mariona Rebull*, in order to confuse any possible inquisitive eyes, to my excitement I discovered that the implacable portrait it sketched of merciless competition and barbaric exploitation by the captains of industry of the time coincided exactly with my own personal observations. Thus my precocious, burgeoning anticlericalism was joined by hatred for the bourgeoisie that supported the Church: a bourgeoisie that I then thought was condemned to die shortly, a victim of its own crimes, contradictions, and abuses.

On the other hand my short but fruitful stay in Madrid had corrected and broadened my narrow, limited perspectives. The territory where I usually lived, centered on home and university, was a miniature reproduction of a compact, well-structured world to which aliens and the marginal had no access. The poverty and helplessness that dominated the areas on the outskirts of Barcelona were totally unreal to me: fleeting, almost dreamlike images of wooden and tin shacks, snotty-nosed, barefoot children, pregnant women, overcrowding, squalor, heaps of excrement, glimpsed from the window of

the train that took us to Torrentbó. Strict sanitary control kept these inhabitants far from the places I frequented: their intrusive, vaguely threatening
presence was upsetting and, conscious of this, they humbly sought to be invisible. On my return I could see these things in a different light: less restrained by shyness, I wanted to repeat the experience of my explorations in
new places and contexts. If the slum areas in the suburbs seemed difficult to
reach, the mixed, colorful, bubbling districts to be seen in the lower reaches
of the Ramblas or from the sixty-four tram on the final stretch to the beaches
and the old skylift in the port filled me with less panic. My plans to poke my
nose into the dense, effervescent reality of the Barceloneta and the Barrio
Chino and to discover there an intellectual vital energy not offered by the insipid areas where imagination and sexuality did not thrive were first tentatively realized on my own, but were then helped after my return from Paris
by the release of my friend Carlos Cortés from the Montjuich fortress. He
was the best person to show me into a milieu that none of my previous
friends even wished to penetrate. While in jail with common criminals, he
had deepened his knowledge of that world by getting to know its customs
and slang. I was very excited by his first-hand accounts of a hermetic universe very close to the one I would later find in Genet: his description of the
queers going to Mass all made up with their combs and mantillas, of the
blind girl led there by her mother on visiting day to suck the prisoners' pricks
for a handful of coins, have not faded from my memory. Ignorant of all that
extended beyond the sterilizing walls of my education, I didn't even know
the terms he used: pimp, grass, fix, bugger, fence. My friend had put together
a glossary of underworld phrases, which he generously lent me years afterwards and which I used openly while writing *La resaca*. Alone or with Carlos, I carefully explored the bars and dives on the back streets between Conde
de Asalto and Atarazanas: the Criolla had disappeared after being frequented by the author of *Journal du voleur*, but other haunts exuding filth
and dirt still justified the reputation of that Barcelona opposed forever to the
homogeneous, paternalist, limp ideal of its petty bourgeoisie and the magnetic attraction the city held for writers like Genet or Bataille. Cigarette girls,
blackmarketeers, cripples, dope peddlers, vile, ill-lit bars, adverts for per-

manganate baths, contraceptive shops, grotesque sights from the Bodega Bohemia, rooms let by the hour, six-peseta brothels, the entire Hispanic court of miracles imposed a brutal reality that burst the bubble around me with one blast. The public whorehouses of Robadors and Tapias, the opulent, sometimes obese shapes of the women queuing on the benches, their legs wide apart, half-naked, preoccupied, in a posture of innocent bestiality, attracted me not only because of a consciously perverse Baudelairean aesthetic but because of their tangible, disturbing promiscuity. As I said, after my time in Madrid, I had lost all reserve or fear with prostitutes: entrusting the hidden part of my body to lips, mouths, hands capable of providing me with more enjoyment than my solitary manipulations also in reality justified my repeated visits. To complete the picture of my adventures I must add that at this time the need to clarify my position after the wretched episode with Lucho encouraged me to overcome my anxiety and worries and accept the offer of going to bed with known homosexuals from some bar in the area. But my clumsiness and frigidity with them, just the same as I would have experienced, I imagine, with a fussy, well-off girl, convinced me it was useless to persist in that direction; with a mixture of disappointment and relief—a relief slightly tinged with sadness—I strengthened myself for a time in the soothing, analgesic idea of an evident if errant "normality."

My fervor for slum areas, which urged me on for years, was incomprehensible and even shocking to most of my friends. Monique has always been right to reproach me for my immediate acceptance of impoverished places and situations that would be unbearable for her without an explicit Christian or Marxist will to change them. The charge is true to a certain extent and I will return to it at another time. But this provisional, selfish adaptation to a reality experienced by others as unjust and oppressive, partly originating in my unquenchable curiosity for what is different, alien, and beyond assimilation—curiosity with both political and literary meaning—nevertheless had other elements of personal authenticity beyond any would-be love of the picturesque or the "low life." In 1955 when Jaime Gil de Biedma recorded in the pages of his *Diario* one of our sprees in the company of a drunken, gypsylike, sinister bootblack or ex-legionnaire, emphasizing my "excessive *mauditisme,"* he leaves out an essential fact: my sexuality—except on very few occasions on the female side—was never bourgeois or polite. As I told him on one occasion when we sat chatting in the early hours in a car opposite our front door, I was never attracted by writers, intellectuals, or, simply, well-brought-up people wearing ties. My halogenous fantasies were then developing along lines that did not exist in Spain: lacking the physical, cultural model of bodily form that would come naturally to me years later, I sometimes chased, under the influence of alcohol, after a sad, degraded shadow, with predictable frustration, bitterness, and failure. This half-baked relationship through hash and the bottle never got beyond posturing. But even at these times, which were depressing and humiliating for me, I didn't try to deceive myself by hypocritically confusing the levels. The motive for my streetwalking was not just to satisfy in some way or another my desire for sex. The urban milieu into which I sank and its creative phantasmagoria sharpened my perception of things, opened up new, juicy bits of reality.

That summer I spent the time left by the hasty writing of my novel in fruitful wanderings through the Distrito Quinto and the bars in the port. My manuscript was almost ready and in September I typed it out. The granting of a passport—previously rejected brutally just as with the heroine in Menotti's *The Consul*—had been just a matter of patience for some time: while I corrected the typed copies of *Juegos de manos* I completed the forms and complied with all the necessary formalities. When I finally received it, I deposited the novel at the offices of the Destino publishing house before the time limit expired for the Nadal prize. My father was resigned to the idea of my trip to Paris: he prepared a letter of introduction for distant relatives, he put me on guard against the dangers and temptations of the city. The French are very immoral, my son; you must have a temper of steel to resist them. With a tiny offering from Grandfather—his only source of income, after the financial disaster, was now his pension from local government—and the profit from the resale of my books—the forbidden novels printed in Argentina—I went to Paris in October, to await there, at a distance, the favorable or unfavorable result of my first incursion into literature.

F OR YEARS CROSSING *the frontier by train would be an op-pressive rather than an exciting experience for you: the dull yet persistent impression of going through no-man's-land, and of being under close watch, strengthened as most passengers abandoned the train, you left Figueras, plainclothes inspectors severely studied passports, the landscape became sad and empty, walls were in ruins, buildings near to Port Bou assumed a gaunt, threatening air, the station itself became a broken-down, inhospitable place, with a strictly barracklike atmosphere: traces of a recent past were still to be seen: barbed-wire fences, sentry boxes, watchtowers, protective* cordon sanitaire, *fear of infiltrations by the maquis, omnipresent police: grey caps, braid, three-cornered hats, sinister offices, corridors with benches where you must wait: perhaps the room where on the 26 September 1940 a group of fugitives, countryless men and women, stayed for hours and hours begging and crying before the impassive officer who, seated at his desk, made routine invocations of the text of the decree that prevented their admission into the country, of his duty to take them under escort to the frontier where administrative internment in a camp awaited them, to hand them over to those they were escaping from: all that he, the man with the traits of a Jewish intellectual, vaguely Trotskyist because of his glasses, a member of the group, had foreseen for years: better to halt the game there, take advantage of the truce at night, absorb the dose of morphine carefully kept for the eventuality: although you knew nothing of him and nobody then cared for the exile's tomb, a trace of the old horror—like that insidious whiff in the well-aired room of the dead man after they have taken out shoes, ties, hats, that miraculous syrup against coughing with which he tried to cure himself, all the pathetic faded details that identified him—still remained, you now think, on the dark station in that apparently deserted, barren town where you impatiently awaited, suitcase in hand, your departure from Spain.*

W ITH MY FATHER's card in my pocket I came out of the underground station in search of that Beauséjour boulevard where my relations from the Gil Moreno de Mora family had lived since their childhood: a beautiful villa like so many in the district, draped in a mossy haze, horse-chestnut yellows, closed lace curtains, stuffily silent and discreetly senile. The ring of the bell, almost mute as if contaminated by the rampant anemia, caused a brief flurry on the top floor: minutes later, one of my aunts, old, tiny, and dressed in black, came to the door and, after enquiring who it was, escorted me along a carpeted staircase to their rooms with white, ghostly, covered furniture. She had just come from a visit to her sister, a nun in a local convent where she carried out her daily worship, and asked after my father, his delicate health, poor Julia, my plans and studies and the reason for my trip. She had carefully noted down in pencil my name and my brothers' and sister's, at her age she forgot everything if she didn't write it down at once in her little exercise book; perhaps, as I later suspected, she wanted to have us there one by one in her rosaries and prayers so rich in indulgences and other spiritual benefits. This was my one and only visit to their house and the residential district where they lived. Fifteen years later, in their eighties and one of them ill with cancer, my aunts sent one of their nephews to Italy to ask the famous, charismatic Father Pius whether they would be safer in Paris or Spain in the case of a Chinese Communist invasion: the oracle's reply favored the desire of the family to move to the peninsula where they perished, I think, just after their arrival, relieved and happy to have escaped the cruelty and horrors of the Asiatic hordes.

Apart from these anachronistic relatives and two French girls who had studied in Spain, the only person I knew when I arrived was a schoolfriend of José Agustín, who had also been expelled by the Jesuits, and with whose family we had kept in contact after one of his sisters married my uncle Josep Calsamiglia. Alberto Blancafort was learning musical composition, aspired to be the leader of an orchestra, and lived with a Swedish girl in some attic or small hotel in the Latin Quarter. Thanks to him, I assimilated the work of a group of composers whom I have listened to ever since: he played Erik Satie's *Gnosiennes* and *Gymnopédies* on the piano, and eagerly reread the partituras of Milhaud, Poulenc, and Béla Bartók. Alberto mixed with a group of Catalan musicians, artists, and writers who had lived in Paris for some time, and I soon got to know some of them. Guessing that my scarce funds would not allow me to keep on paying for the hotel room where I was staying, he immediately offered to find me somewhere to lodge. He said he knew an old spinster in the Septième Arrondissement who rented rooms cheaply to students: he himself had lived in one of them before moving in with his girlfriend and he could introduce me.

Mlle De Vitto's flat was on the ground floor of a silent cul-de-sac off the rue de Varenne: the owner or, more correctly, the tenant was a tall, straight, mustachioed woman, untidily dressed, with a strange, rather warlike air, especially with the extravagant hat that made her look like a transvestite *bersagliere* or an officer in the Garibaldi volunteers. In fact, she had been a soloist or singer in a distant era of fame and splendor that she remembered nostalgically in contrast to her present straits. Faded diplomas, old printed invitations to one of her recitals, the blurred photo of a memorable soirée in honor of those wounded at the front, presided over by Clemenceau or Pershing according to her successive, embroidered versions, hung on the dusty wallpaper or rested on the shelves, consoles, mantelpieces crowded with figurines, jugs, and bric-a-brac. Several cats moved around that melancholy scene with svelte indolence, sometimes perched on their mistress's shoulder, sovereignly inured to her slobbering caresses, with bristling, emblematic power radiating outward as if from an ancient magical print or engraving of witchcraft. Mlle De Vitto was not satisfied with her modest role of subletter: the guests she took in had to share her musical tastes, have refined artistic sensibilities, and listen devotedly to her repertory of past triumphs. She tried to disguise her boardinghouse to outside acquaintances by inventing classes in opera singing and tonic sol-fa: she would often clear her throat before softly humming the first bars of an aria or lightly running her fingers across the piano keyboard. Art, the great Art to which men and women used to dedicate their lives, was about to perish. *Regardez autour de vous, mes pauvres amis, il n'y a rien, mais absolument rien.* Alberto and I nodded in agreement while she, enthralled by the evocation of her own magnificence, condescended to talk to us, in suddenly hoarse tones and with a nervous twitch in her cheeks that revealed her impatience and greed, about the price of the room. Settled in her house, accepting the rules of the game of a daily conversation with her either by myself or with another lodger, a delicate, ethereal Uruguayan pianist, I awaited Alberto's visit to go to one of the places in Saint-Germain or the Latin Quarter where he used to meet his friends. Just after my arrival, my friend gave me the address of the now-defunct Foyer de Sainte Geneviève, near the Pantheon, where I could have lunch for the same price as in the university restaurants without having to show the student-card that I didn't possess. When we were queuing up there one day, trays in hand, he introduced me to the Catalan poet Palau Fabre, who had been in exile for years, and his friends, the actor Sacha Pitoeff and his Argentinian wife. Palau Fabre, whose bitter rebellion against the bourgeoisie and nationalist intransigence reminded me of Great-uncle Ramón Vives, had broken ties with his well-off family and preferred an austere but free existence in Paris to tolerating a regime like Franco's that, apart from the many reasons that made it hateful to me, was vigorously oppressing his culture and language. His moral attitude, reflected in the bare simplicity of his daily life, filled me with admiration. The violence of his poetry, marked with the inimitable stamp of Rimbaud, helped me to understand the drama and frustration of that remote, rebellious relative who was ignored and hated by his own family circle. Palau Fabre had met Artaud before he was interned and enthused about his work. I remember he once took me to his tiny attic on the Isle-Saint-Louis and recited some of his texts to me. As I was not yet suffering the sterility of my Marxist phase—Karl Marx, *éternel voleur d'énergies*, Rimbaud would have written a century later—I was moved by his reading. Palau

Fabre was an original character, a kind of sniper within a cultural panorama that was fatally being politicized. When I decided in 1956 to make Paris my definitive place of residence, Artaud, Bataille, Breton meant nothing or next to nothing to that young Spaniard imbued with Marxism, the supporter of Sartre's thesis on commitment. My friendship with him could have given me the opportunity to penetrate the work of some authors that I only discovered eight years later, when I was freed from my ideological blinkers; but our short-lived relationship, cut short by my return to Spain, spoiled that unique opportunity to hew out the path that would lead me to achieve a responsible, personal form of writing.

Alberto's other friends used to rendezvous in the Dupont on the boulevard Saint-Michel, or in the Mabillon or Old Navy in Saint-Germain-des-Près. The latter gave shelter at dusk to a group of rather self-deluding writers and artists whose grandiose work, repeatedly advertised in the café, would never take shape: an Italian poet with the serene beauty of a Botticelli painting; a dramatist, author of a piece to be performed in La Huchette; an operatic Basque, would-be Luis Mariano, self-styled lover of the daughter of an important publisher for whose sake he would on one occasion try to open his veins while sobbing hysterically. The undeniable star in the Mabillon constellation was *el Campesino*: the former Republican general seated on one of the benches at the back, surrounded by a small faithful band, possibly Argentinians or Chileans, relived the heroic moments of the civil war, and reenacted with a fine flurry of waves and gestures the scene of his dramatic break with Stalin. Later, after eating a sandwich or sausage and chips, Alberto Blancafort would sometimes accompany me to a bar on the rue des Canettes where the grotesque survivors of the existentialist fauna had taken refuge: there a solemn, hieratic girl, systematically dressed in black, with her face painted like a mask, declared that she lived in a damp cave with mice and called on the most daring to try her one night in a cemetery. The Pouilly was filled to the brim with *voyeurs*, drug addicts, and drunks. Customers' disputes would often come to blows and the arrival of the *panier à salade* put everybody to flight. The bohemian life of the cafés offered a provincial like me a string of surprises: I met my first flesh-and-blood Communist on the terrace at the Old Navy where he spent the afternoon engrossed in his reading of *L'Humanité*, admiringly translating for his companions and then underlining in pencil the speeches or commentaries of some leading French or Soviet comrade, as if to mark out the main lines of thought and the need to come back to them at a quieter moment. The desire to taste the forbidden fruit led me one night to accompany a Norwegian journalist friend of Albert's to a Communist meeting chaired, I remember, by Auguste Lecoeur, shortly before his expulsion from the Party: the showy display of flags and the broadcasting of hymns—so similar to the patriotic Falangist performances of my childhood—the strident slogans, the disciplined rhythm of the applause at once doused my enthusiasm: I would experience a similar reaction in Cuba during the great revolutionary celebrations—also the fruit of my precocious experience of the art of manipulating the masses under an opposing symbol. My antipathy toward this kind of meeting, strengthened over time and with the loss of my political innocence, thus had an early manifestation independent of the vicissitudes of my ideology or affiliations. If the friends or acquaintances I had during those years when I was a fellow traveler of the Party had forced me to participate in such acts and ritual assemblies, I am sure that my rather reserved collaboration with them would not have lasted long: the victory parades that I observed with my father and brother from the balconies of the ABDECA office would cure me of demagogy for posterity, and inspired me with a healthy distrust of the sincerity of the people's fervent applause.

Inevitably, in my circumstances, I was dazzled by Paris and limited my tourist roving to the areas with historic and artistic sights. My anxiety to be up-to-date, to see, to read, to experience all that was impossible in Spain made me go from the second-hand bookshops in the Latin Quarter and on the quaysides of the Seine to the tiny cinema on the rue de Messine where I gulped down, in cycle after cycle, the films of Pudovkin and Eisenstein, prewar French films, a choice sample of Italian neorealists. I discovered all at once Beckett and the Impressionists, Genet and Prévert, Schönberg and Ionesco's first works. I had never felt so happy as during those weeks when, with my stomach sometimes empty and my head full of plans, I walked for

hours to tame the city. An intense desire to adapt myself to France, to be sub-
merged in its culture and language, impelled me to polish my pronunciation
and to erase the stigma of foreign extraction. If I compare my present care-
less, opaque French—largely the result of the defensive instinct of my Spanish against the prolonged daily assault from other languages—with the
French I used to show off then in my conversations with the natives, I can
only draw the sad conclusion that that was the shining peak of my life as a
French speaker, and that I have gone backward like a crab rather than advancing. The twenty-year-old's zeal to master the vocabulary and accent of
others would be repeated again at different intervals and moments in my life.
The auditory enjoyment inherent in the first stages, the sudden power of
novelty, perhaps explain this strange whim: the fact that the uncodified,
changeable dialect of Arabic today stimulates my appetite to dominate it
while the languages learned previously wither in the attic of routine familiarity. At distinct stages in my existence I would be impregnated with French
and American English, only to dedicate myself later in my forties to a tardy
assault on Arabic. Spanish was reduced almost entirely to an instrument of
literary toil and inversely would attain a unique status: to be my opponent in
intricate unarmed combat, the sensual ferocity of which would give way after *Don Julián* to a happy love affair.

After a few weeks the money I had brought from Spain began to decrease
at an alarming pace. In order to extend my stay in Paris until January, I decided to restrict my daily diet to lunch at the Foyer de Sainte Geneviève. At
night, if I didn't manage an invitation to a roll from some friend or acquaintance, I went to bed fasting or found frugal satisfaction in biscuits. A contemporary photograph shows me as skinny, emaciated, wrapped up in my expensive overcoat on the day two Colombians from the Guadalupe College
landed in Paris and invited me to a banquet that I judged to be Rabelaisian.
Several of Alberto's friends collected paper, rags, and lost property for a junk
merchant on the rue de Saint Jacques: the work wasn't excessive and it paid
for a day's food, but a mixture of tenacious snobbery, sloth, and weakness
kept me from that exploitation of the student world some considered
manna. Forced to choose, I preferred to tighten my belt another notch and

go to bed with the cautious, parsimonious forethought of someone who has learned to keep a chunk of bread dipped in mustard from lunchtime in his pocket.

My slow physical decline was worrying Mlle de Vitto: she thought she knew why I was skin and bones and tried to worm my financial situation out of me in order to cushion my eventual disappearance from her list of "pupils." Perhaps I was expecting a check from my family? Did I hope to be awarded some scholarship? When she gave me my post, she stood over me with one of her cats on her shoulder tacitly inviting me to open my correspondence. As I did not give in to her blackmail and locked myself in my room to read it, she waited for me to come out to ask if there was a pleasant surprise or if it was really good news. Dismayed and somewhat annoyed by evasive answers, Mlle De Vitto cleared her throat as she reminded me I must pay the rent before the end of the month if I wanted to carry on my so-called lessons with her.

In early December I had received Castellet's letter: he told me he was to spend a fortnight in Paris and wanted me to help him find a room. I passed on his message to Mlle De Vitto and she was so worried by the dreadful state of my finances and also the dramatic desertion by another of her guests that she received the news like a blessing. She wanted to find out about that *signor* Castelletto: his family background, education, artistic inclinations, whether he had means. My replies seemed to satisfy her and his arrival was anxiously awaited. I can remember how the visit from one of the Old Navy dreamers, would-be leader of the surgery team at the Neuilly American Hospital, had dazzled my hostess, who was convinced for some hours she had met a great authority from the medical world whose wealth and influence gave him the natural role of adviser and patron to me. After the portentous Galen vanished, Castellet would briefly be the man of her dreams. When he finally came, Mlle de Vitto welcomed him with open arms: my friend's serious, distinguished manner surpassed all her expectations. With his help I was able to pay off the rent I owed and wait for the award of the Nadal prize while acting as his guide and critic through the world of books, films, and plays. Castellet knew a Catalan art critic who lent me an old radio set on Twelfth

Night. For a while we searched in vain for the wave with the Barcelona station that was broadcasting live the result of the voting: we found it only to learn that my novel, the favorite according to bets laid by people at the dinner, said the commentator, had just been eliminated in the penultimate vote. Minutes later the award would be given to an unknown woman whom no one would hear of again a few months after her book's publication.

DAYS BEFORE MY return, Luis and José Agustín wrote to me about what had happened: as soon as the voting started, the rumor spread among those present that my work was "leftist" and had "prerevolutionary overtones," a fact that was enough to explain its disqualification. At home they all followed the drama of the prize on the radio: Eulalia "was beside herself and in tears" and lost her temper with the winner; Father and Grandfather were reconciled for a moment and greeted the news with despair and despondency.

Back in Barcelona, hopeful and impatient, I rushed to see the publishers at Destino who were quick to remind me of the limits and restrictions of reality: they said they were interested in the work, but in present circumstances it was difficult to publish. As their relationships with the then all-powerful general director of the press were going through a delicate phase, the mere act of presenting it to the censors would, they added, not only be useless but counterproductive. If I could rely on some serious patron, it would be better to have recourse to his services: once it was approved by Juan Aparicio or the minister himself, they would include it in their collection.

As I had no friend or supporter with influence in the ministry, I went and saw Dionisio Ridruejo, whom I did not know personally but whose reputation for honesty and independence of judgment converted him a priori into an ideal intermediary. Although he had been on the edge of the system for some years, Ridruejo had not yet made a definitive break and maintained a series of connections with his former comrades in arms. At the time he was directing a private radio station in Madrid, where he gave me a friendly welcome when I arrived in his office with the manuscript of the novel. He promised to read it in order to have an informed opinion and to be able to defend it before a minister as soon as he had the opportunity. A few weeks later, after telling me some of his strictly literary criticisms of the novel, Ridruejo informed me with a smile of his conversation with Arias Salgado. The Minister for Information and Tourism—famous for his theory that, because of his provident leadership, Spain was the country in the world with the fewest souls condemned to the eternal tortures of hell—had explained to my go-between his most noteworthy criteria on the matter: namely, that a novel was only worthy of publication "if husband and wife, joined in legitimate matrimony, could read it to each other without mutually blushing and especially, he had emphasized, *without being aroused.*" I don't know if the joint reading of *Juegos de manos* made the ministerial couple blush or filled them with desire or whether, absorbed in his numerous good works, Arias Salgado had the leisure or curiosity to read it; the truth is that, despite Ridruejo's good offices, the novel remained stagnating at the ministry for several months and it would probably have slumbered there until the final destruction of the regime if there hadn't been a new, more direct intervention in the meanwhile.

On the advice of Fernando Gutiérrez, I had explained the problem to José Manuel Lara. Thanks to his well-known sympathies for the person and work of Franco, the Planeta publisher was in a better position than Ridruejo to defend my book successfully: he had been told by Gutiérrez that I was preparing another book and he felt obliged to intervene and get me out of the jam in return for my promise to let him see the manuscript of *Duelo en el paraíso* first. I promised, and to my great relief my novel was soon authorized with a few cuts that were fortunately unimportant. I returned to Destino with the *nihil obstat* of the censor and signed the contract for publication during the summer of fifty-four, although for planning reasons, it only appeared at the beginning of the following year.

Apart from writing the novel pledged to Planeta, my reentry into Barcelona life was achieved between my discovery of the floating dive on the Shipyard and my presence at Castellet's literary seminars. After the closure of *Laye* and the failure of our attempts to create a new magazine, the original nucleus of founders broke up: Sacristán went to finish his studies in Germany; Gabriel Ferrater was traveling through Europe; Barral, about to get married, was meeting to a large extent the requirements of his industrial surname. Benefiting from his friendship with the director of the Institute for Hispanic Studies in Barcelona, Castellet organized a course on criticism and the novel that brought together a group of young students who had entered university after my premature departure: my brother Luis, Joaquín Jordá, Salvador Giner, Jordi Malaquer, Nissa Torrents, Octavio Pellissa, Sergio Beser, and others whose names I don't recall gathered in one of the rooms in the old flat on Valencia Street to discuss critical realism, commitment, and Marxism. While I was away in Paris, the circles in which I had moved had suddenly been politicized. Octavio Pellissa, from a family that belonged or had belonged to the Party in Republican times, did not restrain her Communist ideas even in public. Through Castellet or one of his friends, magazines like *Europe* and *La nouvelle critique* began to circulate secretly. Terms such as surplus value, objective conditions, correct line, formal freedoms, democratic centralism thus gradually entered our vocabulary. Equipped with a solid array of arguments, we submitted daily reality to the restructuring process of the brand-new doctrine. The songs of Yves Montand, Léo Ferré, Atahualpa Yupanqui were often listened to communally with liturgical solemnity and all aroused our enthusiasm. With the zeal of the converted, I took advantage of some short holidays to spread my newly acquired ideas among the farmers and peasants in Torrentbó: I was horrified by my playboy privileges and informed them that the revolutionary struggle had begun that would soon put an end to their serfdom and exploitation. Alfredo and his friends must, I imagine, have listened with condescending skepticism to my halting speeches and my naive voluntarism that had little in common with the other elements of their daily experience. From the start my sentimental adherence to Marxism, although largely dictated by my desire to atone for the original sin of my class and my family's odious past, met with difficulties and insoluble obstacles. I remember very clearly the day someone slipped me a packet of back issues of the clandestine Spanish C.P.'s cultural magazine: with the nervous delight of someone about to taste the forbidden fruit, I eagerly began to read but was straightaway flung into profound consternation by the contents. It was the time of the cold war and the thaw after Stalin's death had not yet begun. Violent language, bristling with invective and insults, stigmatized not only the behavior and ideas of authors known for their Francoist sympathies but also some of the foreign writers and intellectuals that I most admired: Gide, Camus, Malraux, Sartre himself were pinpointed as hyenas and jackals, agents of the Pentagon, faithful lackeys of the bourgeoisie. This stream of unfounded accusations, tied together like a bunch of cherries, evoked the dogmatism and poverty of the salvoes against freethinkers, Masons, and Jews in Father Ripaldo's catechism and other such manuals. A sensation of déjà vu made me break off my reading with a feeling of bitterness and displeasure. But, convinced that it was an error capable of treatment and determined not to allow the trees to prevent me from seeing the forest, I just made a comment to Castellet and my friends—as surprised and upset as I was—on my total disagreement with the magazine's editorials and the absurd accumulation of insults. Consciousness of the need for a radical change in Spanish society both politically and socially, and of our moral duty to participate in the process, kept our illusions intact.

Parallel to the literary seminar in the institute, we got together periodically in a place called the Bar Club a few blocks away. The discussions and conversations there were predominantly political. Commentaries on the international situation—the last lashes of McCarthyism, Guatemala, the defeat of the French in Indochina—took up most of the sessions. Octavio Pellissa took the opportunity to underline the manifest moral and material superiority of the socialist regimes: racked by its internal contradictions and struggles, faced by the unbreakable strength and solidarity of China and the Soviet Union, the capitalist world would finally collapse by itself. One day, very excited, we were visited by a mysterious person who had come from Peking: the guest in question, whose name was not revealed to us for obvious security reasons, described a few events and anecdotes of his journey without recourse to flights of propaganda. Although we were disappointed by his coldness, we listened devotedly, unaware that this anonymous man, Julio Cerón, was the diplomat and future founder of the *felipes*, the Popular Liberation Front. I saw him again ten years later, after he left prison, when he was confined to a town in Murcia where I went to meet him, I remember, in the company of Ricardo Bofill.

Through common friends, our group had entered into contact with two young writers based in Madrid: Rafael Sánchez Ferlosio and Carmen Martín Gaite. The former had published a remarkable novel, *Industrias y andanzas de Alfanhuí*, which overwhelmed me: at twenty or so he had a style rich in shades of meaning and suggestion and without any apparent difficulty had reached a density of expression that I would only forge as a goal after painful struggles and conflicts at the time of writing *Don Julián*. Ferlosio and his wife had just come back from a trip to Italy and willingly accepted my invitation to rest in Torrentbó. That was the first of a series of reciprocal visits over the space of two years. While I dedicated my energies to the novel pledged to Lara—on whose advance I was relying to return to Paris—Ferlosio entrusted me with the manuscript of a rather Kafkaesque work of his that he too wanted to submit to Planeta. *El fontanero*—this was the novel's title—was probably just a stage on the path that was to lead from *Alfanhuí* to the marvellous adventure of *El Jarama*; but even taking into account the fact that it was a minor work, its irony, rigor, and sharpness stood out against the barren Spanish landscape of the time. Months afterwards, when Ferlosio had shelved his idea of publishing it, we both exchanged confidences on our respective interviews with the publisher. In the case of *Duelo en el paraíso*, he warned me in his very Sevillian accent that children weren't a commercial subject but advised me to present it for a prize and generously undertook to publish it. The conversation with Ferlosio, as related by the latter, was more colorful and spicy: Lara greeted him with "You write well, extremely well; almost too well!" and, after giving some good advice on the theme of novelistic ingenuity, assured him that one day he might become a worthy rival of Pombo Angulo—if he followed it.

My contact with Ferlosio, which was then broken off by my self-exile in Paris, was of great significance and value to me at the time: in pleasant contrast to the self-sufficiency, vanity, and exhibitionism of the majority of his colleagues, he was proof that a serious writer need not take himself seriously.

An eccentric loner, full of ironic humor, he professed absolute contempt for the theatrical emphasis and lofty solemnity of the fashionable clowns. Always sincere and unconditional in his literary opinions, he did not hesitate to attack currently accepted ideas: I can remember very clearly the day he heard me and Castellet cite *La colmena* as a paradigm of an objective novel and he suddenly exploded to say that Cela was a tyrannical author who didn't even allow his characters the right to breathe. His analysis was not hypothetical and inappropriate like ours: *El Jarama* was already underway and he knew very well what he was saying. For me, above all, Ferlosio incarnated the creator who is resolved to live literature like a prison sentence or a benefaction, not as a way to make a fortune. His later silence—so like that which would in turn affect Genet—would confirm his conception of writing as an extremely volatile, serious act—beautiful and unexpected like falling in love—the experience of which forces whoever lives it to be quiet if the gift suddenly abandons him and he does not wish to fall into the unpardonable, common crime of wordmania. In opposition to the verbal pollution of ordinary publishing, the moral courage to shut one's trap and swallow one's own words is and will be moving evidence of personal faithfulness to an existence that is enjoyed and suffered by the writer like slow, gentle self-consumption: a new, torn Prometheus who can no longer offer the harrying, persistent eagle the bait of his miraculously recreated liver.

T HE PLACE WAS one of those special scenes, like the central square in Marrakesh or the Small Market in Tan-
gier, that immediately appeal to the imagination and are mysteriously transmuted into the written word: a rectangular pontoon about fifty meters wide,
with a hut with a sloping roof, reached by a small bridge. To walk there from
the tram terminal in Barceloneta the visitor had to cover more than a kilo-
meter past the quays and port paraphernalia by the breakwater: a journey
undertaken mostly by fishermen, mussel gatherers, or owners of the boats
being careened or repaired. When the weather allowed, the Shipyard's customers would sit in the open at the tables the owner had set out near the coils
of ropes, fishing lines, and bilge-heads. From there, while they drank a coffee and brandy or a beer, they observed the general movement of the boats,
lighters, tugboats, swallows, and fishing vessels; the jetties and docks of the
maritime station; the rusty towers of the cable car; the seagulls' swooping
flight, at times still as if suspended in the air, about to dive down upon their
victim. The pontoon swayed gently when the police launch or the Americans with their outboard motors sailed by and the thick mooring ropes
would creak painfully in an almost animal-like whimper. Present in the
mind's eye, like actors in a live show, the regulars will always be the same:
Alonso the boss, tubby, small, with blue, melancholy eyes, usually half-
opened, an angelic air, and a eunuch's tone of voice; Amadeus, with his
cheerful smile and beret to one side, a great drinker, fond of humming ha-
baneras; Miss Rosi, well into her forties, fat, a furious smoker of Bisontes,
with her bag on the table, "just like a whore" she would say mischievously to
herself. Mussel gatherers and sailors play a game of cards, joke and swear at
each other, watching the shipwrights at their daily tasks out of the corner of
one eye. Moving in between them, weighed down with buckets of water or

ready to patch up the cracks in a boat's hull with pitch and oakum, one man walking unshod, wearing just torn shorts, commands your attention.

From your first visit to the Shipyard, he has attracted you. Raimundo is of average height, athletic build, with muscular legs and arms, unkempt dark brown hair standing on end, hairy-chested, a wild mustache. His face is tough but energetic: his sparkling dark eyes, the whole of his character and physique, radiate powerful animal magnetism. Along with these physical features—which for the first and only time you will appreciate in one of your fellow countrymen—the laborer in Alonso's service enjoys others that you will eventually learn to discern in the natives of that Sotadic Zone described by Sir Richard Burton, the frontiers of which extend from Tangier to Pakistan: a degree of coarseness in appearance not without charm; instinctive warmth and availability; a proud rejection of the ways and means that open the doors to social climbing in the industrialized countries. Although apparently not belonging to a foreign or alien community like Parisian immigrants from the Sotadic Zone, Raimundo nevertheless represents absolute marginality: he cannot read or write, has no normal family or fixed abode, his past seems cast in a shadow that you will not penetrate despite your efforts: he married or moved in with a woman who had his daughter; he lived for a time in Fernando Poo; he was a sailor and stoker on a merchant ship; for an obscure reason, he spent some time in prison. His explanations change according to the circumstances, as if obeying the artistic imperatives and requirements of the narrative; now he is a widower, now he isn't; the mother-in-law who falsely accused him of incest with his own young daughter will later be transformed into his own mother; the deed that sent him to jail changes color, texture, skin with a chameleonlike versatility. Although he was born on the Costa Brava, his surname isn't Catalan and sounds gypsyish. His ancestral distrust of *el payo* would in this case explain his defensive attitude to life, his tenacious, deep-rooted individualism. Whatever its origins, the fact is he lives alone, sleeps on some sacks in a cubbyhole on his floating palace, never has visitors or leaves the port area; he has lost or has been robbed of his identity papers. When you spot his coercive, magnetic violence you do not even think of resisting and, for the first time in your life, you take on your uncertain addiction with an unblemished feeling of happiness. The social, cultural abyss existing between you fulfills, will fulfill in the future, that differentiating role, fascinating closeness to what is alien and unknown usually corresponding to the complementary dissimilarity between the two sexes. Your friend's world, a thousand miles from the one you have inhabited till then, becomes a kind of drug for you: you will be chained to it for months. Raimundo's wild appearance, the broken-down palafitte that is his home and lair, justify your daily visits to the Shipyard from the other end of the city: the gleaming smile on the sunburnt face when he spies you in the distance and the rough, embarrassed gestures with which he greets your modest presents will be your reward. Although he doesn't suspect the real nature of your feelings, he feels visibly flattered by your interest and, as you are pleased to discover, tries in turn to keep it alive: exoticism has a mutual impact and if he embodies for you the elemental and the forbidden, your upbringing and involuntary snobbishness also captivate him. At nightfall, when he finishes his labors and the bar lights are reflected and sway in the dark, oily glow of the waters, you both drink beer and cognac in one corner beneath the owner's impenetrable, Buddha gaze. The strange couple you make doesn't attract anyone's attention there. The Shipyard's regulars have already become used to your presence: Miss Rosi flirts till very late with the mussel catchers and the fishermen and one day when she is offended by a cutting remark and threatens to depart, suddenly standing on a show of dignity, Alonso interrupts, hoarse with emotion, to assure her that there "she is appreciated, loved, respected, admired, and well-regarded"— a phrase divulged by you in the Bar Club that will become the usual farewell formula of the members of the group when months later they write to you in Paris. The night visitors to the floating bar usually come by taxi: owners of boats being careened, couples, the bourgeois in flight from domesticity. In Madrid you learned to take your alcohol or quell it with hash bought in the port. Raimundo's tongue loosens as the number of drinks increases and, somewhat tight, you say good-bye on the gangway when it is closing time. The long walk back along the jetty toward the San Sebastián Baths and the Barceloneta tram-stop helps to clear your head and clean up your appearance in the likelihood that your father is awake waiting for you to come home, awake in his gloomy bedroom on Pablo Alcover.

One night when you pretended to be more drunk than you really were you walk back along the quay and climb up to the hole where your friend sleeps: your desires to lie next to him, to feel the heat of his body close to you, were stronger than your shyness and physical inhibitions. But the liberating gesture you expect from him—and he is genuinely surprised by your reappearance—will not materialize: the intimacy you secretly long for was anyway unthinkable for him. The aggressive, showy virility of your friend is not, as you will later discover with the sons of the Sotadic Zone, a sign of complicity aimed primarily at sex: Raimundo doesn't even sense that your attraction to him is mainly physical. He just covers you affectionately with his only blanket and after making sure you are comfortable, he stretches out to sleep about a meter from you on his wretched, inhospitable mat. While he snores loudly, you meditate lucidly on the fact that you are experiencing an impossible, nameless passion; that the lack of correspondence between your impulses and the type of body that invites them condemns and will condemn you, you then think, to cruel, inexorable solitude. A gesture or initiative from you seems sacrilegious. What would your friend's reaction be? Don't you run the risk of a harsh, humiliating rejection? The subtle tissue of the uncertain bond that links you can, you know, be shattered by one rash slip. The repulsion aroused by the vile term "queer," the weighty family stolidity you carry around, suggests resignation and prudence. The happiness you foresee in spite of everything has been decreed out of bounds: it is better to leave things as they are and prolong your emotions with impunity in cowardly, anonymous discretion.

The almost holy terror you felt during puberty at the photo of the two strapping lads locked in embrace, almost union, as they wrestled, overwhelms you again in your sleepless night at the Shipyard with that pervasive force that, although haphazard and suppressed, will shoot to the surface one day and sweep away the defenses and barriers by virtue of the inescapable law that, as Ibn Hazm beautifully says, "destroys the toughest, unleashes the most consistent, demolishes the sturdiest, dislocates the stoutest, settles in the recesses of the heart and makes the forbidden legitimate." What most impresses you as you remember the episode in Marrakesh, from a vantage point of those thirty years, is the incredible loyalty of your mental apparatus to a particular spatial framework as well as to qualities, features, and parts of the human body that, beyond parentheses, haziness, and oblivion, independent of your love and its adjacent feelings, will nevertheless be for you, in the words of the Arab-Andalusian poet, "culmination of your desires and peak of your delights." You now view that impotence with Raimundo as the necessary tribute for your birth in an unsuitable cultural and social environment. The deflection that would later mark you out would take place far away and in opposition to the initial boundaries of your life when, settled in Paris and happy in your relationship with Monique, you would again suffer the attacks and pursuit of that ancient, disturbing image: the successive reincarnations of the template spied in other brash, instinctive, hospitable bodies the invasion of whose intimacy you would welcome as you joyfully vindicated the figure of the mythical don Julián.

The failure of your nocturnal approach does not interrupt your friendship: during 1954 Raimundo will be the brightly burning, radiating center around which your existence gravitates. You visited him daily, by yourself or with your friends: Carlos Cortés, the regulars at Castellet's gatherings, will spend many an afternoon with you at the Shipyard, cradled by the creaking of the mooring ropes and the intermittent lapping of the water disturbed by some passing launch. While you drink, you talk about literature or conjecture about the imminent, irreversible fall of the regime, you furtively spy on his movements, the easy rhythms of his daily tasks: the complicity that exists between you is a closely guarded secret and nobody but you will grasp his cryptic allusions and jokes. Sometimes, he goes with you at dusk to the bars and cafés in the Barceloneta: the world later drawn by you in *Fiestas* suddenly assumes, as a result of his presence, a brutal, wounding reality. Your friend's contagious, physical energy draws around him a motley retinue of hags, gypsies, drunks, and beggars. He is the indisputable king of that court of miracles seduced equally by his magnetism and eternal vitality.

Before and after your second visit to Paris, you will visit the brothels and whorehouses of the Barrio Chino with Raimundo, introduce him to one of the prostitutes who go out with you, and you, all three, walk along hand in hand, with the obese, painted woman in between, until it was good-bye time on the sordid steps to some *meublé*. Imperceptibly, as with Lucho, your friend had gradually been changing into a literary character independent of the real model with whom you struggle daily. This change in status implies a tacit distancing from the latter, the end of your previous subordination to his overwhelming, oppressive personality. The day when for some reason he fell out with Alonso, you left the scene of the Shipyard with him and followed him to the places where he briefly worked as bath attendant, fisherman, and lifeguard. His rough, marginal existence—unprotected, plain, no property—moves you and is appealing; but the spring of his liminal power over you has broken. After a year Raimundo has become living evidence of the truth written in your novel: someone to show to friends as additional proof of authenticity. When Monique first visits Barcelona you will include on the program for her stay a compulsory visit to the port: Raimundo seems happy to see you with a friend and the three of you are photographed against the backcloth of his former workplace. Later on you carefully examine the photos and notice on his face the signs of sudden ageing and tiredness, the traces of the illness that is destroying him. But you were absorbed in Monique, her immediate warmth, and did not pay the necessary attention, you didn't pick up the ominous signs of his approaching end. With that cruel indifference inherent in the loss or decrease in physical interest in people we once desired, you live the moments of your amorous happiness far from Raimundo and his host of pariahs. Ten days after the event when you find out about his death, his terrible, lonely, drunken agony in the taverns and bars in the port, only then will you shed a few useless, belated tears. Your letter telling Monique what happened, just before you finished military service in 1956, reveals real grief and a crushing sense of guilt and remorse: your retrospective shame at having changed your friend into a fictional hero only to abandon him to his horrible fate; a sharply painful awareness of your selfish, privileged position. The distressed reference to his calloused hands, converted into tools, is not accompanied however by any mention of the past splendor of his body and the way it intoxicated you: splendor and intoxication that, now relived in memory, redeem the harsh wretchedness of his fate, eliminate your crude versatility and, just as in the times when you went to the Shipyard to catch a glimpse of him, confer on his welcoming smile, darkened by his fierce mustache, a warm, consoling impression of everlasting life.

S LOW COGNITION AND *apprenticeship of your body un-*
dertaken with that delay so essential for you in everything
profound: dizziness, immersion, whirlpool, the secret vortex of which is within
you: silent descent to the abyss, animal pull: desire for annihilation, mysteries of
joy and pain, harsh, exciting Stations of the Cross: gradual, step-by-step appro-
priation of the mental scatology you had foreseen: martial images of force and
subjection, limbs cruelly tied, bright sheet lightning, refined happiness: suffering,
beatitude, rapture close to the poet's mystical experience that confer on the search
for the germinal nucleus of power a discreet halo of sanctity.

Sudden discovery: you are only shell, not knowing the fiery reality at the center:
cautiously sounding out the core from which bubbles the magma of filth, incin-
erated matter: orgiastic crater of slippery, seminal lava: plethora, unquenched
thirst, essential density: mere indication of what is hidden, of the burning pressure
sheltered in the chasm: deepening your knowledge of it, polishing, purifying, es-
tablishing the hidden laws of an intimate, personal vulcanology: enigmatic rela-
tionship of the causal, inductive image, the persistent probing of glorious suffering
with the sudden, rhythmic swoon: cliff, precipice of jaws opened up within you,
yet hardened and resistant to awareness of its illuminating clarity.

In an after-dinner conversation, at the time when Monique and you frequented
the rue Saint-Benoît, the discussion had turned to the sexual peculiarities ana-
lyzed in a book by Stekel or another similar author specializing in such matters:
the story of a devotee of a brothel who always went there with a case filled with

twenty-three kilos of chains: some of your guests smiled or made facile jokes about the individual when Marguerite Duras interrupted you with that intense, serious voice that has seduced and seduces those around her.

I find it admirable, *she said*, to have such a perfect awareness of oneself to determine the exact weight of the chains, to arrive precisely at this figure of twenty-three and not twenty-two or twenty-four, for knowledge to the milligram requires a long, painful novitiate that only the purest people have the courage to confront.

I N THE MONTHS before my next trip to Paris, my friendship with Luis became closer: the secretive, reserved adolescent I used to come across at home had been transformed since entering
the university into a serious, questioning, intelligent youth as passionate as I
was about literature and politics. Our daily exchange of ideas and opinions,
respective discoveries in the field of literature, laid the basis for a relationship
that, with time, would be fruitful and indispensable to us both. Luis also
wrote with a surprising maturity that he acquired suddenly: from the publication of his first story in a Barcelona magazine, any sensitive reader would
realize that here was a real author. Our narrative routes, with two or three
years' difference in the decade of the fifties, display in their contrasts and sim-
ilarities the artist's broad margin of freedom in relation to his conditioning
and origins: the existence of an active, corrective will opposed to the inertia
and fatalism of necessity.

In a well-known passage Freud,* the author of *Moses and Monotheism*,
formulates a hypothesis according to which, when a child discovers that his
parents are normal human beings, he creates a "family novel" in order to
compensate in some way in his imagination for his cruel disappointment as
he enters life: he invents at will a family that is out of the ordinary in its virtues and its defects, where he can shelter from the unhappy discovery and
thus deaden the shock produced by the depressing intrusion of reality. This
"family novel" constructed in unpleasant, inhospitable circumstances would
be the germ of all fictions later developed by the writer: the acorn bearing the
tree of his future work. If literature, as Pavese said, is "a defence against the

---

*This and the two following paragraphs come from my essay, "A Family Reading of *Anta-
gonía*," published in *Quimera*, 32.

offenses of life," the neurotic child's first defensive act would shape the whole of his novelistic constellation: a kind of secret code to his affliction and his temptation to struggle with the pain until it is eventually cured.

Although not all neurotic children become writers and not all writers' fiction is the fruit of precocious, compensatory fantasy, there is not the slightest doubt, as Marthe Robert has pointed out in writing about Flaubert, that the initial impulse that generates, fertilizes, and structures the work of some creators comes from a *Familienroman* conceived in an effort to overcome a disappointment or protect oneself from an attack. The literary vocation, both mine and my brothers', brought out of a social and educational milieu that was a priori not very favorable to the cultivation of literature perhaps cannot be explained without the existence of an anguished need to recover from early traumas and disappointment. The primitive "family novel" we forged could merely have remained latent at the obligatory stage of self-delusion: that was my first, irresistible temptation in childhood and adolescence, which I could only get through by writing dozens and dozens of trashy novels with a kind of obsessive persistence. My decision at the age of twenty to be a writer and make a tardy offering to literature was to a certain degree the result of arduous, complex negotiation: the carefully delineated deal between my distressing awareness of reality and the balancing counterweight of my mythomania. A slow, difficult process that, from *Juegos de manos* to *Señas de identidad*, was gradually to purge me of the latter as I moved toward a style stripped of all "novelistic" trappings: the painful conquest of my own voice, the destruction of the *Familienroman* on the altar of personal honesty and subjective authenticity.

That a similar stimulus and initial situation—the gradual decline of our family's social status, rejection of the father figure, the sudden, brutal disappearance of our mother—have had such a different influence on myself and my younger brother should give some hasty and often dogmatic adepts of psychoanalysis a cause for reflection. Starting from identical roots and parameters—hatred for our class's traditional values, distance from the Catalan language on our mother's side, patriotic and religious indifference, search for a lay substitute for Catholicism in the ideology that stiffened the clandestine struggle against Franco, a precocious conception of literature as the only sure value—the path we have subsequently followed has marked dissimilarities: if it would be easy to prove the existence of numerous common keys to works like *Duelo en el paraíso*, *Fin de fiesta*, and *Las afueras* or even draw parallels between the odd chapter of *Señas de identidad* and sections of *Recuento*, still the direction by both of us in the last fifteen years will be radically opposed: while the world of my childhood slowly abandoned my writing and was replaced by other mental scenes, myths, and ghosts, Luis's creative work has remained anchored there. In my case the break was not only internal but physical, with the family milieu of my early years, with my birthplace, with Catalonia where I had always lived as a foreigner, with Franco's oppressed and oppressing Spain, in order to forge my work and source of energy. In opposition to all this, immersed in a French, Arabic, or North American environment without ever being totally integrated in any of them, I was morally and physically stateless but fatally united to the language in which I expressed my first feeling of "difference" and through which I could be saved. My brother's work expresses faithfulness to truth, an unshakable will to leave a record of the past, to temper his sudden disillusion and destructive impulses with a deep, fertile sense of creative pity. Since *Antagonía* can be read, at least at some levels, as a lucid chronicle of the largely Castilianized or independent bourgeoisie of Barcelona, of its contradictions, crimes, nostalgia, real unhappiness, impossible dreams; or the cultural, historical landscape of Catalonia whether the Emporda or Tarragona, the old quarter of Barcelona or the genial madness of the Sagrada Familia, nobody before had recreated all of this with so much talent, power, understanding, and objectivity.

This early awareness of our vocation as well as a premonition of our respective theatres of action is already clear from the few letters from Luis that I have saved from our spasmodic correspondence. While his narrative tastes centered on Conrad at the time, mine reflected the influence of Faulkner and his young followers in the South. During the autumn of 1954, when I finished writing *Duelo en el paraíso*, my brother had not yet joined the clandestine C.P., but his group of friends began to enter its orbit. The nights I didn't go to the Shipyard I went out with them, exploring the alleys by the Arco del Teatro and the promiscuous side street next to Escudillers. The desire to exhaust the limits and possibilities of nightlife, the generous, regular consumption of liters of Coke with rum or gin were part of our vital rejection of Francoist and bourgeois forms of life. Whether on their own initiative or contaminated by my influence, Luis's companions had also discovered the delights of the underbelly of the city and for several years—until the *gauche divine* appeared with its elegant haunts in the hills at the beginning of the sixties—the idea of night and alcohol would be almost exclusively associated for us with visits to a series of very mixed, sordid establishments between the Ramblas and the Paralelo. Our favorite places for some time would be the Pastís—with its progressive clientele drawn by the Piaf in the background and the Marsellais exoticism of the couple who ran it—and the nearby Cádiz bar—packed with prostitutes and North American blacks—whose lively descent into the lowlife evoked Hollywood images of Hamburg, Singapore, or Tampico. Later on, when we were fed up with the Gambrinus, Bodega Bohemia, and other axes of the Fifth District, we moved our quarters to the Andalusian Tavern and other bars near the Cosmos hotel where I would soon stay with Monique.

About this time a short and rather old story of mine appeared in the *Destino* magazine and the editor gave the illustrations over to a distant cousin of ours. María Antonia Gil was a niece of the pious Catholic lady I had greeted on my father's orders in her mansion in the Bois de Boulogne: I had probably met her years before when her mother died; but her telephone call telling me of the arrangement with the magazine took me by surprise: not only was I unaware of her artistic abilities but in the rigid Barcelona stratification of the time, in which her rich, aristocratic family was horizontally layered above ours, such a form of communication was outside the usual channels. Since her parents died María Antonia had been sharing the family flat in Balmes Street with her two sisters, and she invited me to dine there, to the great satisfaction of my father, who was flattered by my new, unexpected link to the most prestigious branch of his family. Luis's future wife was on my side immediately; clearly depressed by the traditional, conservative circles in which she moved, she readily accepted my invitation to go out for a few drinks at night and cheerfully joined the pilgrims in their worship of the Barrio Chino.

Our nightly topography wove a kind of cobweb from the bars and brothels of the Barceloneta to the cafés and bawdy houses of Tapias Street. With María Antonia, Cortés, and Luis's friends we followed the usual route, stopping off to visit different places like stations on a profane, happy Way of the Cross. When the Planeta prize was awarded to Ana María Matute that year, I had met at a public ceremony Ignacio Aldecoa and a girl of my age, Josefina Dalmau, the author of a novel that remained unpublished, I'm not sure why. Both enjoyed the nightly visit with me to the Shipyard and when he went back to Madrid she soon became a friend and was gradually integrated into the group. The oscillation from literature to alcohol, from enthusiasm for the lowlife to political commitment, reflected very clearly, at least in my case, the action of the conflicting, heterogeneous currents influencing our lives. Crawling through the dirtiest, most wretched areas in the city, rubbing shoulders with criminals and prostitutes, smoking hash, were transformed into a kind of militancy. The instinctive, gut aversion to the world from which I came found an opportune outlet in those places, which were the opposite side of the coin. Such an attitude, shared by the small bourgeois nucleus of our incipient class of progressives, seemed far from orthodox from a Marxist perspective. Manuel Sacristán's return from Germany, with his impeccable doctrinal baggage and his geometric reasoning, would soon call into question that confused, unsettling example of decadence and depravity.

W HEN I RETURNED to Paris in January of fifty-five I was not feeling my way as on my first visit but instead had a very precise plan of action: while my objective in living outside Spain was still in force—and consequently I had to resolve somehow the requirement of a modus vivendi compatible with writing—the idea of establishing regular contact with left-wing intellectual circles in France, in order to harness their moral and material support for our nascent struggle against Francoism—often nurtured in the Bar Club get-togethers with Castellet and his friends—infused my deferred, obsessive trip with an urgency and interest that were not entirely selfish. Once I had solved my lodging problem in a bourgeois edifice on the rue de l'Université next to the Gallimard publishing house, I looked for ways of making links with some of the magazines and journals that for months had been satisfying our political and cultural appetite, furiously stimulated by the diet forced on us by the indefatigable Juan Aparicio's censorship department. Someone, I think it was Palau Fabre, had told me about Elena de la Souchère, whose solitary zeal was then responsible for the few reports and news items about Spain in the left-wing press, and I went to meet her in the *France-Observateur* offices, on the top floor of the building that would later be occupied by *L'Humanité*. At that time Elena was a pale, lean, angular woman in her forties with sober but elegant, clear-cut features, wearing a tight, severely tailored suit with shirt and tie. She spoke in correct Spanish, with well-rolled r's, as if she were on the defensive against the twang of so many French or francophile speakers. As I learned immediately, she lived very modestly in a small hotel in the area, belonged to no party, and opposed Stalinism and Franco with equal gut conviction. Her sources of information on the peninsula were chancy and sporadic: so she welcomed my proposal to keep her informed about the changes and events I thought were being hatched. She asked me to write an article on the consequences of censorship for Maurice Nadeau's magazine,* encouraged me to publish reports under a pseudonym in *Les Temps Modernes*, and, eager to broadcast my points of view as a young intellectual *from the inside*, she invited me to set them out before Claude Bourdet, don Julio Álvarez del Vayo, and the Yugoslav ambassador. This generous, disinterested support of hers for the Republican cause—motivated beyond a doubt by her family background—would nevertheless conflict from the start, as usually happens in Spain, with the reserve, distrust, and lack of understanding of its immediate beneficiaries. No one to my knowledge—with our left officially in power—has yet recognized Elena de la Souchère for her years of selfless journalistic labors in support of democracy or has thought to invite her to the country to pay her a much-deserved homage. Gratitude has never been a Spanish virtue and backbiting, silence, and oblivion are our usual reward for any action undertaken without desire for self-promotion. My experience of the political struggle against Franco has shown me those who were in some way involved in it and those who stepped in and reaped the benefits were generally not the same people: on the one hand, the Ceróns, Amats, and Porqueras; on the other, the old technocrats now sitting in government offices and antechambers. While some showed their faces when it was dangerous or inconvenient to speak up and sometimes paid a very high price for acting or telling the unsavory truth, others waited patiently in silence for the time to move their pawns forward from comfortable, profitable positions. Acting as she did outside the parties, an independent person like Elena aroused fear and hostility from left and right: closely watched by the Spanish police, as I would later substantiate myself, my Communist companions spread the most absurd fairy tales about her. I can clearly remember the day when one of them, a very close friend at the time, informed me in all seriousness that he knew on good authority that she was working for the CIA. Such an obviously false accusation was the first of many confidentially whispered in my

---

*"La littérature espagnole en vas clos" appeared months later in *Les Lettres Nouvelles* signed with just my initials.

ear in the years when I was a loyal, disciplined fellow traveler. With a worrying, confusing regularity one of the "cadres" or lesser intellectuals with whom I was in contact would utter the same or similar denunciations against Pallach, Miguel Sánchez Mazas, and Trotskyist militants. The left-wing French writers I met didn't get any better treatment in private; but, with the pragmatism evident in the double-talk of their ethics, the ones who placed the deadly labels in their intimidation exercises asked me to ask the help of those they were discrediting and obtain their signatures in support of some press campaign in the despised bourgeois news media against Francoist repression or in favor of an amnesty for the political prisoners in Burgos or Carabanchel. When the break occurred between Claudín and Semprún and their comrades in the Party leadership, the same charges rained down on them and indirectly on me and I was reminded of that simple, good-hearted, gentle friend who "revealed" to me with an ineffable smile Elena's secret connections with North American espionage: an ignoble, angelic image, difficult to remove ever since.

The obsession of Communist parties and revolutionary groups with labelling those who differ from them as "lackeys of imperialism" or "agents of the Pentagon" does not date back, as I thought for a time, to the particular historical conditions in which the Marxist and non-Marxist working-class movements were shaped and structured before the victory of the Bolshevik revolution: it is a response to a series of social and psychological factors that, as I would be shown by a reading of Blanco White, have their roots through the centuries in notions of orthodoxy, absolutism, and infallibility—the fruits of Saint Paul rather than Marx—firmly anchored in human nature. "Individuals organized professionally in an orthodox body will resist and sanction with every means any attempt to dissolve the vital principle behind their union. And as a consistent political body, an orthodox Church will easily realize that nothing binds groups of humans together better than their opposition to the rest. . . . Hence the fact that condemnation of the latter is the real essence of orthodoxy."* A rigidly hierarchical party will thus have recourse, as Blanco prophesies, to the simple expedient of marking out those

*See my edition of the *Obra inglesa de Blanco White* (Buenos Aires, 1972), 256–263.

who are not in communion with them with some vile or sectarian label, to bewilder and exhaust them, forcing them to ignore the real reasons for their disagreement and to nervously and rather guiltily refute their presumed identification in deed or word with the worst, most implacable enemy. The future designation as "intellectual bourgeois agents," "shameless pseudoleftists," and "minor agents of capitalism" bestowed by the great Cuban leader in 1971 on Sartre and a group of writers politically aligned with him would again confirm the deep-rootedness of the old custom, but I was not then surprised or upset. My involvement in the political world in my first years of hardened self-exile had revealed the abuses of such a mechanism ad nauseam and I was, you might say, inoculated against such terror.

The interest aroused by my approaches to journalists and politicians hostile to Franco had given me the naive conviction not only that our intellectual struggle was on the right track but also that, as I heard my Communist friends repeat, the demise of the regime was at hand. In the heyday of wishful thinking, I sent a coded letter to the members of the Bar Club, bringing them up-to-date with my contacts and activities; but the code was transparent as I deduced from the anxious reply they sent me. Whatever the truth of that, Elena de la Souchère's first notes and articles on the cultural opposition to Francoism, partly put together with facts and details I had supplied her with, filled me with optimistic satisfaction. The belief that we were not alone, that our guerrilla war against the censors was sympathetically supported abroad, encouraged me to redouble my efforts. During my stay in Paris, the censored text of *Juegos de manos* had come out and Castellet's review of the novel, underlining its non-conformist, critical tone, guaranteed that it would find readers skilled at reading between the lines. For the same reasons, less literary than political, Elena de la Souchère and Palau Fabre made friendly overtures to different publishers with a view to eventual translation.

Busy with my anti-Francoist activities, my initial provincial absorption into French culture waned slightly. The idea of being naturalized French, changing nation and language, gradually lost interest for me, sacrificed to my new plan to carry beyond our frontiers my friends' modest daily struggle for an open, untrammeled culture. My casual acquaintance, I'm not sure how or when, with a couple of very young intellectuals contributed to my timid, inexperienced detachment from the official clichés of Paris and its great names: Guy Debord and his companion at the time, Michèle Bernstein, lived in a hotel on the rue de Racine adjacent to the boulevard Saint-Michel and published a journal called *Potlatch*, organ of their tiny Situationist International. Bitter, implacable enemies of the whole literary establishment—enveloped in internecine quarrels and ferocious splits that at times humorously mimicked Breton's terrorist language and the Stalinist trials—they possessed an all-embracing curiosity and an acute, demystifying vision of things. Their admiration for the *Palais Idéal du Facteur Cheval* and delight in visiting places and settings as far as possible from the tourist routes and famous monuments and vistas matched my developing taste and provided an intellectual justification that it lacked. In their healthy, consistent contempt for everything bourgeois and well-off, Debord and his friend used to visit the Arab cafés that were then located in the rue Mouffetard and the back streets of Maubert-Mutualité next to the Seine and one day they took me by bus from the Gare de L'Est to the proletarian suburb of Aubervilliers and a dive frequented by old Spanish Republican exiles, whose walls and owner I think were filmed by Carné and Prévert in their beautiful film on the poor children in the district. The subtle dovetailing of their tastes and mine, strengthened with the passage of time, conferred a baptismal, initiating value on that first tour with them around districts that I would soon assiduously trawl on my own: that compact, aged, broken-down Paris, shot through by canals, viaducts, railways, and rusty underground arches, which, from Belleville to Barbès, is crowded in a perspective like an illustration of an "Industrial Landscape" from an old, dog-eared children's picture encyclopedia. The harmonious, elegant, cosmopolitan metropolis that dazzled me on my first visit—the famous second home of all artists, so lauded by the "lost generation" and their Latin American followers—would gradually lose its primitive attraction at the expense of a bastard halogenous urban environment, polluted and fertilized by the clash and interweaving of so many different cultures and societies. When it was already dark I crossed the rue d'Aubervilliers with Debord and his companion and walked along the giant meccanolike boulevard de la Chapelle, far from thinking that one day the mere idea of crossing the Seine to meet someone in the intellectual districts of the Left Bank where I then lived would seem to me as remote and unappealing, say, as going on safari in Kenya: my almost animal longing for the Sentier and its continuous creative improvisation would later not allow me any other excursions except to those luxuriant, teeming areas where I truly found my feet, guided by my initiator's prophetic instincts.

S HELLS, PEEL, SLOUGHS *cast off along your road to a future, defunct career as an official intellectual: dedicated to what? to promoting a blissful tomorrow or petty self-interest? an ambiguity preserved for years and then observed, from the barrier, on the smiling faces of the heralds of a progressive society: an ethical squint, profitable dividends, the application of bastardly means to the realization of noble ends: it is possible to split yourself in two as if you were someone else and to ruthlessly examine the insidious, larval simony: to be successful, like so many others, in cultivating the tragedies of history, ennobling your person under the shadow of an attractive, rallying cause: the mythical civil war, famous million deaths, distant, vanished heroism: your presence at the slow, infectious, step-by-step climb upwards: a journey plagued by color blindness, sudden attacks of silence, opportune losses of sight, mystification: calculations, strategies, advantages happily cut off in time in an obstinate war against yourself: rhythmic gestures, hollow smiles, the swaying raised arms of the double or robot who, perched on a stage of moth-eaten fame, would later epitomize in your eyes the abject pettiness of the impostor.*

I RETURNED TO SPAIN proud and happy with my mission, as if bathed in the pleasant but illusory power of the late afternoon sun. The certainty that I had built the first bridge between our group and the European intelligentsia, that I had laid the bases for close, fruitful cooperation, gave my escape to Paris, I thought, a collective transcendence, and I was thus in a way transformed into a kind of ambassador. My closeness to the non-Communist French left—clustered around Sartre and *France-Observateur*—started from the assumption that our commitment would develop outside the parties, in an open, pluralist discourse. As I soon realized, such a position was on the naive side and did not take into account present circumstances or the ponderous inertia of reality. When someone breaks with a coherent, compact set of beliefs that can be as much religious and metaphysical as social, political, and moral, their first almost irresistible temptation is to seek refuge in a system with intrinsically similar characteristics, although on the surface they are opposed in conflict. As a result of a series of reflexes and habits rooted in his internal makeup, the deserter from a church will often be very attracted by the language, structure, and hierarchical model of the rival church. Suckled as a babe in a belief in a unique all-embracing key to explain the world, in a closed, self-sufficient frame of references, in infallible, dogmatic truth, he will abandon the ranks of the doctrine thus inculcated only to embrace with equal fervor and absence of critical spirit the system of the irreducible but symmetrical adversary of his first official credo. In a country like Spain where debate and the free contest of ideas had disappeared with the civil war and its ferocious settling of accounts, the political common-ground inherent in democracy was difficult to implant and lacked the magnetic power to attract the new generation of intellectuals and university students. Decimated by Francoist repression, the Socialist and Republican left vegetated in the land of pious hopes and had no practical contact with the evolution of the country. In the eyes of a youth tempted by action and radicalism, groups like Reventós's and Pallach's suffered from a weak reformism. In such a climate, the Communist party with its well-disciplined, iron structure, splendid ideological cohesion, and heroic resistance to police raids and persecution seemed to many to be the only viable alternative. The political fluctuations and doctrinal squabbles of the members of the Bar Club were unfortunately real: enemies of the authoritarian national Catholicism of the regime for ethical and ideological reasons, nevertheless we did not have our own program and strategy beyond these feelings of rebellion and disaffection. Sympathy for Sartre's revised interpretation of Marxism was not translated into concrete actions: totally cut off from the working class and its struggles, we still did not belong to the ennobling Gramscian category of organic intellectuals. On his return from Germany, Sacristán was to find fertile ground: a group of youths with beliefs close to his own who wanted to turn them into joint action with all the forces present in the revolutionary process.

In the months following my second trip to Paris, Luis, Joaquín Jordá, Pellissa, and other members of Castellet's literary seminar contacted Sacristán and formed the first Communist Party cell in Barcelona University with him as the leader. Although I was not informed personally of this collective adherence—my "bohemian" life and inveterate taste for the Barrio Chino no doubt aroused the fear and hostility of their conscientious mentor—I soon learned what was happening through my daily contact with Luis. I remember very clearly the day Sacristán and the other members of the group came separately to our house to hold one of their cell meetings, and when they were all there, the former hinted with a smile that my presence was not required. These meetings in Pablo Alcover upset my father and aroused his suspicions. The stiff, rather Prussian good humor of Sacristán, the mystery surrounding conversations officially dedicated to matters related to the university, inspired a hazy but accurate presentiment that there was a snake in the grass. Several times, on those afternoons, he popped into the room where

I was working on the manuscript of *Fiestas* to communicate his anxieties to me: I can see him now, thin, honed down to the fragile birdlike profile he acquired in those years, clutching at his grimy dressing-gown and ever-present rosary beads. What did I think about those meetings? What were they discussing for hours and hours with that strange, bespectacled professor? My soothing replies did not succeed in allaying his suspicions. Politics only brings unhappiness, my son, he would say suddenly, interrupting the conversation: remember the Republic and the suffering it brought me and Mother. And again, as he left my room, I could hear him wandering along the dark passage, whispering to Eulalia, curtly asking Grandfather for the daily newspaper, only to return to the subject for the nth time: if they are talking, as they claim, about topics in their course, why did they close the dining room door and break off their conversations when he went in to look for the yogurt spoon or ask if they needed anything? Soon afterwards the cell-members stopped meeting in our house, no doubt realizing the risk of a possible indiscretion on his part.

From this time to his death, my father would live in a state of anxious preoccupation about our political ideas. Although my brothers and I avoided all discussion of the subject, his hunch that things weren't going as they should, that we secretly professed harmful, obnoxious doctrines, never gave him a day's peace. Neither our formal, external respect for Catholic dogma nor the pious lies with which we wrapped everything related to our ideas and private life succeeded in sweeping away his dark, persistent foreboding. With an absentminded innocence, which at the time made us laugh, he would butt in to comment on international political events from principles based on homespun pedestrian common-sense, exempt from the irreproachable, rigorous dialectic that then sustained our own: the friendship between the Chinese and the Russians, he maintained, was not going to last long; as early as the time of Genghis Khan the latter had fought against the yellow peril, and sooner or later they would become aware of this, for, however Communist they might be, all in all they were still Europeans. While we listened to him with haughty condescension, we were far from believing that a few years later facts would prove him right and, in spite of our supposedly scientific laws and peremptory arguments, the break forecast by him would happen and the official bard, Yevtushenko, would publish a poem in *Pravda* evoking the heroic knights of Muscovy hated because of their blue eyes and white complexions by the threatening swarm of Asiatic hordes, and we were heartbroken when we read it. Today, when I look back and recall our blindness to historical, ethnic, and geographical realities and conditions captured by an eccentric bourgeois like our father, such petulance makes me smile: to submit the rich complexities of the world to a single-voiced reading, to exclude from the analysis of reality dreams, feelings, defects, secret drives of human beings seems not only a monstrous reduction of the latter but also incredibly puerile. The head-shrinkers with their single official ideology, in leaving out of their projections and analyses man's irrational elements, were unwittingly contaminating all their schemas with delirious irrationality: what they threw out of the door slipped back in again through the window and penetrated to their marrow; hardly had they built the protective, sanitary wall of the ideal city where the new man would reside than they would see arise there the cruelties, misery, madness, and extravagances of the old barbarian against which they initially fought.

My father's premonitions about the risks of the new and for him odious ideas we defended would be sadly confirmed before his death by a campaign in the regime's news media against my "anti-Spanish" activities in France and, especially, by the predictable arrest of Luis. Immersed in a conservative milieu both in the family and society where our ideas and behavior caused a scandal, he would be singularly ill-equipped to support us publicly against the avalanche of insults, judgments, and condemnations that rained down on us, having to do it as he did in the teeth of his dearest and deepest convictions. His well-intentioned letter to Franco, written during Luis's imprisonment—recalling his life and beliefs as a right-wing Catholic, his widowhood, and the unhappiness caused by the war, the traditional religious system in which he had brought us up—the revelation of which by José Agustín would make me blush with shame, now seems to me, after some years, both moving and pathetic to the extent it reflects his loneliness and the painful conflict of his ideas and feelings. At the time our mutual lack of com-

prehension—not imputable only to him—prevented me from pitying the
isolation in which he lived and the corrosive harshness of his fate. His recourse to that other tyrannical, castrating Father whose ubiquitous, all-
embracing presence extended over us and eclipsed his own, reveals crudely
and sharply the correlation of strength between the two and the weak, vi-
carious nature of his parental authority: the impotence, senility, frustration
of a nominal progenitor obedient to the one who really ruled and shaped our
lives from the pinnacles of absolute power. From then on my hatred for the
Other, the recipient of the humiliating letter, would be transformed into a
real mania: compulsive desires to stamp on, almost crush, like a furious, energetic, punctilious post office worker, the pile of letters with his grotesque
effigy reproduced to infinity on the stamps; hopes of being present some day,
as would happen fifteen years later and in North America, at the death rattle
of a cruel, sordid, and prolonged death agony.

The reasons, or rather the doubts, that prevented me from following
Luis's example and asking for Party membership, would be difficult to specify. I was intellectually mature enough; at the same time as other Barcelona
friends I had read Dionys Mascolo's article in the special issue of *Les Temps
Modernes* on the left, and his lucid, persuasive argument that the need to ex-
tract the minimum common denominator from all the nonconformist, rebellious positions and attitudes must inevitably lead to the assumption of the
"universal need for Communism" had made a strong impression on me.
Both Castellet and myself felt tempted to take the step and Jaime Gil de
Biedma later reached the point of asking to join only to be turned down for
the same intolerant criteria that caused Cernuda's persecution in wartime. In
my case, my inhibition probably fed on some anti-Soviet reading in my adolescence about the Moscow trials and a frequently unfortunate experience
with Communist militants who defended socialist realism to the death.
Fleeing as I was from a world where I felt alien and marginal, I was unconsciously afraid of being interned in another where these feelings of difference and disagreement could be reproduced. But the chance, and perhaps
decisive, reason would be, at least externally, a meeting set up for me and
Castellet with the person who was to act as our Virgilian guide into the heart

of the organization. The contact chosen by the C.P. turned out to be Juan José Mira, a writer barely in his forties, who had won, if I remember correctly, the first Planeta Prize with a detective novel. Mira sublet, I think, one of those dismal, oppressive flats on the Ensanche, furnished on purpose, one would say, to imbue visitors with an insidious feeling of unease and give them repeated nightmares. He welcomed us in his dressing-gown, jovially, and after a brief exchange of pleasantries, he went straight to the point. He was aware, he said, that we were well disposed toward the Party and had been charged to meet with us on a regular basis in order to clear up our problems and uncertainties. After such an alarming prologue he opened a cupboard stuffed with clandestine journals, which, being negligently arranged, suddenly fell noisily on the carpet. He looked through the scattered publications and gave each of us a copy of *Mundo obrero*. He pointed out an extensive, solid speech by Bulganin, illustrated with his photo, and asked us to read and think about it at our leisure, so that we could discuss its "political and philosophical" content with him at a later meeting. But unhappily for our guide there never was another meeting: we had hardly left the flat in a sleepwalkers' daze than the astounded catechumens threw the bemedalled marshal's stodgy prose into the nearest drain and disappeared from sight forever. Soon afterwards, the mighty Bulganin would fall into "the dustbin of history" and from then on neither of us—nor probably Mira himself—would hear of him again.

As one might have expected, even before the change wrought by Sacristán's arrival, the Bar Club political discussions and my French contacts attracted the attention of the police. Just before my new trip to Paris and Monique's first stay in Barcelona, I received a telephone call from an inspector of the Social Political Brigade, famous at the time for his unswerving persecution of Communists. Antonio Juan Creix and his brother Vicente played a leading role in the regime's repressive apparatus and their harsh, suspicious nature made them rightly feared by the different "families" of the clandestine opposition. He said that he wanted to discuss a personal matter with me and, although the point of his call was perfectly clear, I feigned surprise and with rather rash, provocative cheerfulness I made a date for the fol-

lowing day in the Pastís. When I arrived at the appointed time, he was already waiting for me and, from the owner's tight-lipped, impassive gaze, I
deduced that he had questioned her about me. Antonio Creix was a sturdily
built man of average height; he wore a Bogart-style raincoat, and had one of
those mustaches so characteristic of his profession, as painted carefully and
artistically by Arroyo in his recent, polemical picture. Our conversation,
spelled out in a letter sent to Monique via an intermediary, centered at once
on my meetings with Elena de la Souchère: somebody from Paris had informed him of our interviews and my visits to the editorial board of *France-
Observateur*. Creix handled his information with ease and self-confidence,
pleased to demonstrate that no movement, even abroad, had escaped the police's eagle eye. As I saw, he was especially interested in tracking down the
sources where my friend obtained her information: did I know that my relationship with her could cause me unpleasant consequences? Was I aware
that she was planning a visit to Spain? Although I protested my innocence
and pretended I had only spoken to her about literature, he insisted that I
must inform them if she came to see me in Barcelona, even perhaps under a
false identity. His aim was not to arrest her nor to harm her in any way, he
added, but to talk to her, show her the real country that she did not know, and
make her realize that her articles suffered from serious prejudices and a total
lack of rigor. On the subject of the anti-Spaniards who obsessed him, Creix
expressed absolute contempt for the Catalan, bourgeois opposition while his
hatred for Communists revealed an obvious sickly fascination: his ashen face
would suddenly light up when he spoke about them and take on a more human expression. Later on he changed the subject and chatted about the literary, cultural world, of how exposed we writers with some weakness or de-
fect—he didn't specify which—were to blackmail, to being changed into
enemy agents without realizing it. While we walked up the Ramblas, he
asked me to sign a copy of *Duelo en el paraíso*; he then bid good-bye with a
pleasant but curt warning that our exchanges could be quite different if I
went back to my old ways.

That first police warning bell would be followed by others that fortunately weren't serious either. As a result of an organized foot-stamping by

our group in the Calderón Theatre at a Luca de Tena play in which a cruel, heartless Communist slumped to the ground after being executed shouting "Death to Spain!" to the applause of a bourgeois audience fond of that kind of creation, Luis, Castellet, and a dozen friends who turned up spontaneously in the police station to accompany one of the protestors arrested by a plainclothes inspector would be rounded up later in their homes and released hours afterwards, having made statements about the events. As I had been forewarned by Creix, I didn't follow the rest out of the theatre although, as I soon discovered from Castellet, he interrogated him during his questioning about my nocturnal habits and sexual inclinations. My recurrent, distressing nightmares of persecution related to Spain date back to this time: a mental scenario of denunciations, secret hiding places, harassment, frenetic flights from the police resulting from some dark, vaguely dishonorable crime, a scenario that would not disappear when I uprooted myself from the country nor even after Franco's death. The sequence with the Reverend Charles Lutwidge Dodgson at the Police Headquarters in my novel *Paisajes después de la batalla* is the faithful transcription of one of its versions in which sex and politics, exhibitionism and revolutionary militancy are subject to sarcastic attack by a chorus of inspectors whose dress, features, and manner recall those who, with the sensitive intuitions of bloodhounds, showed off *avant la lettre* the perverse eventuality of my *defects* and *weaknesses.*

T HE CHAIN OF events that would unexpectedly favor
my plans to leave Spain—at least that Spain in the grip
of an arbitrary, anachronistic, sterilizing regime that I hated with all my passion—began to come together throughout the summer of 1955, in a period
of personal frustration and political doubts when I devoted my free time and
efforts to writing *Fiestas* astride the Bar Club and the Shipyard. Soon after
the publication of one of my first books, I received a short note from the
North American Hispanist John B. Rust in which, after expressing his appreciation of these, he offered to negotiate the possible translation of *Juegos
de manos* with one of the New York publishing houses open to European
narrative; he added that he had passed my novels to his friend Maurice Edgard Coindreau during the latter's visit to Sweet Briar and that the French
translator completely shared his point of view. I was filled with surprise by
the reference to Coindreau's praise: although I knew his excellent versions
of the great North American novelists—Dos Passos, Hemingway, Faulkner, Steinbeck, and Caldwell—I did not know he read Spanish and had
been interested in our literature from his youth. Rust had previously sent me
a questionnaire about my tastes and the influences on my novels and my replies included a group of authors, starting with Faulkner, that I had often
read in Coindreau's translations. Some days later I received a letter from the
latter whose generous, magnanimous praise of my work filled me with elation. In his support for the judgments advanced by Rust, Coindreau not only
overwhelmed me with sincere and copious praise but offered to translate my
novels and suggest them to Gallimard. To a raw provincial writer like me,
dazzled by the novelists he translated and the prestige of the publishing
house for which he was assessor, the letter seemed like a wonderful dream,

too beautiful to be real. It was a singularly propitious stroke of luck that my enthusiasm at the time for Faulkner and young Southern narrators like Carson McCullers, Capote, or Goyen coincided with Coindreau's likes and interests. He still taught French literature in the Princeton Romance Languages Department, but traveled to Europe every year, and he suggested it would be convenient to meet in Paris where he would be staying for a few days at the beginning of October so he could introduce me to his publisher.

In our correspondence during those months, which unfortunately I haven't preserved, Coindreau showed his delight at discovering in the novels of a young writer brought up under Francoism the impact of an author like Faulkner whose work he had defended from the start against the hostility and lack of understanding of the majority of his colleagues. His prologues and studies of him had cleared a path for first a group of pupils and then a pack of imitators to follow in his footsteps and throw themselves into mapping out imaginary geographical landscapes directly or indirectly inspired by his at once realistic and fantastic vision of the decrepit society of the South. Today, when despite my continuing admiration for Faulkner I haven't read him for twenty years, I feel that it is fortunate his influence on me was only a brief, if intense infection activated particularly by the work of Capote and McCullers, before I discovered the much closer reality of the committed art of Pavese and Vittorini. As shown by the example of Latin America in the last twenty years, the powerful fascination exercised by his universe has not only had positive effects: if, on the one hand, it has allowed the creation of novelistic worlds as seductive and attractive as that of García Márquez, the immediate, devastating success of the latter has given rise, on the other, to the fortunate but doubtful formula of "magical realism," a luxuriant plantation of epigones, grandchildren or descendents of the author of *The Wild Palms* who have transplanted or tried to transplant the hallucinating world of Yoknapatawpha—seen through the multicolored lantern of Macondo with its levitations, witches, wise grandmas, miraculous girls, downpours of blood, and galleons moored in a silk-tree wood—not only to the heart of the *selva* or the Indies but also to lands as parsimonious and unfriendly to that kind of portent and marvel as Cantabria, Aragón, and Galicia. Nothing so easy and tempting as to transpose into a language often as opaque as Spanish Faulkner's long, heavy sentences stripped of all prosody, rhythm, and suppleness: if we add to that an area as well-defined as that county on the lower banks of the Mississippi complete with ordinance surveys, a transfer of the Macondo reincarnation, we can capture with hindsight of time the grandiose extent of its influence and, willy-nilly, the ravages of contamination. But Coindreau couldn't guess then what the first swallows of Faulknerism would herald in a long exhausting summer, the end of which is still not in sight. He had spotted, with his most delicate literary scent, before anyone else, the seminal value of a work that, through him, was going to change the direction of our narrative fiction. That first meeting of ours in the Pont Royal hotel would also be the beginning of a close, fruitful collaboration that would extend from his versions of *Juegos de manos* and *Duelo en el paraíso* to *Señas de identidad*. I discovered then that Coindreau's initiation into the art of translating had been Valle-Inclán's *Divinas palabras* and that only the accidents of his university career in the United States had deflected him from our language and made him discover at its source the work of the "lost generation." His return, after more than thirty years, to the love of his youth would not be limited to translating five of my novels but would extend to those of authors like Sánchez Ferlosio and Marsé, who would penetrate the French literary world thanks to his influence and prestige.

After I arrived in Paris at the beginning of October I went to Gallimard, the publishers, where I had an appointment with Coindreau. I asked for him at the receptionist's desk in the entrance lobby: the receptionist informed me that he had just left and that he expected me in his hotel in the afternoon, but that the secretary from the translation service wanted to see me. I waited nervously and soon a young woman appeared on the linoleum-covered stairs; she was sunburnt, had very short hair, and I can remember her smile very precisely. Monique Lange told me in rudimentary Spanish that her boss Dionys Mascolo wanted to talk to me and asked me whether I spoke French. *Je le baragouine un peu*, I replied with false modesty. I followed her through a labyrinth of stairs and corridors to the spacious office looking out over a beautiful interior garden where her boss was waiting for me. Mascolo welcomed me with a simple show of affection: Coindreau had written to him recommending my books and, he said, he wanted to take advantage of my visit to inform me of the usual clauses in the contract. However, the dialogue veered off at once toward Spain, where my interlocutor had just been on holiday with Marguerite Duras, Vittorini, and a small group of friends. Their attention had been caught by the country's development even under a system as authoritarian as Franco's; but unfortunately their ignorance of Spanish and lack of contact with intellectuals in the country prevented them from penetrating to the heart of things as they would have liked. What did I think of the situation? Could I see, as they had, some hopes of change? For a good hour I set before Mascolo my violent anti-Francoist feelings: with my naive optimism of those days, I explained to him that the new generation of intellectuals and university students was opposed to the dictatorship and was adopting more and more open, radical positions. In spite of our isolation and the fear provoked by the harsh repression of the postwar period, the young generation was beginning to open its eyes and was planning actions in support of its demands in harmony with the clandestine trade union opposition. Attributing to our tiny group's experience an impact it never had, I forecast that the country would very soon enter a phase of revolutionary agitation. Mascolo soaked up my words with rapture on his face and when our conversation ended, expressed a desire to see me again. Monique, who had remained in a discreet middle ground, asked me whether I would be free to have dinner with her the following day: I've also invited Jean Genet, she added straightaway to persuade me. I accepted and wrote down her address, that number 33, rue Poissonnière, that would soon become my refuge and haunt: the "permanent" abode that has for almost thirty years appeared on my official documents.

As Monique revealed later, Mascolo exclaimed after I left his office: "This is the Spaniard we have been waiting for." After that, infatuated with him and influenced by his ideas and opinions, she interpreted this comment as an order. With her typical lack of self-confidence she put forward Genet's name and its power of persuasion to ward off a possible rejection. My political vehemence and Belmonte-like appearance impressed her: after I leave, she asks the receptionist whether she thinks I'm interested in women. Geneviève says yes. Monique isn't so sure: my gaze reveals no personal emotion beyond my hatred for Franco's system and existence. Anyway, she decides, my coming conversation with Genet will clear up any doubts.

On the night of the dinner, the eighth of October, I leave the Bonne Nouvelle underground, immediately locate the Rex cinema opposite the old offices of *L'Observateur* where I met Elena de la Souchère months before, look for the adjacent building, not in the boulevard but in the street, take the lift to the third floor, walk to the second door on the left, and ring the bell. Monique comes to welcome me and introduces me to her guests: a fair-haired, bearded young Englishman named Peter and, bald, slight, beardless, wearing corduroy trousers and a leather jacket, Genet. I am intimidated by his presence and my intrusion among these strangers but, happily, Genet only seems interested in Peter, with whom Monique is having a passing relationship after her divorce. He asks him about his likes and dislikes, slyly makes fun of him, tries to make him confess that he has at some time felt repressed or secret attraction for a male friend or companion. He denies this, which amuses and excites Genet, leaning on the couch next to Monique. Suddenly he turns to me and asks point-blank:

"What about you? Are you a queer?"

In my confusion, I reply that I have had homosexual experiences—something that until then I had never revealed in public—and it helps me to clear things up with Monique, toward whom I already instinctively feel warmth, but my boldness—I suppose I blushed when I answered—makes no impression on him at all.

"Experiences! Everybody has had experiences! You talk like an Anglo-Saxon pederast! I meant dreams, desires, fantasies."

Genet doesn't speak to me again that night and, with a mixture of disappointment and relief, I understand I have not passed the test. I let him ironically court Peter while, during the dinner and afterwards, I devote myself entirely to Monique.

When I try to recall my first images of her these always hinge on the strange, unexpected aura of her smile: an open, warm, generous smile, tinged with melancholy, which is exclusively hers and is impossible to forget once it has been noticed and internalized. Throughout my life I have not come across another endowed with such expressive intensity: relaxing, warm, moving, and yet imbued with a mysterious fragility. Even at the harshest moments of our troubled and sometimes painful coexistence, the mere evocation of her smile has been enough to instantly sweep away bouts of sulking, break down ideas of moving apart or splitting up, recreate the disturbing emotion that overcame me the day I really discovered her and found out I was the fortunate recipient, making me relax and unwind, bewildered, intoxicated by pure happiness.

From that night on, despite Genet's interference and his overbearing personality, a reciprocal feeling was established between us, the nature of which is difficult to capture. Monique in some way broke down the cautious, prickly, defensive barrier that comes between women and me, with the exception of a certain kind of prostitute. Although my affection is not yet physical, her body does not leave me unmoved nor does it inspire fear. The unmentioned but obvious relationship with Peter does not favor our coming together, it will however make me understand that my arrival has introduced a small change in her life and scale of priorities: when it's time for me to go, in a conspiratorial gesture aimed at me, she bids farewell to him rather abruptly, as if telling me that the way is clear. When I realize what has happened, I am in the street with Peter, too late for the underground or bus and without the means to permit the luxury of a taxi. We have no alternative but to walk back to the Left Bank together and we silently walk the long distance; I'm still agitated by the memory and novelties of the evening while, by my side, he seems absorbed by the bitter, gloomy thoughts of a displaced gallant.

During the next few days Coindreau and I resolve some of the problems and difficulties posed by the translation and sign the contracts drawn up by Mascolo, which Monique has typed out. My long-standing, persistent goal of settling in Paris is now within reach but I have to return to Spain to fulfill several months of military service or be dubbed a deserter and be forced to cut all my ties with my brothers and friends and reject the country, if not definitively, at least for several years. Convinced of my usefulness as a link between our group and the European intellectuals we take as our model, unenthusiastic about selfishly deserting the struggle we are engaged in, I prefer to sacrifice myself for a time and return free from burdens and obligations. Monique, to whom I explain my problems of conscience, supports my decision and, although our connection is still hesitant, promises to come and see me in Spain. I see her daily, alone or with one of her friends: Mascolo, Marguerite Duras, Florence Malraux, Odette Laigle. In her initial flush to introduce herself and seduce me she spread out her radiant, showy visiting cards like a fan: not only is she an intimate friend of Genet but also someone as unapproachable as Faulkner writes to her affectionately and is her daughter's godfather. Her close friendships, in fact, range over a list of writers I have read and admired: she wishes to know if *je suis ambitieux*—I understood *un vicieux* and, comically, I hurriedly soothe her—whether I am worried, like many of her colleagues, more about the desire to make a career than by writing as such. Her moral vigilance in a matter she judges to be fundamental— from her privileged vantage point she has been able to witness ad nauseam the vanity, stratagems, envy, and wretchedness of the ever-grotesque literary tribe—will be a tremendous help, during our first years together, in curing my initial propensity to snobbery and the obscene flattery of fame: a long, difficult battle with myself in which her rigor and the simultaneous example of Genet will prevent me from becoming one of those smug, dropsical self-sufficient barrels who, with telegenic ubiquity, exhibit themselves daily on the peninsular Parnassus.

Gradually, as an already tender but delicate and uncertain relationship strengthens, she reveals details and mysteries in her biography: her Jewish origins, childhood in Indochina, conversion to Catholicism and immediate loss of faith, discovery of Indian poverty, return to Paris, friendship with Genet, impact of the journeys to Spain, joining the Communist Party. Her humor, frankness, and natural emotion sweep aside my restraint and afford me a warm immediacy I am ready to reciprocate. Used to the narrow, trivial, tight-lipped behavior of Spanish middle-class women of the time, her straightforward language, her total lack of embarrassment and fear of the ridiculous, surprise and attract me. After she finishes at the office we go out for a walk, I show her my favorite spots by the Mouff', the canals and cafés in Aubervilliers discovered by Guy Debord. Encouraged by her spontaneity and candor, I confide in turn my inhibitions and hang-ups with women. Till now I've only been able to fuck whores, I tell her. We all dream about being whores to the man we're interested in, she replies.

In order not to force things, Monique tactfully prolongs the ambiguity of our bond. Although we kiss and act as if we are lovers in public, we aren't yet, and she organizes the day so we say our farewells in a public spot. We have tacitly agreed to postpone the experience for a few weeks, until she comes and visits me during her end-of-year holidays. As she later tells me, this leap into the unknown, strongly discouraged by some of her friends, seems like a real act of madness; but, determined to win the bet, she comes to see me on the agreed date, even at the risk of failing and biting the dust. When we say good-bye on the twenty-third in the Gare d'Austerlitz we both feel confused and excited: our relationship is precarious and fragile; any unlucky or chance event could still destroy it, wipe it out.

During the weeks after my departure, mainly spent in Torrentbó, I correct the *Fiestas* manuscript and read the books by Genet, Leiris, Violette Leduc, Elio Vittorini that she sent me; I listen time and again to the records we listened to together in Paris. My letters contain weighty Sartrian reflections upon Genet's committed attitude toward the FLN rebellion in Algeria in opposition to the silent, indifferent complicity of the "mandarins." I am ashamed and worried by my social status as a "young gentleman"—emphasized by time spent with Alfredo and the peasants: I am objectively *une ordure*, I write to her; I belong unwillingly to the camp of *les ordures*. What can I do to avoid this? Even if I were to enlist in the Communist Party like her, my position would not change since the economic structures in the country would still be the same and unjust class differences could only be abolished by a hypothetical revolution. If I showed a real interest in their fate, didn't this imply the risk of stifling them with my paternalism and thus contributing to their acceptance, however provisional, of their state?

When, after a month and a half of letters and telephone calls, she disembarks in Barcelona, I wait for her at the end of the platform in the old station for trains from France: Monique walks toward me laden with suitcases, smiling with the sensitive, receptive expression I anxiously expect from her. I booked a double room in the Cosmos hotel whose position in the middle of Escudillers and vaguely suggestive *meublé* appearance appeal to me: Gil de Biedma strongly recommended the "nuptial bedchamber" where he once spent a glorious night; but it is let and we move into another more modest room. Luis, María Antonia, and several friends come to meet her and celebrate the occasion. We have lunch in the Amaya, drink, and go for a walk round the port: when we return to the Cosmos at night we are slightly tipsy. We both explore our nakedness tentatively: her skin is firm, soft, welcoming and my much-feared frigidity melts away at her touch. Happy and excited I penetrate her time and again, get lost between her breasts, belly, and lap. Joined to her body, I unhurriedly find the necessary gestures and movements, I share with her the beautiful, leisurely intimacy. The telephone rings and we leave it on the hook: we live isolated in our fiery bubble, disconnected from the outside world.

For five or six years, the relationship begun among the loud colors of the Cosmos bordello will experience its ups and downs and quiet interludes, but will not fade away: Monique will also be, at the sexual level, the omnivorous center of my life. We will love each other, fall out, deceive each other, and then have reconciliations like any couple in Paris, Italy, Barcelona, Andalusia: we try each of the four beds in a solemn, anachronistic hotel in Cartagena; make love naked on the burning sand dunes on the Guardamar beach spied on by a local lad. The sumptuous, baroque scenes of virility, all-consuming passion, violence, do not disappear entirely from my dreams, but remain silenced, vegetating in a kind of back room, as I discover later to my distress; when the opportunity arises they will reappear and dominate me.

Exhausted but happy, we dine out very late on elvers and red wine. To justify my absence from home, I explained to my father that I was going to Calafell for a few days and, from this date, the term *calafell* acquires for Monique and myself the Proustian dimension of *faire catleya*. During the day I show her the Shipyard and Barceloneta taverns that I had toured with Raimundo; at night, we go to see the blacks dancing in the Cádiz and drink manzanilla in the Andalusian Inn. María Antonia and Luis usually come with us, and during one of these soirées we meet up in the last bar with Gil de Biedma and a stranger, Jaime Salinas, who has been exiled since the war and is walking on Spanish soil for the first time. Monique then declares an irresistible passion for gays and dykes: the ones she meets in Barcelona with their heavy makeup, hysterical agitation, titters, and to-ing and fro-ing confirm for her Genet's age-old opinion that the Spanish variety are undoubtedly the most comic, saddest, sauciest, and grimmest in the world. On that and subsequent stays, the port, the Ramblas, the Barrio Chino, and the pompous, counterpaned nuptial couch in the Cosmos will be our exclusive, absorbing haunts. Our only incursions into the well-off bourgeois districts in the hills will be to Pablo Alcover and the Barrals' flat, where we had a date with Castellet on one of their literary Tuesdays.

My father is disconcerted by the Frenchwoman who inopportunely crosses his path, however much she shows off in his honor the very limited and at times mistaken repertory of polite formulas she memorized in his language in far-off schooldays. Eulalia belies my fears, likes her immediately, and looks after her during and after lunch with gushing emotion. Grandfather stays in his corner leafing through the newspaper or scratching his scalp. The ghostly, ageing, decrepit scene in the house impresses Monique: after a few hours there, she tells me, she feels as oppressed as I do and has the same desire to escape.

The meeting in the just-married Barrals' flat, though enlivened by Ferrater's shining presence, suffered from that mundane literary itch *d'être à la page* illustrative, for a Parisian woman used to Genet, of our incurable provincialism, but it did later enable the publisher not only to introduce in Spain some of the names revealed by Monique but also to establish, thanks to her, the basis for a fruitful and stimulating close relationship with Gallimard that will climax in the future Formentor Conversations and the creation of the innovative but ephemeral International Prize for Literature.

When Monique says good-bye, our life has changed. I must turn up some days later at the Mataró barracks to fulfill a sergeant's apprenticeship in the so-called University Militia, but we agree that after that's finished we'll meet in Paris and spend a few months together in daily contact to see if the experience suits us. In the meantime, our correspondence, her telephone calls and visits will, we hope, keep alive the warmth of a relationship that, without either of us suspecting it at the time, is going to have a lasting, definitive influence on our destiny, character, and ideas.

T HE RECORD OF the months after your first meeting in Barcelona is minutely detailed in the correspondence you maintained and its reconstruction poses no difficulty. The majority of your letters are from Mataró from January to July in fifty-six, and the continuous flow is only interrupted by her brief, infrequent visits. Rereading them, almost thirty years later, one often sees praiseworthy frankness and openness alongside some character traits you would struggle against afterwards: the adolescent tendency to embellish or magnify all that happens to you, which, had it not been soon lopped off, would have swept you into incurable mythomania; the vanity of the well-heeled young leftist, which, paradoxically, you would cast off thanks to an excessive if healthy creative pride: the fact experienced day in and day out that, as your addiction to literature intensified, you weren't modest enough to feel flattered by the fame and honors that sustain that activity; that the giddy adventure of writing discovered in *Don Julián* finally constituted something alien and even opposed to worldly glory: a new expression or an unexplored territory of your sexuality.

Your dialogue at a distance reveals the cautious pleasure of those walking to an amorous encounter between dunes and shifting sands. The plans you forge for the future are fragile and transitory: on your return to Paris, you book in alone to a small hotel on the rue de Verneuil and you spend the weekends together. Each of you preserves your freedom and neither aspires to the exclusive possession of the other. While you remain separate you must "cheerfully" accept minor infidelities. When Monique tells you the details of the adventures she had on some of her trips, both before and after getting married, you write to her that you have never loved her so much or felt so

proud of her independent, fearless qualities. You list your mediocre ambi-
dextrous *calafells* and encourage her to relate hers in turn. Her parallel story
with a friend in common and the unexpected, painful problem it throws up
force you to deepen your thoughts on the subject: the word "whore," used
with moral connotations, repels you. Everybody, women and men, has
changing fantasies and desires about the other sex, independently of their
emotional ties. The notion of deceit, you tell her, is reactionary and confused;
you don't feel betrayed by the fact she has been with another man; real betrayal would have stemmed from any attempt to hide it like a bourgeois wife.
This does not prevent, logically enough, a tingling jealousy; but it is a bearable unease that is even pleasantly melancholic. Taking into account your
hatred for traditional female passivity and frigidity, you are impressed and
excited by her Don Juan qualities. Sometimes you tell her about your dreams
of fucking her and don't leave out, on occasion, the presence of some Alge-
rians you went drinking with in Mouff' and their sudden, disturbing promiscuity. You have entered the Mataró barracks at the beginning of the year
and your description of the tedium and brutalizing absurdity of life there
takes up a large part of the letters:

> This morning, Mass. A terrific ceremony: the priest flutters about the al-
> tar to the sound of drums and cornets like a prima donna. On the other
> side of the yard, surrounded by armed guards, the prisoners attend the
> service bareheaded, and prostrate themselves on bended knee during the
> Consecration. The priest, childish and angelic like a doll, preaches the
> sacrifice and resignation appropriate to Lent. Rather moving. I was look-
> ing at the prisoners—some have been inside for years—the priest, host,
> noisy military band, the officer's gleaming sword. Everything beautiful
> and well-ordered: morality, religion, God, etc. How I remembered,
> loved, and missed Genet!
>   The Thursday procession was really beautiful! Helmet, machine gun,
> one, two, slowly keeping in step behind the God-child to the rhythm of
> the band. In front of us, the First Communion girls with their candles and
> little white wings and priests, priests, still more priests while we sweat

blinded by the sun and its reflection in the bayonets, one, two, one, two, and I am stupefied, exhausted, with the distressing impression I am an ape.*

To tell the truth, your life is not always as harsh and depressing as you paint it. Even in a system as rigid and hierarchical as the army and under the diffuse but real oppression of the dictatorship, typically Spanish disorder, arbitrariness, and incongruities palliate what in other latitudes could have been inflexible Prussian regimentation, opening up gaps and breathing spaces, pleasant like holes in Gruyère, in a life at first sight constrained, stifling, and airless. The daily routine and discipline of a Francoist barracks—imagined with anguish and horror by the French friends you write to—contain a series of whimsical imponderables, improvisations, and fantasies that only those who know the Spanish character and its weak points can assimilate unsurprised. Monique has been telephoning you regularly since you arrived with the twenty-sixth Badajoz Infantry Regiment and these calls from a Frenchwoman not only give you the enviable status of a deserving, tough Hispanic conqueror but also create a palpable atmosphere of expectation and lust among the officers: while one lieutenant tries to gain your esteem with a view to an eventual trip with your "fiancée" and some French girlfriend, followed by a cheerful, carefree spree by all four, another suggests the possibility of obtaining through her one of those Parisian magazines that today would fall from the hands of any eight-year-old, so insipid are they, but which then aroused in repressed, frustrated soldiers an excitement difficult to imagine. Discreetly courted by your superiors, you use the situation to get out of the most painful duties in your life as a sergeant—processions, reviews, marches—by invoking the exotic need to stay by the telephone in case of a call from Paris. Francoism was also like this and had little in common with the iron, monolithic, totalitarian regime that exiles and Republican sympathizers used to describe and evoke from afar: despite your religious

*Neither of the two letters quoted, which I have translated from the French, carry a date although this can be deduced from the text: the procession mentioned in the second relates to the festival of Corpus Christi.

agnosticism and well-known disaffection from the regime, the long-distance telephone calls from an invisible, suggestive French fiancée conferred on you a special, privileged halo within the regiment.

Neither would the experience of those months in Mataró be purely negative: the contact with the soldiers and prisoners would allow you a glimpse of areas and hidden corners of Spanish reality that you could have penetrated in no other way. In one of the stories in *Para vivir aquí* you capture your fleeting vision of the unjust, irrational world of prison: the assortment of pathetic or eccentric individuals brought together by an accident of fortune in the barrack cells. You can remember the poor peasant who deserted when he received a letter from his father demanding he join in the reaping; the Lombrosian deserter whose sorties out always ended up in the whorehouses on Robadors Street; the queer detained there for the sole crime of being one, and whom the officers in their drunken parties would order out of the cell to sing and dance in front of them dressed and made up like a woman; the lad who dictated a letter to you with only this address, "To Pepe who sells melons on the Side of the Road," and you never persuaded him that without more exact details the letter would never arrive; finally the day a small, stunted recluse wrapped himself up in his friend's soft, clean sheet, masturbated, and ejaculated over it, provoking the wrath of the others and a noisy attempt at lynching.

Your indignation at the abuses and outrages of the system, restrained within the barracks, is poured out in every line on the pages of your correspondence. But the events of February 1956—the first open political crisis within the regime—and subsequent police measures—the arrest of Ridruejo, Pradera, Múgica, Miguel Sánchez Mazas—force you to take extreme precautions. Thanks to some friends who travel, like Jaime Salinas, and are willing emissaries, you inform Monique regularly of all that is happening: you tell her how blacklists of oppositionists are circulating in Barcelona, those who must be neutralized if necessary, and your name appears there as "the C.P.'s intellectual link with abroad." Although these are only alarmist rumors, you and your colleagues take them seriously and for some days you break off all contact and meetings. "In such circumstances," you write, "I honestly don't know what awaits me: I cannot even make plans: will I complete my military service without any problems? Will they grant me a visa?" Fortunately things go no further and, after Ruiz Giménez's dismissal, life returns to its normal channels. However, foreseeing future obstacles, you establish alternative methods of communication through intermediaries while awaiting her next trip.

Monique's frequent calls and visits to Barcelona have repercussions on the hypocritical, evasive but irritating relationship you maintain with your father. The would-be trips to Calafell and prolonged absences from home and barracks reveal the kind of bond that offends his Catholic principles. While María Antonia's family background and religious upbringing put her beyond suspicion despite the frequency of her meetings with Luis—to such an extent that years later he will point out to you that both needed great strength of character "not to fall into temptation"—he has no doubts about your clandestine affair with a Frenchwoman. But, as you are quick to notice, if Monique is "the divorced Jewess" with whom you are living in sin, your cohabitation seems to have taken a weight from his mind and does not arouse the same reproaches as it would have in your brothers: his secret, unavowed apprehension that you were homosexual, incubated and latent since the episode with Grandfather, might have robbed him of hours of sleep, and even with her matrimonial separation and "Jewish blood," Monique seems a lesser evil to him. His easygoing views about her and confidences to Luis and José Agustín make his ambiguity transparent. When his younger sister meets Monique's mother by chance in Puerto Alcudia, her very favorable opinion of her and her bourgeois position alleviate his fears that you are in the hands of someone on the make and lead him to accept the accomplished fact: although without the blessing of the Church, your partner is "normal." His death, eight years later, will protect him from confronting a truth much harder to handle than his brutal discovery of your Communist sympathies: the development and flowering in one of his sons, despite his precautions and defenses, of that monstrous seed of disorder, aberration, and deviance from the maternal side that was the obsession of his life, although he had laughingly, in vain, tried to exorcise it.

A HIGHLY FORTUNATE COINCIDENCE *of lasting consequences for you determined that the company to*
which *you were sent as a sergeant was mainly made up of Murcians and Anda-
lusians. Until then, circumstances had imposed on you a reluctant distancing from
them: fleeing the injustice and greed of their land, they came to the industrial regions in the north of Spain hoping to find work and a roof over their heads, only
normally to meet exploitation very much like that from which they were fleeing.
Overcrowded, next to the gypsies in the slum belt surrounding Barcelona, they
were marginalized and discriminated against by the indigenous population,
marked out with the insulting label of* xarnegos. *The wretched conditions in
which they camped out and the continued persistence of their migration had often
led you to wonder about their situation in their native provinces; however, apart
from the odd chance encounter on one of your forays into the slum areas, you never
had an opportunity to mix with them or consider their problems. The negative
opinion held by your social milieu, including the nationalist sectors, was based on
their ignorance, laziness, and excessive birthrate when it was not preoccupied with
their supposed enthusiasm to join the Civil Guard and other repressive branches
of the army and the police. As Albert Manent's friend had said at the university,
"without those Andalusian guards they send us from Madrid, Catalonia would be
free."*

*Your company's soldiers came from the most forgotten areas of the steppes of
Spain. Their social and cultural defenselessness, the jokes that the others sometimes
played on them, very naturally predisposed you in their favor: you remember as if
it were today the time when two of them went out for a walk, as they used to in
their villages and as men still do in the whole of North Africa, with their little fingers entwined, and the laughter and sarcastic comments their innocent gesture*

gave rise to. Transplanted into the city directly from their farms and villages, some seemed frightened by the traffic and the bustle, crossed the road clumsily, and gazed in amazement at the much freer, casual ways of the local boys and girls. Catalonia was their El Dorado and the majority cherished plans of settling down there. Almost all had a friend or a relative in Somorrostro, Pueblo Seco, Casa Antúnez, or La Verneda; but knowledge of the situation their fellow countrymen struggled with daily did not discourage them. As they would gradually reveal to you in your conversations with them, the poverty of the Barcelona hovels implied an escape from an even harsher, more inhuman poverty that apparently gave no sign of softening.

This discovery inspired you with the desire to travel to their land. The recruits with whom you would break regulations when you had the chance by going out for a drink together would talk to you with real feeling about their villages: Mazarrón, Aguilas, Totana, Pulpí, Huercal Overa, Garrucha, Lubrín, Níjar, Carboneras . . . The story of their life there, its beauty and backwardness moved you. Although your obsession after leaving the army was to depart from Spain as soon as possible, Monique wanted holidays in the sun: impressed by the stories of your friends, you suggested a trip by bus through the coastal towns of Murcia and Almería; she was delighted with the idea. When, free at last of your military duties, you welcomed her as before on the station platform, your space to be happy would no longer be the Barrio Chino or the Ramblas or the shiny, soft bed in the Cosmos. Impatient, excited, wanting to drink, make love in new settings, you caught the train to Valencia, on the way to Guardamar, Cartagena, and the distant beaches of the luminous, longed-for south.

Purifying bath, brilliance of epiphany: fleeting images interweave, visual maelstrom, expansive happiness: a prolonged operation to thread in a veiled order, the torrential flow of still photos: violently dislocated strata, bare, clean stretches of whitish land, erosion refining down ochre stones subject to slow, millennial torture: thirsty tracks, scattered oleanders, stunted vegetation, the ubiquitous sun: a light that seems to vibrate and thicken while the bus wearily clings to the leaden tar on the road: flattened hovels, shining firmament, repressed, ephemeral attempts at greenery: pervasive sensation of beauty and wretchedness, cruel, un-

shod, ragged existence, heartless mineral splendor: the exhausted tranquillity of mountains with tight rumps, sharp, broken backs, and heads embellished by a painter's capricious palette: skin rash, pink sores, sinuous scars, whitish gashes: desolation, severity, magnificence, corrosive pain, diaphanous splendor: an instinctive, spontaneous affection for the sumptuous, orphaned landscape, sharp realization of the enjoyment of your identification, blinding recognition of your spatial frame: affinity, immediacy, harmony with an almost African land that endows the journey with the initiating aura of a second, deferred nativity.

As bitter as crab apple: that's how the boy defines his own region, the boy who, lying on the sand next to you, vaguely flourishes his arm toward the harsh, burnt countryside, the beach blurred by the mist, the plain, white town sunk in the lethargic depths of the siesta: ravaged, bloodless land, abandoned mines, ruined chimneys, blackish profusion of slag: evidence of past euphoria aggravating the unwelcoming impression of poverty: horizontal lives, yawning caves, calcareous desolation, ancestral stubbornness: women in mourning, prematurely worn out, laden with pitchers next to the freshet: sleepwalking peasants, strings of mules, sad, silent men peacefully sheltering under a sunshade: no change nor likelihood of change: solitude, repetition, monotony, desire to escape, to throw the dust off the soles of their shoes: emigration to Madrid, Barcelona, France, wherever: the price of a bus ticket and a suitcase with their only inheritance: their brutal life-sentence and also their hope.

A drowsy, decrepit, colonial city: police dressed in drill and wearing white tropical hats: horse-drawn carriages sway indolently: the marketplace bustles promiscuously: the Simón hotel with its ancient rooms.

Discovery of rhythms, smells, voices, sweet apprenticeship in idleness: tentative exploration of the urban scene, horror and fascination intermingle, inner civil war, insoluble contradiction: plurality, alternating current: creative, spermal spark, product of a simultaneous collision: an exercise in ecstatic contemplation of a world that in another way wounds your defenseless moral sensibility.

The harsh, guttural or singsong accent of the south, through which your love for your language will perhaps mysteriously be filtered: territory conquered inch by inch, listening to the dull tones of resignation and poverty, gradual dual apprehension of a possible belonging and of the uncertain, chance nature of the doubtful identity granted to you.

Your indifference to Spain—that incomplete, fragmentary entity, which is sometimes obtuse and pigheaded, at other times brutal and tyrannical—in whose negligent bosom you have grown, will suffer the impact of the brief, fruitful trip through the region of Almería: to your youthful tiredness with the pobre, brut, trist, dissortat *native town beautifully evoked by Espriu, and to the dreams of escaping to some place in the north where the people are* neta i noble, culta, rica, lliure, desvetllada i feliç *will be counterposed henceforth to the image of a radiant, captive landscape whose power of attraction will divert your compass and draw it toward the tormented configuration of its tracks, hills, and steppes: your first holidays with Monique, on the eve of your journey to Paris, will thus be cause for an unforeseen, fertile combination: source and subject of nostalgia, compensatory vision of a frustrated homeland, glimpse, hint, forerunner of a world that is still fantastic but already present in your mind, silent, near, lying in wait for you.*

Design by David Bullen
Typeset in Mergenthaler Granjon
with Weiss display by Wilsted & Taylor
Printed by Braun-Brumfield
on acid-free paper